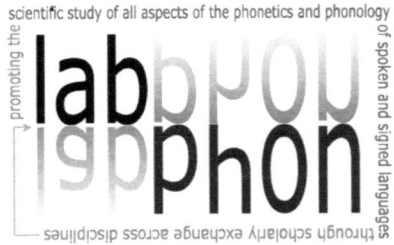

Studies in Laboratory Phonology

Chief Editor: Martine Grice
Editors: Doris Mücke, Taehong Cho

In this series:

1. Cangemi, Francesco. Prosodic detail in Neapolitan Italian

Prosodic detail in Neapolitan Italian

Francesco Cangemi

Language Science Press
Berlin

Language Science Press
Habelschwerdter Allee 45
14195 Berlin, Germany

langsci-press.org

This title can be downloaded at:
http://langsci-press.org/catalog/book/16
© 2014, Francesco Cangemi
Published under the Creative Commons Attribution 4.0 Licence (CC BY 4.0):
http://creativecommons.org/licenses/by/4.0/
ISBN: 978-3-944675-01-5

Cover and concept of design: Ulrike Harbort
Typesetting: Francesco Cangemi
Proofreading: Tom Gardner, Martin Hilpert, Michelle Natolo, Stephanie Natolo, Benedikt Singpiel, Siri Tuttle, Tamara Schmidt

Storage and cataloguing done by FU Berlin

Language Science Press has no responsibility for the persistence or accuracy of URLs for external or third-party Internet websites referred to in this publication, and does not guarantee that any content on such websites is, or will remain, accurate or appropriate. Information regarding prices, travel timetables and other factual information given in this work are correct at the time of first publication but Language Science Press does not guarantee the accuracy of such information thereafter.

Contents

1 Introduction   1
- 1.1 Intonation between exemplars and abstraction 1
- 1.2 Prosodic detail 7
  - 1.2.1 Modelling perception of speech 7
  - 1.2.2 Phonetic detail 11
  - 1.2.3 Prosodic detail 15
- 1.3 Neapolitan Italian intonation 18
  - 1.3.1 Neapolitan Italian 18
  - 1.3.2 The Autosegmental-Metrical framework 20
  - 1.3.3 Neapolitan Italian intonation 22
- 1.4 Structure of this book 24
  - 1.4.1 Production and perception 27
  - 1.4.2 Intonation and tempo 28
  - 1.4.3 Sentence modality contrasts 29

2 Melodic detail in production   33
- 2.1 Introduction 35
  - 2.1.1 Background 35
  - 2.1.2 Hypotheses 38
  - 2.1.3 Phonological analysis 39
- 2.2 Method 43
  - 2.2.1 Corpus 43
  - 2.2.2 Measures 44
  - 2.2.3 Indices 46
- 2.3 Results 48
  - 2.3.1 Alignment 48
  - 2.3.2 Scaling 49
  - 2.3.3 Shape 49
  - 2.3.4 Summary of results 51
- 2.4 Discussion 53
  - 2.4.1 Contour shape in other contrasts 53

Contents

		2.4.2 Enriching inventories or grammars?	58
		2.4.3 Segmental and suprasegmental phonology	61
	2.5	Conclusion	65

3 Perception of melodic detail — 67
- 3.1 Introduction . . . 67
- 3.2 Experiment 1 . . . 72
  - 3.2.1 Background . . . 72
  - 3.2.2 Hypotheses . . . 73
  - 3.2.3 Method . . . 74
  - 3.2.4 Results . . . 77
  - 3.2.5 Discussion . . . 78
- 3.3 Experiment 2 . . . 79
  - 3.3.1 Background . . . 79
  - 3.3.2 Hypotheses . . . 81
  - 3.3.3 Method . . . 82
  - 3.3.4 Results . . . 83
  - 3.3.5 Discussion . . . 86
- 3.4 General discussion . . . 87
  - 3.4.1 Possible task improvements . . . 87
  - 3.4.2 A broader research question . . . 89
- 3.5 Conclusion . . . 90

4 Temporal detail in production — 91
- 4.1 Introduction . . . 93
- 4.2 Material . . . 94
  - 4.2.1 Corpora . . . 94
  - 4.2.2 Forced alignment . . . 98
- 4.3 Experiment 1 . . . 99
  - 4.3.1 Background . . . 99
  - 4.3.2 Hypotheses . . . 101
  - 4.3.3 Method . . . 102
  - 4.3.4 Results . . . 103
  - 4.3.5 Discussion . . . 105
- 4.4 Experiment 2 . . . 106
  - 4.4.1 Background . . . 106
  - 4.4.2 Hypotheses . . . 107
  - 4.4.3 Method . . . 107
  - 4.4.4 Results . . . 108

		4.4.5	Discussion	110
	4.5	General discussion		114
		4.5.1	Universality and specificity	115
		4.5.2	Tempo (and intonation)	116
	4.6	Conclusion		117

5 Perception of temporal detail — 119
- 5.1 Introduction — 120
  - 5.1.1 Two views of tempo — 120
  - 5.1.2 Hypotheses — 123
- 5.2 Method — 125
  - 5.2.1 Operationalization — 126
  - 5.2.2 Material — 127
- 5.3 Results — 127
  - 5.3.1 Orthogonality hypothesis — 129
  - 5.3.2 Nesting hypothesis — 129
- 5.4 Discussion — 130
  - 5.4.1 Design-related issues — 130
  - 5.4.2 Epistemological issues — 134
- 5.5 Conclusion — 136

6 Conclusion — 139
- 6.1 Summary of findings — 140
  - 6.1.1 Intonation — 140
  - 6.1.2 Tempo — 142
  - 6.1.3 Production and perception — 143
- 6.2 Tools for prosodic detail research — 145
  - 6.2.1 Automatic Speech Segmentation for Italian — 145
  - 6.2.2 Multi-parametric continuous resynthesis — 146
- 6.3 Theoretical implications — 148
  - 6.3.1 Exemplar prosody — 148
  - 6.3.2 Substance, form and function — 150

Bibliography — 153

Name index — 174

Subject index — 179

1 Introduction

> *Los ponientes diversamente rojos que miro cada tarde serán en el recuerdo un solo poniente.*
>
> J.L. Borges
> *Historia de la eternidad*, 1936

1.1 Intonation between exemplars and abstraction

In the last century, the overwhelming majority of linguistic theories on perception of speech relied on the assumption that, in order to access meaning, listeners convert the incoming audible signal into abstract mental representations. In this perspective, which can be referred to as *abstractionist*, representations are a necessary device to cope with the extreme variability of speech productions. Variability is an intrinsic characteristic of speech: due to individual physiological differences, the same word uttered by two different speakers will be acoustically different. Even two repetitions of the same sentence uttered by a same speaker will never be exactly identical: paraphrasing Heraclitus, we could say that you cannot step twice into the same (speech) stream.

The abstractionist approach to perception of speech has been applied to recognition and categorization of linguistic units of different levels, from activation of and discrimination among sound-based lexical representations (*word recognition*) to the problems of invariance and variability of lower level units (such as syllables and segments: *speech perception* proper). In both cases, it is posited that mental representations only contain "substantial" information, which is necessary to distinguish one representation from the other. Information which does not contribute to establishing a contrast between two representations, such as the pronunciation details discussed above ("accidental" information, usually referred to as *phonetic detail*), is not included. These simplified representations are stored in the listener's memory, and used to recognize new incoming signals. In order to perceive speech, the listener must reduce the richly detailed signal into a simplified abstract representation, by separating substantial and accidental information. This reduced representation can then be compared (and matched) with the representations which are already stored in memory. Reduction of a rich signal into a simple representation (or, in other words, separation of substantial and accidental information) is the key to generalization: to exemplify at the level of word recognition, listeners are able to recognize words produced by new unknown speakers because speaker-specific information is filtered out.

As this brief account shows, the abstractionist approach to perception of speech is strongly rooted in the linguistic, philosophical and psychological thinking which permeated the West until the first half of the last century. We avoided on purpose the use of terms such as category, feature, phonetics, phonology and normalization. But if we cast our account of the abstractionist approach into the frame of Western thinking before the 1950s, connections become visible. Focussing on word recognition, we could say that listeners map the continuously variable phonetic signal onto a discrete and abstract phonological representation, thus accessing entries in the mental lexicon. Each word in the mental lexicon is represented as the association between a meaning and a phonological form, which is in turn solely and thoroughly characterized by the contrastive features which permit to distinguish it from other forms. Entries in the mental lexicon are categories in the monothetic sense, in that they are defined by a set of singly necessary and jointly sufficient features. Perceiving speech entails the extraction of these phonological features from the signal, thus normalizing all phonetic variation. As an example, imagine that a listener is presented with the signal represented acoustically in Figure 1.1.

According to the abstractionist approach, in the mental lexicon of Italian native speakers there is an entry, the word *cane*, which links some semantic information (which we can assume to be equivalent to English 'dog') with an abstract phonological form. This form is characterized by a set of singly necessary and jointly sufficient features. These could be represented by acoustical, articulatory or perceptual information, and arranged as a linear string or as a superposed score. Let us simplify on this specific point and assume they are represented by the ordered string of the phonemes /k,a,n,e/. If the actual phonetic signal is compatible with this abstract phonological representation, the word <cane> is recognized. Crucially, in order to establish the compatibility of the phonetic signal with the phonological representation, some properties of the signal are ignored or only partially attended to. The transcription /'kane/ does not allow us to

1.1 Intonation between exemplars and abstraction

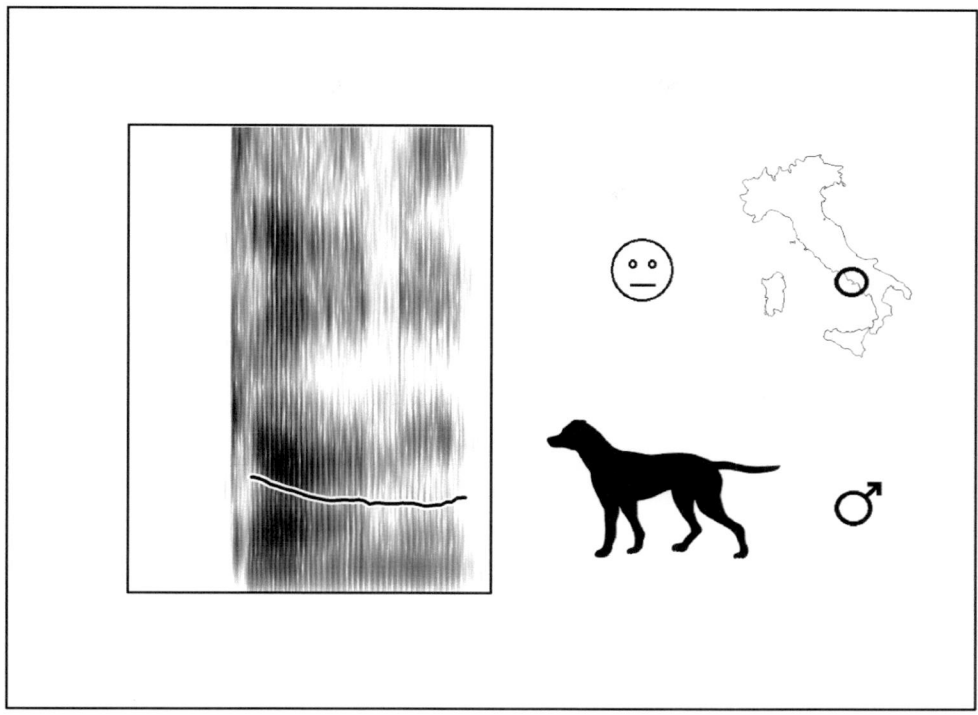

Figure 1.1: Spectrogram and fundamental frequency track of the Italian word *cane* 'dog' as uttered by a bored male native speaker of the Neapolitan regional variety, and (part of) the information which can be extracted from the signal.

recover the information that the word has been uttered by a male speaker. Other features in the signal might cue other information, for example that the native variety of the speaker is the Neapolitan one. Some speakers of this variety tend to articulate low vowels with the tongue in a slightly retracted position, and final unstressed vowels are also slightly centralized. A closer phonetic transcription of the utterance above, specifying at least the position of the tongue during the vocalic portions, would thus be [ˈka̠ːne̽]. The signal could also be richly specified along other dimensions, such as those cueing speaker's attitudes or emotions. However, as far as word recognition is concerned, all this information must be filtered out through a normalization process. The listener will still have access to the information that the speaker is a male, that he learnt Italian in the Neapolitan area and that he is somehow bored, but word recognition will be carried on by

1 Introduction

the abstract representation /'kane/ alone. This representation does not contain any information which is not necessary to establish a contrast with other lexical representations. Indeed, in line with the strongly minimalist assumptions of early phonological theories, these abstract representations are as bare-boned as possible.

The idea of monothetic classes, which Western thinking inherited from Aristotle, and the clear-cut distinction between rich phonetic signal and minimalist phonological representations, which can be traced back to Trubetzkoy, represent the two pillars on which the abstractionist approach rests. However, in the last fifty years, both have been vigorously shaken by developments in philosophy, cognitive psychology and linguistics. The starting point of this renewal process can be identified in Wittgenstein's research on family resemblances, which questioned in the first place the relationship between language, reality and thought, but were eventually interpreted as providing an alternative to the long-standing monothetic approach to category structure. He showed that at least some concepts are difficult (if not impossible) to define by using a finite set of singly necessary and jointly sufficient features, as in the famous example on the uses of the word *game*. Some games are played for recreation, some as a profession, and some out of addiction; they can rely on muscles, brains or luck, and not all of them have scores, teams or winners. The different members of the category of games are instead linked by the propriety of sharing *some* of the relevant features, none of which is necessary, and which never appear all together in any of the members.

The cognitive interpretation of Wittgenstein's investigations inaugurated a season of intense research on the structure and the formation of categories, which was mainly carried out in the 1970s by experimental psychologists working on memory and learning. The rejection of singly necessary and jointly sufficient features had major repercussions on category *structure*. Monothetic categories are flat, in the sense that each member is equally representative of the class (as in the case of even numbers); categories based on family resemblances, on the other hand, have an internal structure. The members which share more features with the others are more representative (or prototypical) of the category: chess is more representative of games than Russian roulette, and robins are more representative of birds than hens. Eleanor Rosch's work on such prototypicality effects on memory and learning show how researchers' attention was shifting from abstract categories and features, as in the monothetic view, to members. The complementary line of research on category *formation* went even further, by focussing on the role of concrete individual instances. The idea that categorization of a new stimulus depends on the analysis of its features and on the match with stored abstract sets of features was challenged by Lee Brooks' non-analytic approach to categorization. In his view, categorization is achieved by retrieving from memory the items which are most similar to the new stimulus. The most radical version of the main assumption behind this approach, then, is that each experience leaves an individual trace in our memory. Crucially, these traces or *exemplars* are not reduced to a set of abstract and contrastive features - they rather are detailed and embodied episodes.

These developments had a deep impact on models of perception of speech. If categories are not defined by a set of singly necessary and jointly sufficient features, and if memory is a collection of individual detailed traces rather than of abstract feature sets, an exclusively abstractionist model of speech perception becomes untenable. Word recognition cannot be modelled as the result of activating a single abstract form in the mental lexicon, because storage units are detailed episodic traces. Moreover, the abstractionist approach requires, between audition and recognition, a normalization stage in which phonetic variation is separated from phonological information. And just as the postulate of monothetic classes and abstract memory was questioned by work in philosophy and cognitive psychology, recent developments in linguistics challenged the postulate of a clear-cut separation between phonetics and phonology as monolithically dealing with gradience and categoriality, respectively. Work on the interface between phonetics and phonology shows that knowledge of sound structure might rather be spread along a continuum, ranging from the fine-grained and continuous varying phonetic end, to the coarse and granular pole of lexical contrasts. By the end of the last century, then, both the psychological and linguistic assumptions behind abstractionist models were challenged.

As a result of the recent insights on episodic memory, a new approach to linguistic knowledge emerged. Its basic principle is that linguistic categories are the result of the accumulation of individual experiences, and that linguistic structures emerge from language use. This paradigm has been applied by Joan Bybee in the study of a wide array of phonological, morphological and diachronic issues. Coupled with the insights on phonetic grounding of phonological contrasts and applied to the problems of speech perception and word recognition, this approach gave rise to a new generation of models for perception of speech, usually referred to as *exemplar-based*. Models of word recognition inspired by this approach assume that listeners store phonetically detailed traces of individual events, which include both information which is necessary to lexical activation and information which concerns non-lexical contrasts, such as talker identity or

1 Introduction

context-based effects. By assuming that memory traces include detailed phonetic information, there is no longer need to account for normalization as in abstractionist approaches, and phonetic variation becomes a resource for robust categorization, rather than a source of noise for the perceptual system.

Abstractionist and exemplar-based models of perception of speech rely on a set of clearly opposed assumptions, as we tried to illustrate in the paragraphs above. However, the dichotomy between the two should not be emphasized beyond necessity. For one, exemplar models do not rule out the possibility of generating abstract representations, if only as a by-product of the activation of multiple individual traces. And abstract representations could be enriched so as to contain more phonetic information than the one exclusively required to establish phonological contrasts. Indeed, a vast amount of experimental evidence shows that both phonetic detail and abstract phonological categories play a role in speech perception and word recognition; integration of both perspectives into *hybrid* models has been pursued since the beginning of the new century. The speech signal contains information at different levels of granularity, and we cannot rule out the hypothesis that insights from both approaches might be necessary to account for them all. Modelling how listeners perceive speech and handle information at different levels (e.g. lexical *vs.* pragmatic contrasts), or the same information in different contexts (e.g. clear addressed speech *vs.* multi-party noisy conversation), might require more than a single analytical tool.

In order to develop a truly effective hybrid model, we should have a grasp of how linguistic information is processed along various dimensions and in various contexts. However, the striking majority of the studies informed by the abstractionist-exemplar debate deals with speech perception and word recognition alone. But words, syllables and segments do not exhaust the range of possible linguistic units. Some fifty years of intense research on prosody have shown that it is possible to find structures in the relationship between signal and meaning above the word level, as in the case of accounts on how modulations in fundamental frequency (henceforth $f0$) cue contrasts on the pragmatic and informational level. If a phonological approach to intonation is possible (and even necessary, as suggested by a vast amount of evidence gathered in the last thirty years), the issue of how intonational categories are formed, accessed and instantiated must be asked as well. However, little is known about storage and retrieval of larger chunks of speech, such as phrases or entire utterances.

In this book, we defend the thesis that the study of categoriality and gradience in intonation would benefit from insights coming from the debate on abstractionist and exemplar-based approaches to speech perception and word recognition. Our aim here is not the formalization of a model of speech perception for form-function relationships at the prosodic level. Similarly, we do not explore how chunks of speech above word level are processed, even if we recognize that these two issues would be instrumental in the development of a truly integrated hybrid model. We will rather focus on how current phonological models of intonation may benefit from research on phonetic detail, by investigating the potential role of such detail at the prosodic level (henceforth *prosodic detail*) in a model of abstractionist inspiration, namely the Autosegmental-Metrical framework. Under this light, our main research question is how rich phonetic specification of phonological categories for intonation should be. Or, in other words, we question whether phonological categories in this model should be reshaped in such a way as to permit an enrichment with more phonetic information.

In the following sections, we will flesh out the title of this book, by providing our working definition of prosodic detail (Section 1.2) and a brief account of intonation in Neapolitan Italian (Section 1.3), the variety from which experimental data are drawn. Before turning to the experimental chapters (Sections 2–5), we will detail the structure of this book (Section 1.4) and comment on some of the methodological choices overarching individual experiments.

1.2 Prosodic detail

In spite of its relative recency, the concept of phonetic detail has already been used in a possibly confounding variety of senses. A thorough review of the history of its uses falls outside the scope of these introductory pages. However, since its exportation on the prosodic level is instrumental in setting our main research question (see Section 1.2.3), we will at least provide some background and clarify our use of the term (Section 1.2.2). In (Section 1.2.1, we briefly review the two major shifts which characterized research on perception of speech in the second half of the twentieth century and which prepared the ground for the rise of the notion of phonetic detail: from infra-lexical to lexical units, and from abstractionist to exemplar-based approaches.

1.2.1 Modelling perception of speech

Research in the relatively young field of *perception of speech* deals with how listeners represent and process speech, and how they manage to map the variability displayed by the continuous signal onto stable and discrete units (Jusczyk & Luce 2002). As we have seen above, different approaches to this main issue are possible. In abstractionist frameworks, a further line can be drawn between

1 Introduction

early work on speech perception and subsequent studies on word recognition, according to the size of the units under analysis. *Speech perception* proper focusses on psychoacoustic processing of speech sounds, that is on units linking substance and form but devoid of independent function, such as segments and syllables. *Word recognition*, on the other hand, deals with units associated with lexical meaning, thus focussing on activation and discrimination of lexical representations (Luce et al. 2003). In the following, we argue that shifting attention from speech perception to word recognition permitted a shift in perspective from abstractionist to exemplar-based approaches. This, in turn, blurred the line between speech perception and word recognition themselves.

1.2.1.1 Speech perception

Early studies in perception of speech were strongly influenced by the empiricism of late American structuralism and taxonomic linguistics (Harris 1955; Chomsky 1965; see Matthews 1993 for a review), which considered the observable acoustic phonetic features as the ideal starting point for a structural description of languages. In this frame, it comes as no surprise that early research on perception was mainly focussed on the phonemic level, thus equating perception of speech with speech perception. Moreover, in the late 1940s, the new spectrographic techniques started to show in full detail the acoustical complexity of speech. The alleged basic units of speech in theoretical linguistics, i.e. phonemes, were found to be highly variable.[1] Phonetic variation was ascribed to two main sources, which we might label as *indexical* and *allophonic* (Luce et al. 2003) or talker variability and contextual variability (Johnson & Mullennix 1997), and which result in the lack of *constancy* and *invariance*, respectively (Jusczyk & Luce 2002).

First, phonemes were found to have different acoustic proprieties in different segmental environments (Delattre et al. 1955, among others). From an articulatory point of view, allophonic variation and subsequent lack of invariance in acoustic features are a natural effect of coarticulation. Sounds are not produced in strict sequentiality, but rather with a certain degree of overlap in the articulatory movements required for their production. Second, even in the same segmental environments, a given phoneme can have strikingly different phonetic

---

[1] As a result, the linguistic, phonetic and perceptual role of the segment was put under examination. Studies undermining the central role of the phoneme started with acoustic investigations on perceptual units (Cooper et al. 1952), progressed within Firthian and articulatory phonology in the following decades (Firth 1948; Browman & Goldstein 1986), and have been recast in connection with the history of writing systems already since Faber (1992), and more recently by Albano Leoni (2006) and Port (2006).

realizations across talkers (Peterson & Barney 1952, among others). Indexical variation, and the subsequent lack of constancy, are again easily understandable in an articulatory perspective, by taking into account the individual characteristics of a speaker's vocal apparatus. But even if the production of allophonic and indexical variation is motivated, what about its perception? How do listeners manage to map different acoustic proprieties to a same phonological category? As we said in the introductory pages, the problem of mapping phonetic variation onto phonological discrete categories was faced by postulating the existence of a *normalization* procedure. Using either contextual (Ladefoged & Broadbent 1957) or local (Stevens 1960) cues, indexical and allophonic variation in the incoming phonetic signal is filtered out.

1.2.1.2 Word recognition

The concept of normalization seemed to provide an answer to the mechanisms of speech perception, but it soon became evident that perception of speech could not be reduced to perception of consonant and vowels. For a variety of reasons, in the 1970s researchers' interest shifted from the segmental to the word level (Marslen-Wilson & Welsh 1978). Possible reasons for this reorientation might be traced in the advances in visual word perception (Wheeler 1970; see Balota 1994 for a review), or in the ever growing interest of the linguistic research community in syntactic structures, which are instantiated by words. More probably, it is the intuitiveness of the link between form and meaning at the word level that turned words into the main research object, since it provided a bridge between sound and sense, thus allowing the extension of perception into understanding.[2] This allowed research on word recognition to join ends with issues in how memory storage works, through the notion of mental lexicon (Oldfield 1966).

Different comprehensive models of spoken word recognition appeared in the 1980s, such as *Cohort* (Marslen-Wilson & Tyler 1980) and *Trace* (McClelland & Elman 1986). We will not detail here the structure of these models, which moreover have been (in some cases thoroughly) revised in the last years. What is relevant to our discussion is that they both share the assumption that word recognition is mediated by primitive sub-lexical units (phonemes in *Cohort*, features and phonemes in *Trace*), thus qualifying as abstractionist models of word recognition. Abstractionist approaches assume, at various degrees of explicitness,[3] that words

---

[2] Limitations to the role of features and segments as central level of progressing also came, for example, by studies on the understandability of spectrally rotated speech (Blesser 1972).

[3] See Licklider (1952); Peterson (1952); Lindgren (1965). According to Luce & McLennan (2005), with the exception of Klatt's (1979) model of *Lexical Access From Spectra*, virtually all current

1 Introduction

are represented as separate, abstract and idealized "types" in the mental lexicon, using conventional abstract representational formats built of discrete abstract features or phonemes.

1.2.1.3 Exemplar-based models

As we have seen in the introductory pages, on the other hand, according to exemplar theories the lexicon is built by a myriad of phonetically detailed traces, one for every "token" of spoken words, which are formed as words are repeatedly encountered by the listener in her life-long experience.[4] Exemplar-based approaches to perception of speech are not restricted to word recognition, as Johnson's (1997) early work on vowel perception shows. However, the shift from speech perception to word recognition that we discussed in the previous subsection permitted an easier percolation of new ideas from neighbouring fields. Research on visual word recognition (Tenpenny 1995), in fact, had already assimilated insights from non-analytic cognition (Brooks 1978) and early modelling of episodic memory (Medin & Schaffer 1978). Studies on the computational implementation of this approach flourished in the following decade (McClelland 1981; Hintzman 1986; Nosofsky 1986), and provided in the 1990s a testing ground for exemplar approaches to perception of speech.

The first studies in this direction focussed on memorization of voice in isolated words (Goldinger et al. 1991; Schacter & Church 1992; Palmeri et al. 1993; Church & Schacter 1994; Goldinger 1996). Both explicit (recall) and implicit (priming) memory were tested using both clear and degraded (low-filtered) speech. They found facilitatory effects of known voices, which were accounted for by assuming storage of phonetic information relative to talker identity. That is, against the abstractionist assumptions, indexical variation is retained and participates in word recognition. Exemplar-based explicit models were used by Johnson (1997) to simulate, among others, identification of different vowels across various speakers. Each stored exemplar consisted in vowels extracted from read words and

---

models of spoken word recognition are based on abstractionist assumptions. Accounts of visual word recognition based on distributed models of memory (McClelland & Rumelhart 1985) are labelled by Tenpenny (1995) as *weakly episodic*; this however does not diminish the role of sub-lexical units in *Trace*, on which we base our conclusions.

[4] Accepting that every single experience leaves an individual trace entails assuming that storage capacity for human memory is virtually unlimited. Proponents of exemplar-based approaches cite findings from Standing et al. (1970), showing that subject have surprisingly accurate recall rates (above 90%) of vast amounts of pictures (more than 2500) even with short presentation times (down to 1s) and long test times (3 days). Another line is to assume some kind of information reduction, as in the *Alcove* connectionist exemplar model (Kruschke 1992).

reduced to a set of acoustic features (fundamental frequency, first three formants, duration) linked to a set of category labels (the intended word, the sex and the identity of the speaker).[5] The high correct identification rates show that an exemplar-based model can use indexical variation as a resource for speech perception, thus circumventing the need for normalization procedures.

If indexical detail is included in episodic memory traces, words can be accessed without normalization of sub-lexical units. Words are stored as connections between category labels and detailed acoustic traces, and not as abstract strings of segments. Thus there is no need to recover abstract segments from the signal in order to access the higher level of word processing. In this sense, exemplar-based models suppress the modularity between speech perception and word recognition which is posited by abstractionist models. However, as we suggested at the beginning of this section following Luce et al. (2003), abstract representations filter not only indexical (speaker-dependent) details, but also allophonic (context-dependent) phonetic information. In exemplar-based models, indexical and allophonic variation is handled without substantial differences. The distinction is however crucial in abstractionist approaches, since the treatment of allophonic detail is strictly related to the construction of phonological categories. We take up this issue in the next section.

1.2.2 Phonetic detail

Unlike indexical or speaker-specific variation, treatment of allophonic or context-based variation has always been a core issue in phonology. Inspired by the saussurean emphasis on the differential function of elements within a system, early structuralist phonology stressed paradigmatic relations in the individuation of units. That is, phonemes were intimately linked to the notions of distinctiveness and contrast. The paradigmatic dimension was seen as constitutive, but syntagmatic aspects (pertaining to the linear combination of units) were not excluded from the scope of phonology. Since its structural origins, phonology dealt with both contrast and distribution, with both archiphonemes and, crucially, allophones. This long-term acquaintance with syntagmatic and context-based processes might explain why, when exemplar-based models of perception suggested new ways of handling allophonic and indexical variation, allophonic variation received the greatest share of interest in the linguistic research community. Much

---

[5] Following Nosofsky (1988), stored exemplars are activated on the basis of acoustic similarity with the incoming signal. Similarity is calculated using attention weight and euclidean distances between values of the acoustic features. Activation of exemplars, in turn, yields evidence for the category labels they are associated with, ultimately leading to classification.

1 Introduction

of the recent studies on the so-called *(fine) phonetic detail* deal in fact with phonetic information linked to language-specific rather than speaker-dependent variation. In a very broad sense, phonetic detail could be defined as systematic phonetic variation excluded from abstract phonological representations.

1.2.2.1 Context beyond phonemes in word recognition

By qualifying this variation as *systematic*, we draw a line between language-specific and speaker-dependent variation, as we said above, thus excluding indexical variation from our definition of phonetic detail. However, this does not mean equating phonetic detail with allophonic variability in the sense of Luce et al. (2003). As they put it, quoting Ladefoged (2000), allophonic variation refers to context-induced articulatory and acoustic differences among speech sounds belonging to the same phonemic category. But this definition is only viable when focussing on speech perception and word recognition - that is, when the only functional contrasts under examination are those based on phonemic categories, thus at the lexical level. Decades of research on the structures of conversation, talk-in-interaction and prosody, however, have convincingly shown that "meaning is much more than lexical meaning" (Local 2003b). In this sense, perception of speech does not boil down to accessing meaning through the mental lexicon. Crucially to our discussion, then, context-induced phonetic variation should not be exclusively sought at the phonemic level (allophonic variation), but at all levels of granularity in form and substance, with respect to all systematic functional variation (phonetic detail).

A review of the possible roles of phonetic detail is provided by Hawkins (2003: §5.1). Such phonetic information is systematically produced and, at least "in the right circumstances" (Hawkins 2010) as in the case of adverse listening conditions, used as a cue to the perception of various contrasts. Systematic phonetic variation might cue word boundary placement: [s] duration and possibly degree of diphthongization of the second nucleus help listeners in segmenting the phoneme string /katsaɪz/ as *cat's eyes* or *cat size* (Hawkins & Smith 2001). Differences in periodicity, aperiodicity and voice onset time ratios systematically distinguish prefixes and pseudo-prefixes, as in *discover* versus *discolour* (Smith et al. 2012). Variations in speech rate and in articulatory tension provide a set of devices for turn management (see Local 2003a for a review). Apart from localized phonetic information cueing non-segmental contrasts, phonetic detail might also refer to segmental contrasts cued by diffuse phonetic information. This is the case for the so-called short and long domain r-resonances in English: acoustic differences between pairs like *miller* versus *mirror* are not exclusively localized in the intervocalic portion (Kelly & Local 1986). Moreover, when the intervocalic portion is masked by noise, listeners still manage to make reliable identification judgments (West 1999; Heinrich et al. 2010). Diffuse cues are not restricted to r-resonances: see Hawkins & Nguyen (2004) on voicing of coda obstruents and Coleman (2003) on the feature [anterior]. Phonetic detail might also be linked with frequency of use, as in the case of differences in duration of post-stress schwa before non-wordfinal non-labial sonorants. Words with increasing frequency like *mammary*, *memory* or *every*, thus tend to have progressively shorter schwas (Bybee 2001).[6]

Phonetic detail thus encompasses this broader spectre of phenomena, by relying on an extended vision of allophony, affecting both the definition of context (beyond adjacent phonemes on the segmental string) and domains within perception of speech (beyond lexical meaning in word recognition).

1.2.2.2 Present exclusion from phonological representations

As we suggested in our definition above, this systematic variation must be *excluded* from abstract phonological representations in order to qualify as phonetic detail. The use of a negative definition here should not be mistaken for a theoretical weakness. On the contrary, it has the advantage of suggesting a strict link between our current understanding of phonetic detail and the debate from which it originates. As such, negative features are present in virtually all definitions of phonetic detail (or fine phonetic detail, FPD): for example, "the term FPD has come to be applied to anything that is not considered a major, usually local, perceptual cue for phonemic contrasts in the citation forms of lexical items" (Hawkins 2010), or "FPD refers to phonetic properties that are judged non-essential in the identification of speech sounds in a theoretical framework whose limits the exemplar approach endeavors to demonstrate" (Nguyen et al. 2009). As a result, phonetic detail does not exist in its own right, but only as a mirror reflecting a particular thread of evolution in linguistic thinking: we call phonetic detail all phonetic information which *has been* treated as (negligible) detail in abstractionist approaches, but which *is now* treated as (possibly) useful information in exemplar-based approaches.

Let us push the intrinsic historicity of phonetic detail to its extremes. As we said above, we are looking for phonetic information which can be recognized as useful once we move from an abstractionist to an exemplar-based approach.

---

[6] See Hooper (1976) for a use of "schwa deletion" (the binary version of the durational differences reported above) in the perspective of frequency-based morphophonological change. For a recent review on frequency-based "acoustic reduction", see Ernestus (2014).

1 Introduction

This leaves us with the issue of phonetic information which has already been recognized as systematic and useful within *abstractionist* approaches themselves. To exemplify, the essential phonetic exponents of the phonological contrast in voicing (Trubetzkoy 1939) have initially been identified in vocal fold vibration and low frequency periodicity (Jakobson et al. 1952), on the articulatory and acoustic dimensions, respectively. Focussing on the acoustic dimension and on non-final stops, we could say that at this stage the phonological contrast between voiced and unvoiced is cued by presence or absence of periodicity during closure. However, the exploration of the voicing contrast across different languages (Lisker & Abramson 1964)[7] eventually led to the discovery of a great number of systematically produced and perceived acoustic cues to voicing contrasts (Lisker 1986). If we do not usually consider voice onset time as an example of phonetic detail,[8] it is because it has already been accommodated inside abstractionist approaches to speech perception. This has been done by *enriching* the representation of the phonological contrast in voicing for a given language with phonetic information beyond periodicity during the closure.

As we said above (see Section 1.2.1), abstractionist and exemplar models crucially differ in the degree of phonetic information stored in mental representations. However, finding new systematically produced and perceived phonetic information does not constitute an evidence for the inadequacy of abstractionist approach altogether - it does not prove that abstraction plays no role in perception of speech. At best, discovering new phonetic detail can be seen as evidence for the inadequacy of *currently available* abstractionist models. As we have seen in the introductory pages, the sharp divide between bony phonological categories and rich phonetic signal is not an indisputable matter of fact, but rather a theoretical heritage of early structuralism. As such, it can be questioned when new findings are made available, and in the last years it has indeed been questioned by new developments in phonology.[9] In this sense, the notion of phonetic detail has the merit of fostering research from both abstractionist and exemplar-

---

[7] Languages with three-way stop contrasts were instrumental in drawing researchers' attention on cues other than periodicity during closure. Voice onset time, for example, received perhaps its first formalization in early work on Armenian dialects (Adjarian 1899).

[8] On this topic, see also van Alphen & McQueen (2006). For studies on indexical aspects of voice onset time in an exemplar-based perspective, see Theodore (2009) and Levi & Bruno (2010) instead. However, as we argued at the beginning of this subsection, we are now focussing on (extended) allophonic aspects.

[9] Work in laboratory phonology (Ohala 1990; Pierrehumbert 1990; Pierrehumbert et al. 2000) and inspired by optimality theory (Flemming 1997, 2001) are perhaps the best examples of these new developments.

based perspectives. As Nguyen et al. (2009) point out, sensitivity to phonetic detail is not inconsistent with abstractionist models which allow for richer phonological representation, as in the case of Stevens' (2004) language-specific enhancing gestures or of *Trace*'s interactive account of fine-grained coarticulatory variation (Elman & McClelland 1988). Exemplar-based approaches provide an intrinsic account for the role of phonetic detail, since they assume that all phonetic information is stored in long term memory. Abstractionist approaches, on the other hand, must review the early assumption of minimalism in phonological categories, and permit an *enrichment* with phonetic information previously dismissed as meaningless or predictable variation.

1.2.3 Prosodic detail

From an abstractionist perspective, phonetic detail thus offers a vantage point to explore the relationships between phonetics and phonology. It points to the need of including more phonetic information in phonological representations. But if we see the glass half full, once phonological representations are properly enriched, phonetic detail might even represent evidence for abstraction mechanisms themselves. That is, phonetic detail might point to the need of rich abstract representations, meaning that we need both the enrichment *and* the existence of abstract representations. In the following we exemplify this dynamics by focussing on intonation. We discuss how the exploration of phonetic detail at the prosodic level, while apparently providing evidence against phonological approaches to intonation, could actually lead to their validation and refinement.

As we said above, exemplar-based models posit storage of phonetically detailed traces in long term memory. Phonetic details at the word level, such as r-resonances (Heinrich et al. 2010), voicing of coda obstruents (Hawkins & Nguyen 2004) and durational patterns in prefixed and pseudo-prefixed words (Smith et al. 2012), are stored in the individual acoustic traces associated with those exemplars. We have seen that storage of individual traces at the word level entails virtually unlimited memory capacity. But what about phonetic detail spanning above word level and functioning as cue to non-lexical contrasts, as in the case of variations in speech rate and articulatory tension as devices for turn management (Local 2003a)? Should we conclude that memory provides storage for entire utterances as well? In this case, the "head-filling-up problem" (Johnson 1997) would become simply unsolvable.[10]

---

[10] More importantly, positing memory storage for entire utterances would ultimately mean dismissing the whole lexicon-grammar duality, and pulverizing both paradigmatic and syntag-

1 Introduction

1.2.3.1 An alternative to phonology

Exemplar-based approaches do however allow plausible storage of information beyond words and lexical meaning. First, we could not exclude processing and storage as single units of particular chunks above word level, as in the case of idioms (such as *pull strings*) and collocations (such as *prominent role*) (Bybee 2006). And more importantly to our discussion, since exemplars are supposed to include all sort of detailed phonetic information, they could indeed include not only temporal and spectral information useful in accessing lexical meaning, but also melodic information useful in accessing post-lexical meaning. That is, stored exemplars might contain as well time-aligned fundamental frequency contours, and exemplars of a same word with different f0 information might be linked to different categorical labels referring to informational and pragmatic meaning. Recent research on the effects of word frequency on variability in the production of pitch accents is indeed aimed at verifying this hypothesis (Walsh et al. 2008; Schweitzer et al. 2009, 2010b), and will be extensively reviewed and commented in the concluding remarks (see Section 6.3).

With regard to our present discussion, the strongest form of the theoretical implication behind these studies is the rejection of *post-lexical accounts of prosody* assignment (Schweitzer et al. 2010a, 2011).[11] If not all, most accounts of the relationships between sentence-level meaning (e.g. syntactic chunking, information structure, pragmatic meaning) and phonetic information (mainly fundamental frequency, duration and amplitude) rely on the assumption that the prosodic component in general and intonation in particular can be somehow separated from the lexical material which composes a given utterance, at least on a descriptive level. This assumption is central in those approaches emphasizing the role of phonological structures in prosody (Ladd 2008). The best example is provided by the notion of the independence between tune and text, which permeated from Liberman (1979) through Pierrehumbert (1980) into modern AM approaches to

---

matic dimensions in a myriad of isolated points. Even exemplar-based approaches to grammar as emergent structure refuse to venture this far (Bybee 2001).

[11] More precisely, the authors question the usual assumptions according to which "prosody is 'post-lexical' in English" (Schweitzer et al. 2011: 1), "prosody is assigned 'post-lexically' in English" (ibidem) and "accenting is 'post-lexical' in English" (Schweitzer et al. 2010a: 1), meaning that "prosodic realisation is determined by a combination of 'top-down' syntactic, semantic and pragmatic factors (e.g. given/new status), and the phonological context (e.g. how close together accents are)" (Schweitzer et al. 2011: 4). If *post* in post-lexical is not intended in terms of sequential application of generative transformational rules, we could say that by rejecting post-lexical accounts of prosody the authors essentially question Beckman's (1996) claim that prosody is a grammatical structure to be parsed.

1.2 Prosodic detail

intonation (see Section 1.3.2).[12] However, even in approaches which do not posit the existence of phonological structures in intonation and suggest a direct link between phonetic exponents and sentence-level meaning (a line of research that goes from Cooper & Paccia-Cooper 1980 to Xu 2005), or even more so in the so-called superpositional models of intonation (e.g. Fujisaki & Hirose 1982), intonation is seen as somehow orthogonal to lexical material.

Thus, *both* phonological and phonetic approaches to intonation can posit a post-lexical assignment of prosody. On the other hand, negation is not a symmetrical function in this case: exemplar-based models which reject post-lexical assignment of prosody can *only* allow for a phonetic approach to intonation. If we assume that f0 contours are stored as part of the phonetic information of a given exemplar, and directly linked to categorical labels of informational and pragmatic meaning, we can dismiss altogether the notion of an abstract and discretized level of representation for intonation. There is no longer need for independent and abstract tunes, composed by pitch accents and boundary tones, and embodied in the actual text of an utterance. When a listener is presented with a word, a part of its phonetic information (especially the spectral one) will activate lexical meaning, and another part (especially the melodic) will activate post-lexical meaning. In both cases, for phonemes as for pitch accents, abstractions would be at best a by-product of exemplar activation.

1.2.3.2 A resource for phonology

However, evidence of structures in intonation and thus support for phonological approaches have become overwhelming in the last thirty years (see Ladd 2008: §1.3 for a review). In suggesting the existence of a direct bridge between phonetic information and sentence-level meaning, exemplar-based approaches to prosody might actually represent a step backwards. This does not mean that research on prosodic detail is altogether incompatible with phonological approaches to intonation. As we said above, the intrinsic historicity of the notion of phonetic detail leaves open the possibility of refining abstractionist approaches as well (see Section 1.2.2). By enriching our phonological representation of voicing contrasts, for example, allophonic variation in voice onset time can also be framed in abstractionist terms, without the need of dispensing from the ideas of linearity and discreteness. Acknowledging the existence of multiple phonetic cues to a given phonological contrast has indeed been instrumental in the formulation of new

---

[12] According to which "tunes are linguistic entities, which have independent identity from the text. Tunes and texts cooccur because tunes are lined up with texts by linguistic rules" (Pierrehumbert 1980: 19).

research questions, such as in the investigation of trading relationships between perceptual cues (e.g. Repp 1979). Before dismissing abstractionist assumptions altogether, we might well want to push them to their limits, and see whether they lead to new and possibly interesting research questions.

This is precisely the spirit which animates this book. In the following chapters, we will explore how the study of prosodic detail might be useful in reshaping phonological representations for intonation. Unlike the literature on exemplar prosody we reviewed in the subsection above, we start from the assumption that it is both possible and necessary to posit the existence of abstract phonological structures in the study of intonation. For this reason, we will frame our experiments in an overtly abstractionist model of intonation, the Autosegmental-Metrical framework (see Section 1.3). By gathering evidence on prosodic detail on both the melodic and temporal dimension, we will question some of the strictly minimalist assumptions behind this model, and suggest some improvement strategies where necessary. Our purpose, however, is neither to develop a new abstractionist model of intonation, nor to rule out the viability of alternative exemplar-based approaches. We rather aim at showing how research on phonetic detail at the prosodic level might be a resource in the exploration of the relationships between phonetics and phonology.

1.3 Neapolitan Italian intonation

If prosodic detail is language-specific systematic phonetic variation excluded from phonological representations in current abstractionist intonational models, its exploration requires the choice of at least one language and one model of intonation. In this section we provide some basic information on both the variety we draw our data from, Neapolitan Italian (henceforth *NI*; see Section 1.3.1), and the framework we use to interpret them, the Autosegmental-Metrical one (henceforth *AM*; Section 1.3.2). We conclude with a succinct review of AM studies of NI intonation (see Section 1.3.3).

1.3.1 Neapolitan Italian

In this section we provide our working definition of NI, and motivate the choice of its use in the experimental chapters.

One of the most readable signs of Italy's utterly multi-centric history is with no doubt its extreme linguistic diversification. After centuries of overt and covert normalizing efforts, Italian has developed a fairly unitary physiognomy, but only as far as its written uses are concerned. Spoken Italian, on the other hand, is still today a multifaceted object, characterized by a high degree of diatopic and diastratic variation (De Mauro 1970). Whereas written productions of educated Italians from different regions are virtually indistinguishable, some sort of information on geographic origin is often easily recognizable in the majority of oral productions.

The usefulness (and even the viability) of concept of standard Italian varies along the diamesic dimension: if we exclude the case of professionally trained speakers, spoken Italian is most of the times one of its spoken regional varieties (Bruni 1992). Being nested in a multidimensional repertoire, which in its richest form spans over a continuum between dialect and standard Italian (Sabatini 1985), regional varieties are no monolithic entities either. The diastratic and diaphasic dimensions can account for a part of the variation within regional varieties, by separating the two ends of a "popular" regional varieties of Italian, mainly used by dialect native speakers in contexts which would require the use of a national language, and an "educated" regional variety of Italian, used by Italian native speakers in their everyday exchanges (Sobrero 1992). In the following, we will use Neapolitan Italian with reference to such a regional variety, spoken by educated native Italian speakers born and raised in the area around Naples, and with Neapolitan parents.

The choice of using NI in the experimental chapters stems from three main reasons, one relating to the use of Italian in general, and two to the choice of the Neapolitan variety in particular. First, any regional variety of Italian is particularly suited for research on prosody in general and intonation in particular. Some pragmatic and informational contrasts, in fact, such as the question/statement opposition or focus placement, are conveyed in Italian by prosody alone. Other languages can in this case use morphosyntactic devices, such as question particles or verb inversion for sentence modality contrasts (Dryer 2011), or modal particles for informational highlighting, as in German or Russian (Arndt 1960). The use of Italian allows us to concentrate on the prosodic level alone, with obvious advantages in both the preparation of the experiments and the interpretation of the results.

The educated Neapolitan variety, in particular, was first of all selected because of the presence in the literature of a conspicuous amount of studies on its intonation (see Section 1.3.3 for a brief review), which could have served as a solid base for further investigations. Of course, the intonation of other regional varieties has been extensively studied as well, as in the cases of Palermo (Grice 1995), Bari (Savino 1997) and Pisa (Gili Fivela 2004). The choice of Neapolitan was thus mo-

1 Introduction

tivated by our life-long familiarity with this particular variety, which we thought could prove useful in the exploration of phonetic detail. Purely practical reasons, namely related to the recruitment of subjects and the execution of experiments, motivated the choice of focussing around the educated pole of NI.

1.3.2 The Autosegmental-Metrical framework

As we said above (see Section 1.2.3), the AM theory of intonational phonology is the ideal framework for the exploration of prosodic detail such as we conceive it. In this section we motivate this choice in greater detail, by commenting on some of the basic features of the AM approach which are relevant to our discussion.[13]

Ladd (1996) suggested to qualify as Autosegmental-Metrical the approach to intonation based on Pierrehumbert's (1980) influential work on English. Over the years, the framework has been refined, applied to a variety of languages and used for the development of rule-based synthesis and prosodic transcription systems. Thirty years of polycentric and multifaceted contributions to the model have generated a remarkable amount of discussions and disagreements on some specific points, but have also highlighted the basic tenets shared by individual positions in the general framework. According to Ladd, two of these[14] are *sequential tonal structure* and analysis of pitch accents in terms of *level tones*, and are especially relevant to our discussion.

First, the autosegmental (A) component of the theory suggests that "tonal structure consists of a string of local *events* associated with certain points in the segmental string". That is, tonal structure is deeply bound to the segmental string which actualizes the lexical material, yet it can also be treated as an independent abstract entity.[15] The metrical (M) component of the theory is responsible for the main distinction between such tonal events, according to their association with particular positions in the metrical tree (prominent syllables are docking sites for *pitch accents*) and the prosodic tree (prosodic boundaries are docking sites for *edge tones*). Second, pitch accent and edge tones "can be analyzed as consisting of primitive *level tones* or pitch targets, High (H) and Low (L)". That

---

[13] For a thorough introduction to the AM framework itself, the reader is thus rather referred to Shattuck-Hufnagel & Turk (1996); Gussenhoven (2004); Ladd (1996, 2008).

[14] The others notably being (1) the distinction between pitch accent and stress, and (2) local sources for global trends (Ladd 2008: 44, which is the source for the other quotes in this section, unless otherwise specified).

[15] With all probability, this can be regarded as the basic insight behind the "post-lexical prosody assignment" questioned by the exemplar-based approaches to prosody we discussed above (see Section 1.2.3).

is, AM can be contrasted to both theories which analyze intonation in terms of tonal movements or configurations (see among others Bolinger 1951; Delattre 1966; Isačenko & Schädlich 1970; 't Hart et al. 1990) and to approaches which use multiple level tones (Pike 1945; Wells 1945; Trager & Smith 1951).

Crucially to our discussion on prosodic detail, the analysis of intonation in terms of a sequential structure of two level tones relies on clearly abstractionist assumptions. The very existence of a tonal structure, which can be conceptualized as theoretically independent from the segmental string, is already difficult to reconcile with the idea of purely episodic storage. Moreover, establishing phonological contrasts in AM entails a massive reduction of phonetic information. First of all, although virtually all prosodic phonetic features, that is "acoustic patterns of F0, duration, amplitude, spectral tilt, and segmental reduction" (Shattuck-Hufnagel & Turk 1996), are relevant to intonation in AM, very often fundamental frequency alone is taken as the main exponent of phonological contrasts. This is implicit but evident in the defining features of the AM framework we examined above.

Focussing on *f0* is not the only kind of information reduction operated on the phonetic signal. As we said above, the tonal structure is composed by a string of local events, namely pitch accents and edge tones. However, "between such events the pitch contour is phonologically unspecified and can be described in terms of *transitions* from one event to the next" (Ladd 2008: 44). That is, not only phonetic information is reduced to the pitch contour, but the pitch contour itself is only relevant as far as the tonal events are concerned: *f0* movements between an event and the next do not need to be specified, and can be interpolated by rule. But the process of information reduction can be pushed further. If tonal events, as (tones composing) pitch accents and edge tones, can be analyzed as primitive binary level tones, then we can conceive that "tones are phonetically realised as coordinates on the frequency-time axis" (Grice et al. 2005a). Simplifying to a reasonable extent, their position on the frequency axis will be used to assign the tone to the High or Low category, and its position on the time axis will be used to associate it with a given position in the metrical and prosodic tree, thus defining the type of tonal event.

There is of course a multitude of factors which influence the translation of phonetic information into phonological categories for intonation, and which have been omitted on purpose. The main point we aimed to illustrate is that, through information reduction and discretization, the AM framework enables one to "characterize the notion 'possible prosodic structure' independently of the phonetic details of intonation contours" (Gussenhoven 2004: 123). In this respect, AM represents perhaps the most overtly abstractionist approach to intonation. This is the first consideration that motivated the choice of this particular framework for the exploration of prosodic detail.

The second motivation lies in the fact that AM phonological categories are particularly flexible, and are not incompatible with an enrichment in phonetic specification. Thirty years of intense research have provided evidence for the relevance of phonetic information which was not necessarily accounted for in the original Pierrehumbert's (1980) model, starting from the enrichment of phonetic implementation rules in Pierrehumbert & Beckman (1988). This includes work on phonological contrasts cued by subtle phonetic differences in the scaling or the alignment of tones with respect to the segmental string, or in the shape of $f0$ contours between tones, as we will see in the experimental chapters. By operating on pitch accent inventories, on association mechanisms or on stratifications in the prosodic tree, researchers in the AM framework have developed a rich set of tools for including newly discovered meaningful phonetic information, without resigning the basic tenets of abstraction and discretization in tonal structures. Being both overtly abstractionist and open to the enrichment with phonetic information, AM is thus the ideal starting point for our exploration of prosodic detail.

1.3.3 Neapolitan Italian intonation

Intonational studies specifically focussing on NI began with Maturi (1988), following the phonetic approach of earlier studies on Italian intonation in general (Magno Caldognetto et al. 1978). The adaptation of the basic insights of the AM framework to Italian (Avesani 1990) prepared the rich season of AM studies on NI, which started with Caputo (1994, 1996), Caputo & D'Imperio (1995), and especially D'Imperio (1995, 1997b, 2001, 2003),[16] which established a tonal inventory and highlighted the perceptual importance of peak alignment for sentence modality contrasts. In the following decade, work on NI intonation has focussed on the influence of phonetic variability on lexical access (D'Imperio et al. 2007), phrasing (Petrone & D'Imperio 2008, 2011; D'Imperio & Cangemi 2011) and informational contrasts (Brunetti et al. 2010). Useful syntheses of NI intonation can be found in surveys of different Romance varieties (D'Imperio 2002; Grice et al. 2005b; Prieto et al. 2005). Specific points and controversies in AM accounts of NI will be discussed in the relevant experimental chapters; in this section, we limit

---

[16] See D'Imperio (2000: §2.1) for a review including D'Imperio (1996, 1997a); D'Imperio & House (1997).

ourselves to some broad introductory notions based on work from D'Imperio and colleagues (Grice et al. 2005b; Petrone & D'Imperio 2011; D'Imperio & Cangemi 2011) on sentence modality, focus and contrastive topics.

As for prosodic constituency, NI is claimed to have three domains, tonally marked on their right edge. Apart from the intonational and intermediate phrase, as in the standard AM approach, a smaller domain is said to be relevant for NI, namely the accentual phrase. The intonational phrase seems to be always associated with a L% boundary tone: as acknowledged since Grice (1991), questions in some Italian regional varieties have no final rise (Savino 2012).[17] The intermediate phrase right edge, on the contrary, has been seen as the docking site for multiple contrasts, and has been labelled as L- in statements,[18] HL- in questions (D'Imperio 2001) and !H- in contrastive topic statements (D'Imperio & Cangemi 2011); see Section 2.1.3 for a discussion. Moreover, as we will see in greater detail (Section 3.1), in order to account for the acoustic regularities and the perceptual role of the prenuclear region in sentence modality contrasts, Petrone & D'Imperio (2011) suggested the existence of a third level of phrasing, namely the accentual phrase, whose right edge would be specified as L in statements and H in question.[19]

Unlike the original model for English (Pierrehumbert 1980), AM accounts of NI intonation posit a different inventory for nuclear and non-nuclear pitch accents. This stems from a different understanding of nuclearity itself: the traditional positional interpretation, according to which the nuclear accent is the last accent in the phrase, is compatible with languages such as English, in which postfocal material is deaccented. This is not the case in Italian (Swerts et al. 1999) which thus needs a different interpretation for nuclearity. Grice et al. (2005b: 380) thus "take the Italian nuclear accent to be the rightmost fully-fledged pitch accent in the focussed constituent". Any following tonal event within the same intonation phrase is postnuclear. Accents in postnuclear position are acoustically characterized by a compressed pitch range, and are thus considered as downstepped and transcribed with a preceding ! symbol.

Nuclear pitch accent in statements are labelled as H+L* and L+H* in broad and narrow focus utterances, respectively. This distinction is not relevant for ques-

---

[17] In this sense, observations such as "in all of the varieties it is undisputed that it [i.e. the intonational phrase] has a right peripheral tone which may be high (H%) or low (L%)" (Grice et al. 2005b: 373) must be intended as involving typological rather than exclusively paradigmatic contrasts.

[18] However, it has to be noted that the transcription examples for NI in Grice et al. (2005b), besides always omitting L- before L%, sometimes display HL- for statements as well.

[19] For question accentual phrases labelled as HL, see Petrone & D'Imperio (2008).

1 Introduction

tions, which only have nuclear L*+H pitch accents. The H+L* also appears, downstepped, in postnuclear position in statements,[20] while questions may have a postnuclear (downstepped) H*. The situation for prenuclear accents seems more complicated. Whereas Petrone & D'Imperio (2011), following insights from Prieto et al. (2005), label prenuclear accents as (LH*) in both questions and statements, NI examples in Grice et al. (2005b) show H* in statements, optional L* in questions, and even a L+H* on the first stressed syllable of a long focus constituent in a statement. This specific labelling choice shows that the prenuclear inventory is actually richer than the nuclear one, opposite to what happens in postnuclear position.[21]

As this quick survey shows, phonological descriptions of NI intonation are undergoing constant refinement, and a truly comprehensive account is still work in progress. Nevertheless, the knowledge available in the literature on some specific contrasts can serve as a useful starting point for our exploration of prosodic detail in NI. For the experimental chapters directly concerned with intonation (see Section 1.4.2), the relevant introductory sections (Sections 2.1.3 and 3.1, respectively) will provide more detail about the AM accounts of the contrasts under examination.

1.4 Structure of this book

Our exploration of how the AM framework deals with prosodic detail in NI will rely on four experimental studies of increasing complexity. These will be presented individually in the four next chapters (Sections 2–5) and discussed jointly in the concluding chapter (Section 6). The four experimental chapters can be arranged monodimensionally, that is in a sequence, in the sense that the findings of the last constitute the input for the next. However, they can also be organized bidimensionally, that is as cells in a cross tabulation (see Table 1.1).

As we said above (Section 1.2.2), we conceive prosodic detail as systematically *produced and perceived* phonetic information cueing post-lexical contrasts and excluded from present *abstractionist* accounts of prosody. Thus, as for the first

---

[20] This is actually the only context in which H+L* appears in NI examples in Grice et al. (2005b).
[21] Examples from Grice et al. (2005b) show that, in a specular way, prenuclear accents involving a H tone seem to be realized in a wider pitch range than nuclear accents themselves. This applies both to prenuclear accents within the focussed constituent (and thus labelled with the same pitch accent type as nuclear accents, see Figure 1.2) and outside it (thus labelled differently, notably H* in Figure 1.3). In the light of these examples, the discussion on nuclearity, downstep and pitch accent inventory in NI should not be considered as settled.

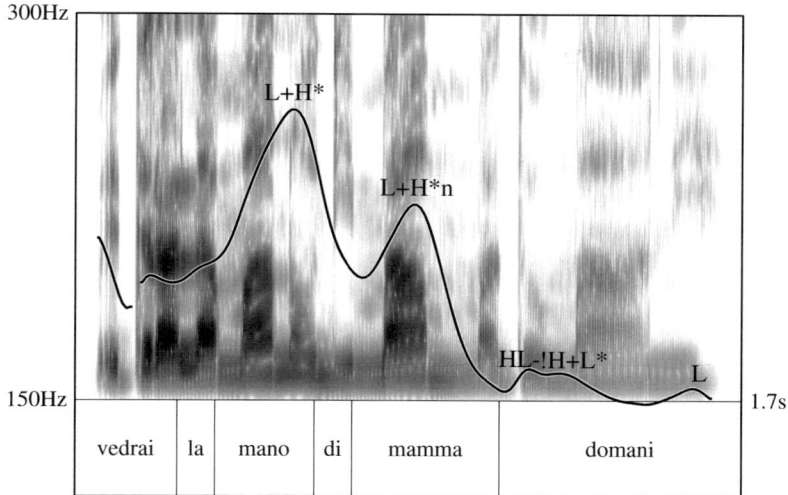

Figure 1.2: The constituent medial fall analyzed as the L component of the narrow focus L+H* accent in Neapolitan. *Vedrai la [MAno di MAMma] domani* 'You'll see [Mom's hand] tomorrow)'. Readapted from Grice et al. 2005b, Figure 13.1, original caption.

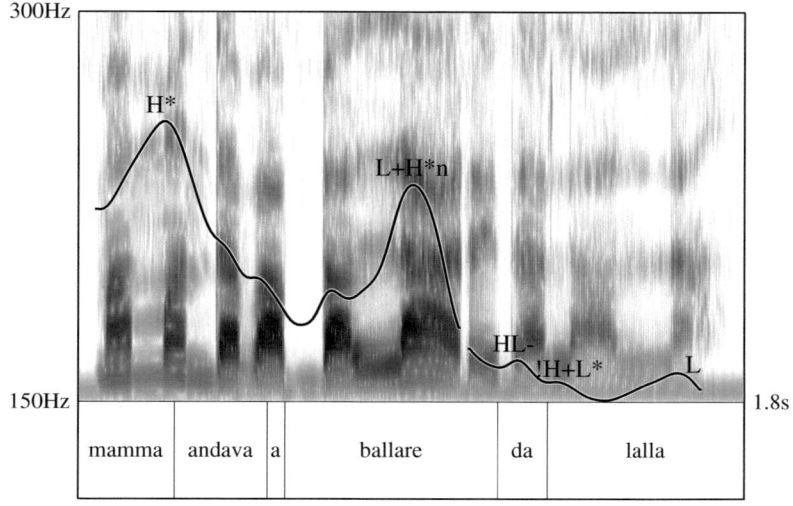

Figure 1.3: Neapolitan: *MAMma andava a [balLAre] da Lalla* 'Mom used to go to [dance] at Lalla's'). Narrow focus declarative with L+H*. Readapted from Grice et al. 2005b, Figure 13.7, original caption.

1 Introduction

Table 1.1: Overview of the experimental chapters.

	Production	Perception
Intonation	Chapter 2	Chapter 3
Tempo	Chapter 4	Chapter 5

dimension of the cross tabulation, prosodic detail must prove relevant in both *production* (Sections 2 and 4) and *perception* (Sections 3 and 5; see Section 1.4.1). The second dimension deals with the phonetic dimensions which undergo information reduction in the framework we chose. As we said above (see Section 1.3.2), in the AM framework phonetic information is pruned twice: first, by concentrating on *f0* contours among the various suprasegmental cues (such as duration, amplitude, spectral tilt, and segmental reduction), and second, by reducing continuous modulations in *f0* contours to sequence of frequency-time coordinates. Our experiments will address both kind of reductions (see Section 1.4.2): we start by testing whether there is systematically produced and perceived phonetic detail which is not captured by the discretization of f0 contours into relevant events and predictable transitions (Sections 2–3; *intonation* in Table 1.1). Then we test whether other phonetic information on dimensions other than *f0* is consistently produced and perceived, focussing in particular on the role of duration (Sections 4–5; *tempo* in Table 1.1) for the reasons we discuss in Sections 1.4.2 and 4. In the rest of the book, the phrases melodic detail and temporal detail will be used to refer to phonetic detail at the prosodic level relating to the intonational and temporal dimensions, respectively, and instantiated acoustically by patterns in *f0* and in duration of linguistic units.

Before turning to the experimental chapters, we comment on some of the methodological choices overarching individual experiments, by grouping them along the two dimensions of the cross tabulations discussed above (Sections 1.4.1–1.4.2), and by providing some brief information on the functional contrasts used in the experiments (Section 1.4.3). The experiments will be followed by a final section in which we summarize our findings (Section 6.1) and group our methodological innovations (Section 6.2) before concluding on prosodic detail and exemplar-based approaches (Section 6.3).

1.4.1 Production and perception

The first remark to be made on the experimental chapters bearing on the acoustic manifestation of prosodic detail[22] is on the nature of the speech material collected and analyzed. While research on phonetic detail in production has used material ranging from highly controlled scripted speech to spontaneous enacted conversations (Beckman 1997), we chose to focus exclusively on read speech.

We agree with Gili Fivela (2008), who points out that controlled and casual speech should both be used in the study of prosody, and that each should complement the other by providing both prospective insights and retrospective validations. Such a virtuous circle, however, could not be set in motion on the study of both production and perception of both melodic and temporal detail without exceeding the frame of a short monography. Our use of read controlled speech should be considered as a mere first step in the exploration of prosodic detail.

As for the evaluation of the perceptual role of prosodic detail, the motivation of our methodological choices require perhaps more elaboration. First, even researchers devoting great efforts to the exploration of phonetic detail acknowledge that "we do not always use available phonetic detail": listeners rather learn about it "when it does not contradict other important cues to communicating meaning" and use it "when it is relevant to the task at hand" (Hawkins 2011: 9). In this context, research striving to prove the importance of phonetic detail has to find the right task and the right cue interaction in order to maximize its visibility. Commenting on this line of research, Nguyen et al. (2009: 8) say that "the goal of current research on FPD is to show that FPD *is* important in speech perception" (original emphasis). As we stated above, our research interests bear on information reduction in phonological accounts of intonation. That is, we are rather interested in *whether* phonetic detail is important in speech perception. Nevertheless, in our perception experiments we will try to maximize the impact of prosodic detail, by suppressing other cues usually available to listeners. It is known for example that indexical variation has a stronger effect in the perception of degraded speech, as in the case of low-pass filtered material (Church & Schacter 1994). In our experiments, this will be achieved by using either excised (Section 3) or resynthesized (Section 5) stimuli.

The experimental tasks used in research on phonetic detail range from identification (West 1999) to word monitoring or word-spotting (Smith & Hawkins 2000), lexical decision (Hawkins & Nguyen 2003) and sentence completion (Heinrich et al. 2010). Given the pragmatic and informational nature of the functional con-

---

[22] Or on its *production*, as said commonly (but perhaps in a not entirely correct way).

1 Introduction

trasts involved in our manipulations, word monitoring and lexical decision could not be used. Heinrich et al. (2010) used sentence completion in order to evaluate the intelligibility of speech in adverse listening conditions and, in turn, the role of r-resonances in building perceptual coherence. That is, the task did not deal with any functional contrast at all. For this reason, the core of our perceptual evaluations will be two-alternative forced-choice identification tasks.

1.4.2 Intonation and tempo

As for information reduction, our experiments will concentrate on the phonological dimensions of intonation (Sections 2–3) and tempo (Sections 4–5). In the first two experiment we will address the reduction of phonetic information relative to fundamental frequency into a discretized string of tonal events, phonetically realized as coordinates along the *f0* and time axes. In an investigation of prosodic detail, this is the natural place to start, since in AM phonetic information relative to transitions between the tonal events is considered as phonologically irrelevant, and derivable by interpolation rules.

Sections 4 and 5 deal with information reduction on a higher level. After dealing with detail along a phonetic dimension which is already taken into account in AM (namely *f0* contours) in the first two experimental chapters, we will shift our attention to phonetic dimensions which are altogether absent in phonological representations bridging phonetic substance and post-lexical meaning. Among these potentially interesting prosodic cues, namely duration, amplitude, (Shattuck-Hufnagel & Turk 1996) spectral tilt and measures of segmental reduction (Ladd 2008) and voice quality (Campbell & Mokhtari 2003), we decided to focus on duration. This is because its effects on post-lexical meaning have been more widely studied (see Section 4.1), and it is more reliably investigated using acoustic data alone, that is the only kind of data which could be collected in our fieldwork sessions in Naples.

The relevant chapters will provide an extensive motivation of our terminological choices (see Section 4 and especially Section 5.1.1), but for the sake of clarity we can anticipate some remarks of our use of duration, tempo, and durational and temporal patterns. We use *duration* in its fairly uncontroversial sense of an acoustic propriety of linguistic units, which can be measured in an absolute way along the time dimension and is usually expressed in milliseconds. However, since "it is not the duration of a single segment but the complex relationships between segment durations that convey information to the listener" (Lyberg 1981), we use *durational patterns* when referring to vectors grouping duration of sub-units inside an overarching unit, as for example in the case of phones within an utterance. In this case, of course, measures can be both absolute and relative to the duration of the overarching unit.

Our use of *tempo*, on the other hand, requires some elaboration. Already in the 1970s, Wood (1973) remarked that terminology in this area was quite uncertain, and that "tempo is not one single, unambiguous concept". However, it is clear that in his account tempo belongs to the conceptual family of measures such as speech rate, rate-of-speech, rate of speech production, speed of talking, talking rate or speaking tempo. Tempo had this meaning since at least Abercrombie (1967), according to which "tempo (speed of speaking) is best measured by rate of syllable succession", and is nowadays prevalently used in this sense (e.g. Trouvain 2004). However, tempo has also been used in another sense which is more adapted to our research interests, notably by Lehiste (1970). In her account of suprasegmental phonetic features and their linguistic function, tempo is seen as the formal dimension bridging durational phonetic information with post-lexical meaning. In this sense, tempo can be contrasted to both intonation (which deals with phonetic information relative to $f0$ contours rather than duration) and length (which deals with lexical rather than post-lexical meaning). In the following, tempo will be used in this particular meaning of a formal phonological dimension which is parallel to intonation, rather than in the more widespread phonetic interpretation consistent for example with Abercrombie's use. It is important to note that this terminological choice seems to entail a particular vision of prosody, in which the temporal dimension is seen as parallel to the intonational one. We stress that we do not commit to this interpretation, and we rather take it as a working hypothesis, which we will actually test in Section 5. That is, we take tempo to design a phonological dimension in order to have the terminological support to formulate the claim that durational differences are phonologically relevant.

As a result, the phrase *temporal patterns* will be used when referring to phonological accounts of phonetic durational patterns spanning over the utterance. In this respect, temporal patterns can be seen as the temporal equivalent of what tunes represent in intonation, namely formal structures which combine primitives into a larger domain. As we said above, however, these terminological choices will be discussed at greater length in the introductory pages of the relevant experimental chapters.

1.4.3 Sentence modality contrasts

Given that our understanding of phonetic detail emphasizes, rather than speaker-specific variation, language-specific variation and thus allophonic detail in its

1 Introduction

broadest sense (see Section 1.2.2), our research on prosodic detail will be based on functional contrasts at the post-lexical level. The majority of our experiments (Sections 4, 5 and 3.3) will use sentence modality contrasts. Sadock & Zwicky (1985) call *sentence type* the "coincidence of grammatical structure and conventional conversational use". By grammatical structures they mean not only specific syntactic constructions, but also "special particles, affixes, word order, intonations, missing elements, or even phonological alterations". The inventory of the possible conventional conversational uses is also very broad, and ranges from making a bet to asking for information or to ordering someone to do something (Lyons 1977). By examining pairs of grammatical structures and conversational uses in 23 languages, Sadock & Zwicky (1985) provide a tentative taxonomy of apparently universal sentence types, grouped in the three macro-classes of declaratives, imperatives and interrogatives. In the following years, the phrase *sentence modality* has been extensively used in prosodic research focussing on a particular contrast between sentence types, namely the one between declaratives and interrogatives which are distinguished through prosody alone. For languages such as Italian, this is the case of the opposition between statements and yes-no questions,[23] as seen above (Section 1.3.1).

Sentence modality contrasts have a sort of privileged status in prosodic research. They have always drawn consistent attention, even before the development of phonological approaches to intonation (Kretschmer 1938, among others), because of the immediacy and the relevance of the functional contrast involved. Other post-lexical functional contrasts expressed by prosody, as in the case of information packaging, are less self-evident and more theory-dependent. That is, whereas segmental phonology is based on lexical contrastiveness, which does not need to be theorized in order to be tested (i.e. lexical contrast is somehow accessible to the epilinguistic conscience of the speaker/listener), research on intonation focusses on the link between prosodic acoustic cues and post-lexical meaning which apparently needs to be structured in a linguistic theory (e.g. sentence semantics, pragmatics, information structure). We will comment on this later on (see Section 2.4.3); for the sake of the present discussion, it is only necessary to say that sentence modality contrasts were used in the majority of the experimental work presented here precisely for this reason. That is, since the investigation of prosodic detail already entails, by definition, the exploration of previously unaccounted phonetic information, we decided at least to concentrate

---

[23] For languages such as English or French, in which statements and yes-no questions can have different morphosyntactic structures, sentence modality contrasts rather oppose statements and so-called "declarative questions".

on the most thoroughly accounted functional contrast (Huddleston 1994; Haan 2002).

The only exception to this general methodological choice is represented by the exploration of the contrast between narrow focus yes-no questions and partial topic statements in Sections 2 and 3.2. Details on the functional aspects of this contrast will be provided in the relevant introductory sections (see especially Section 2.1.3). With respect to the present discussion, the motivation for this choice lies in the extreme substantial (phonetic) similarity between the two contexts, which is in itself an ideal starting point for the exploration of dissimilarities in phonetic detail.

2 Melodic detail in production

An essential ingredient of any phonological account of intonation is the definition of a finite set of units which serve as primitives. The combination of these units into higher level structures is then governed by a grammar which specifies paradigmatic and syntagmatic relationships among those primitives, and yields an abstract representation of well-formed structures. This representation, in turn, serves as the input for the stage of phonetic implementation, ultimately generating an output which is comparable with features extracted from the signal. In the model which served as the basis for the development of the Autosegmental-Metrical (AM) framework (Pierrehumbert 1980: 10), a finite state grammar generates tunes which are composed by sequences of only two tones (the primitives, namely High and Low). Further rules specify the phonetic implementation of the abstract tune, turning a sequence of discrete labels into a continuous representation which can be analyzed in conjunction with fundamental frequency tracks extracted from the signal.

The individuation of a basic inventory of primitives, the specification of the rules governing their selection and combination, and the description of the interface between the phonological and phonetic representation are issues of central interest to every phonological model of intonation, even if the three points can be more or less stressed out in different frameworks. However, these issues are so closely intertwined that drawing a clear line between them is nothing more than a simplifying strategy. Very often, the choices made on a given level end up shaping the account provided for another level. To exemplify, consider Janet Pierrehumbert's early model of English intonation (Pierrehumbert 1980: 29), in which the inventory of primitives is restricted to only two tones, as we said above. Given this highly limited set of primitives, we can expect a high degree of complexity in the grammar providing the rules for their combinations. And indeed we find that the two tones can instantiate different structural positions (i.e. pitch accents, phrase accents, boundary tones) within the tune, and that in some cases one given position can be filled up by a combination of tones (as in the case of bitonal pitch accents). On the other hand, we can expect richer inventories to be matched by simpler grammars. This is the case of Pierre Delattre's account of

French intonation (Delattre 1966), in which the primitives are not two tones but ten tonal movements, quite richly specified, namely with regard to the height of their starting and ending point, and to the shape of the contour between them. In this case, the intonational grammar is essentially reduced to a discussion of the paradigmatic aspects (quite linearly linked with syntactic structure and pragmatic meaning) and of some simple syntagmatic restrictions (as in the case of contextually determined allotony).

Thus, trading relations between richness of inventory and complexity of grammar represent a useful lead when describing and contrasting different phonological models of intonation. It is interesting to note that a very similar conceptual device has been proposed when contrasting abstractionist and exemplar models of speech perception. This opposition can be framed in terms of trading relations between richness of representations and complexity of mapping procedures (Johnson & Mullennix 1997). Under this light, traditional accounts of speech processing would rely on the assumption that listeners derive a "canonical linguistic representation" (thus, a simple representation) through a normalization process (a complex mapping) of the incoming speech signal. The collection of abstract representations of this sort would build up the mental lexicon, in which only linguistically contrastive information is stored. In the alternative view, listeners would store many and highly detailed traces for (or as) individual entries in the mental lexicon (complex representations), and access to category labels and meaning would be mediated by a simple similarity function (simple mapping). The adoption of such an exemplar approach allowed Keith Johnson to propose an account of vowel perception (Johnson 1997) in which speaker normalization is no longer necessary: variability in the signal is not regarded as noise preventing the access to an abstract representation, but is rather seen as a resource for robust categorization.

There is a striking parallel between trading relations in complexity among inventory and grammar (in phonological models of intonation) and among representations and mapping (in models of speech perception). This seemed an ideal starting point for a closer examination of the role of prosodic detail in the AM framework.

2.1 Introduction

2.1.1 Background

In the frame of the AM theory of intonation, phonetic (continuous) *f0* data are translated into a phonological (discretized) tune, composed by the combination of only two tones, labelled as High (H) or Low (L). Intonation contours consist of a string of tonal events linked to the prosodic structure of the sentence: tones can be associated either with prominent syllables (as in the case of pitch accents) or with the edges of various prosodic domains (as in the case of phrase accents and boundary tones). Some tonal events, mainly pitch accents, can phonetically appear as a rise (or a fall) in the *f0* curve. In these cases, they are analyzed as the succession of two tones (L H for rises, H L for falls).[1] In AM, the *f0* path between the two tones which compose a rising pitch accent is not regarded as phonologically relevant. Speech synthesis systems based on this framework (Pierrehumbert 1981; Anderson et al. 1984; Black & Hunt 1996) use a simple monotonic interpolation between the two tones. Nonetheless, data from Neapolitan Italian (D'Imperio et al. 2008) show that, in different pragmatic contexts, the intonation contour of the same segmental string also differs systematically in terms of the *f0* path between the two tones. The curve seems to follow a concave or convex[2] path, depending on the pragmatic context in which the sentences are uttered.

Figure 2.1 displays the spectrogram and the *f0* contour for the sentence in (1) read twice by a female speaker.

(1) Milena lo vuole amaro.
    Milena it wants sour
    'Milena prefers black coffee.'

In the first case (top panel), the sentence is uttered as a statement, while in the second it is uttered as a question (bottom panel). From a phonetic point of view, the most striking difference between the two *f0* contours is visible in the movement associated to the last stressed syllable of the sentence (/'ma/ in *amaro*). In the top panel we find a gradual fall, while in the bottom one we find a slight rise followed by a quite rapid fall. In other words, the local *f0* peak (marked

---

[1] See D'Imperio (1999) for Neapolitan Italian. Similar treatments have been proposed also for Spanish (Hualde 2002; Face 2001) and English (Ladd & Schepman 2003).

[2] Note that, following the common geometrical terminology, the attributes of concave and convex refer to the half-plane *above* the curve, whereas some of the linguistic literature on the topic uses the opposite viewpoint (see Grice et al. 2000; Dombrowski & Niebuhr 2005 for recent examples).

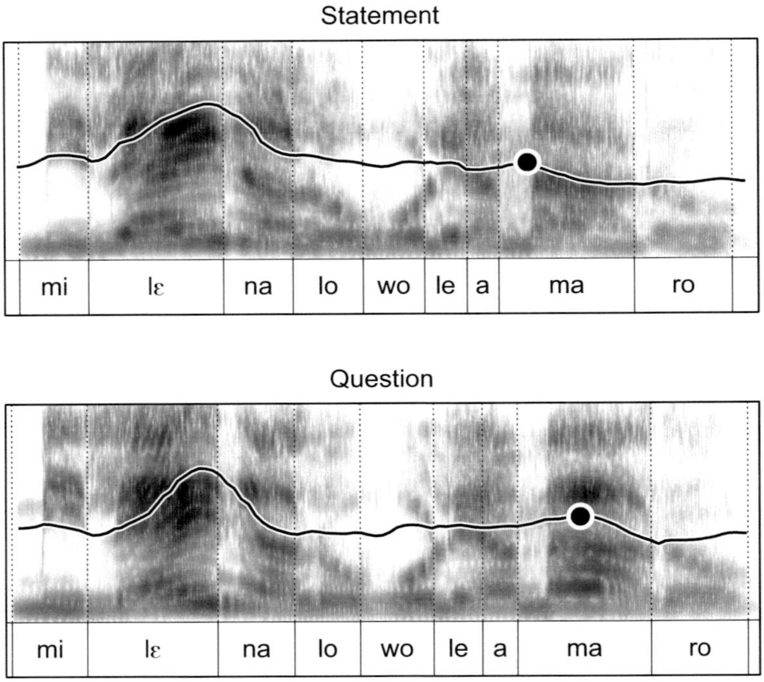

2 Melodic detail in production

Figure 2.1: Spectrogram, *f0* track and phonetic transcription of syllable segmentation of the sentence *Milena lo vuole amaro* uttered as a statement (top panel) and as a question (bottom panel).

with the black circles in the figure) occurs slightly before the vowel onset in the statement, but is found later (vowel-internal) in the question, where it is also visibly higher. Following the usual terminology, the H belonging to the post-nuclear pitch accent is aligned (in time) and scaled (in frequency) differently in the two contexts.

Tone alignment and scaling are the indices usually employed in AM to define the phonetic properties of different phonological units (e.g., of the different tones composing a pitch accent). But if we concentrate on the intonation contour of the first word in the sentence (*Milena*), we notice that the rising movement associated with the stressed syllable has a different shape in the two contexts, namely a concave rise in the statement condition and a convex one in the question (/ˈlɛ/ in *Milena*). This difference, though, does not seem to be related either to the alignment or to the scaling of the two tones: both Ls are in the first half of the stressed syllable onset, and around 225 Hz; both Hs are at the end of the stressed syllable nucleus, and around 350 Hz. Thus, differences in shape of the *f0* contour between the two tones composing the rising pitch accent are not accounted for by the phonetic indices of alignment and scaling employed in AM, and this entails *a fortiori* that shape differences do not play any phonological role in this framework.

In terms of the speech perception models evoked above, we could say that the listener is supposed to ignore the phonetic information provided by the shape of the *f0* contour between tones when categorizing the incoming signal into the different pitch accent options. That is, representations of pitch accents do not include the prosodic detail of interpolation path, which has to be stripped away from the signal during the mapping phase. The autosegmental-metrical model of intonation combines simple primitives using a rich grammar and maps the incoming signal to simplified and underspecified representations, thus qualifying as an overtly abstractionist model. But in this specific case, it appears that the phonetic information retained by the model (scaling and alignment of the tones composing the rise) is less powerful in distinguishing two pragmatic contexts than the information which is discarded (shape of the interpolation between the tones). If shape differences are consistently produced by speakers and consistently used by listeners as a cue to phonological forms with different pragmatic meanings, then the model would need some refinement (by enriching the abstract representations for pitch accents) or even a radical revision (by weakening the abstractionist component).

Building on the results presented in a previous small-scale production study (Cangemi 2009), in this chapter we will compare the traditional AM phonetic indices (namely tone scaling and alignment) with an indicator of contour shape as for their efficacy in discriminating between pragmatic contexts. The analysis of production data will be preceded by a phonological description in AM terms of the materials used in the study (Section 2.1.3), and will be followed by a discussion of the possible impact of our findings on the fine-tuning of the model, in which we will also provide an in-depth review of three studies reporting related findings (Dombrowski & Niebuhr 2005; Petrone & D'Imperio 2008; Petrone & Niebuhr 2014). We will conclude the chapter with a discussion of the role of prosodic detail in the reconfiguration of the relationships between phonetic substance, phonological form and pragmatic function in intonation.

2.1.2 Hypotheses

Before proposing to enrich the description of Neapolitan Italian intonation by adding contour shape information in its phonological representations, we must show that shape differences are consistently produced by speakers and exploited by listeners. The analysis of the perceptual role of contour dynamics (where dynamic refers to properties of $f0$ movements rather than of $f0$ targets) will be postponed to Section 3; in the present chapter we will focus on speakers' productions. Indeed, differences in shape could arise as a by-product of the variation in proprieties of tones which are already traditionally acknowledged, namely their alignment and their scaling. For this reason, our first concern will be to evaluate whether the traditional indices of scaling and alignment are adequate in cueing two different pragmatic contexts. We can prospect four scenarios:

TD: *both traditional and dynamic indices* consistently mirror pragmatic contrasts. In this case, the dynamic index could be deemed redundant, and further elaboration would be pointless.

TX: *traditional indices* mirror pragmatic contrasts, while the dynamic one does not. In this case, observations stemming from the informal analysis of material such as the utterance pair in Figure 2.1 would qualify as statistically aberrant. Again, further elaboration would be pointless.

XD: *dynamic indices* mirror pragmatic contrasts, while the traditional ones do not. In this case, before proceeding to the enrichment of phonological descriptions, a perceptual validation is in order.

XX: *neither traditional nor dynamic indices* mirror pragmatic contrasts. In this case, either the pragmatic contrast is not instantiated in the phonological position under exam (and any further elaboration would be pointless), or a different dynamic index should be tested. A perceptual test could be used to tell apart these two sub-cases.

In what follows, a corpus of read speech will be analyzed in order to find which of these hypotheses is supported. Given the unfortunate condition of a very restricted number of experimental observations available, the operationalization of the hypotheses will be fairly straightforward for this experiment. Indices will be deemed to mirror pragmatic contrasts if the difference between their means across pragmatic conditions is significantly different (see Section 2.3).

2.1.3 Phonological analysis

Though the main concern of this chapter is with the evaluation of phonetic indices to pragmatic contrasts, given the very nature of our investigation a thorough phonological analysis of the materials used in the experiment is in order. Over the last decade, NI intonation has been fruitfully studied using the AM framework: both broad surveys and in-depth studies are available to the reader (see Section 1.3.3). Since the original framework was tailored on the specificities of American English intonation, its adaptation to NI required a conspicuous effort and was achieved through the introduction of various more or less innovative features. While a detailed account of the history of these innovations clearly falls outside the scope of this paragraph, we will motivate the main non-standard interpretative devices used in the phonological analyses that follow.

2.1.3.1 Pragmatic contexts

Figure 2.2 shows the *f0* track of the two utterances already displayed in Figure 2.1, along with a tonal labelling. In the first case (top panel), the target sentence in (3) was uttered as an answer to the question in (2). This means that the pragmatic interpretation of the sentence is supposed to be that of a Partial Topic (Büring 1997), namely the one in (4).

(2) *Come lo bevono il caffè i tuoi amici?*[3]
    how it drink the coffee the your friends
    'How do your friends like their coffee?'

---

[3] The non Neapolitan reader should keep in mind that coffee in Naples is often served already mixed with a sugar-based foam, and that in some cases this is even the "unmarked" option. Polite bartenders and hosts, however, are always supposed to ask for a confirmation before serving coffee.

2 Melodic detail in production

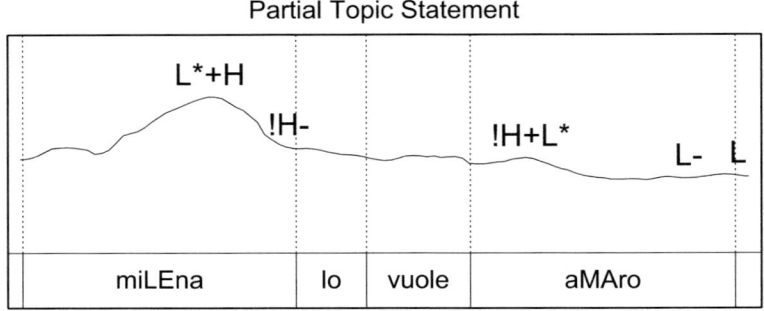

Figure 2.2: Intonation analysis and word segmentation of the sentence *Milena lo vuole amaro* uttered as a partial topic statement (top panel) and as a subject narrow focus question (bottom panel). Capital letters indicate syllables associated with a pitch accent.

(3) *Milena lo vuole amaro.*
    Milena it wants sour
    'Milena drinks it black.'

(4) *Milena lo vuole amaro gli altri   non saprei.*
    Milena it wants sour   the others not know.COND.1SG
    'As for Milena, she drinks it black; as for the others, I wouldn't know.'

The new information in the answer ("black coffee") can be retrieved by analyzing the question, which explicitly puts in discussion how the coffee should be served. However, the answer elaborates on the given information as well: among the original set put forth as the topic of the question ("your friends"), the speaker elects a single element ("Milena") as the subject of the predication. The topic in the answer is thus a subset of the topic in the question: for this reason, in the following we will refer to this context as Partial Topic Statement (henceforth *SPT*).

The other utterance (Figure 2.2, bottom panel) is labelled as Narrow Focus Question (henceforth *QNF*): in this case, the sentence is imagined to fit in a context where the speaker is serving coffee and remembers that one of his guests (possibly Milena) takes no sugar, and then asks whether she is indeed the one who has to be served black coffee. We will come back to the nature of this pragmatic contrast in the discussion of the link between post-lexical meaning and intonational contrasts (see Section 2.4.3).

2.1.3.2 Pitch accents

Two of the stressed syllables in the utterances bear a pitch accent, namely the penultimate in *Milena* and in *amaro*. The first pitch accent in both utterances is nuclear, in the sense that it falls on the rightmost (here, the only) stressed syllable of the focussed constituent (Grice et al. 2005b: 380). This definition applies in a straightforward way to the QNF context, in which the Subject (*Milena*) is indeed focussed. In the SPT context, however, the Subject is not focussed, but is rather interpretable as a contrastive or partial topic. Since partial topics have been shown to trigger post-accentual compression (D'Imperio & Cangemi 2011), they can also be considered as nuclear, and for this reason the pitch accent on *amaro* can be deemed to be post-nuclear and transcribed in both cases using a diacritic for range compression (!). This latter pitch accent is different in the two utterances: according to Grice et al. (2005b), we use H+L* for the statement and H* for the question; this contrast accounts for the phonetic differences in the

2 Melodic detail in production

scaling and alignment of the high turning point, which were already discussed above (Section 2.1).

As for the first pitch accent, the choice of using the label L*+H for both utterances is consistent with the null hypothesis that shape differences do *not* participate in the specification of pitch accents, are not contrastive and can not justify the use of two different labels. For these reasons, according to D'Imperio et al. (2008), the only paradigmatic choices available in this position would be LH* for the non-contrastive topic rise, L+H* for the focussed statement rise and L*+H for the focussed question rise. Given that the assessment of the phonological status of this rising pitch accent in partial topic statements is one of the main aims of this chapter, we believe that when deciding upon this working hypothesis transcription the safest choice is to rely on the phonetic similarity between pitch accents. For this reason, given the scaling and alignment properties of both tones composing the rise, the nuclear accent in partial topic statements will also be labelled as L*+H at this stage.

2.1.3.3 Edge tones and phrasing

Unlike many languages, NI does not mark questions with an high boundary tone, as in the case of many Italian regional varieties (Savino 2012). This accounts for the (mainly phonetic) transcription of L% for both the question and statement; the same holds for the immediately preceding L- phrase accent.

More importantly, both utterances can be analyzed as an intonational phrase composed by two intermediate phrases, namely [(*Milena*)(*lo vuole amaro*)]. The phrase break after the Subject is expected in the case of the narrow focus question, where the Subject is coextensive with the focus domain. For this same reason, the break would not be expected in broad focus questions (D'Imperio et al. 2005; Frota et al. 2007), nor in non contrastive topic statement, as in the answer to the question in (5):

(5) *Milena come lo vuole il   caffè?*
     Milena how it wants the coffee
     'How does Milena drink her coffee?'

However, after the Subject in partial topic utterances we find a strong degree of *f0* compression (D'Imperio & Cangemi 2011), and in some utterance even a short pause; for these reasons, we assume that there is indeed a phrase accent after the subject in both context, which we label HL- in the case of the narrow focus question, following D'Imperio (2002) and !H- in the case of the partial topic statement, following D'Imperio & Cangemi (2011); see Section 1.3.3.

2.2 Method

2.2.1 Corpus

For our study we used a subset of the corpus *Tre Grazie*, first described in D'Imperio et al. (2008). Nine native speakers of NI read 60 experimental stimuli and 38 fillers in a silent room. The stimuli consisted of 5 repetitions of 3 sentences designed without voiceless plosives, which were semantically plausible and syntactically quite similar (6–8):

(6) *Amelia dorme da nonna.*
    Amelia sleeps at grandma
    'Amelia sleeps at grandma's.'

(7) *Valeria viene alle nove.*
    Valeria arrives at nine
    'Valeria arrives at 9.'

(8) *Milena lo vuole amaro.*
    Milena it wants sour
    'Milena drinks it black.'

Target words were all feminine proper names (hence the corpus' name), agents, subjects, trisyllabic, with penultimate stress, the same syllabic structure for the tonic syllable (.CV.) and the same quality for its nucleus (/ɛ/), while a greater flexibility was allowed for unstressed syllable structure (post-stressed .CCV in *Valeria*, joined by pre-stressed V. in *Amelia*). Sentences were presented together with a contextualization paragraph, which had to be read silently; this made possible the elicitation of every sentence with four different pragmatic meanings. For example, the sentence in (8) would be interpreted and uttered by speakers as a QNF with the meaning of (9b) if preceded by the context in (9a):

(9) a. After a family lunch, you're preparing coffee. You know that one of your cousins is on a diet and stays away from sugar, but you don't remember which one. You ask your aunt:...
    b. Is it Milena, the one who drinks unsweetened coffee?

On the other hand, sentences preceded by the context in (10a) would be interpreted and uttered as a SPT, with the meaning of (10b):

2 Melodic detail in production

(10) a. In the afternoon, among friends, your brother is preparing coffee. He asks you whether your friends would like it sweetened or not. You don't know everybody's preferences, but only your girlfriend's. You answer:...

b. As for Milena, she drinks it unsweetened; as for the others, I couldn't tell.

Other contextualization paragraphs prompted a Broad Focus Statement and a Narrow Focus Statement interpretation. In the first case, all the information in the utterance was intended to be new; in the second, the utterance was intended as a statement where the speaker corrects the interlocutor's beliefs about who asked for black coffee (i.e., Narrow Focus is on the Subject).

Given the poor quality of some of the recordings and the focussing on the pitch accents with similar alignment and scaling proprieties for the two tones composing the rise, the experimental material retained for this study consisted of 2 subjects x 3 sentences x 2 pragmatic contexts (QNF and SPT) x 5 repetitions = 60 items total.

2.2.2 Measures

Target words were manually labelled in syllables using a scripted procedure under *Praat* (Boersma & Weenink 2008). The stressed syllable, which always had a CV structure, was also labelled in segments: the labels were *Os* for the beginning of the onset (and of the entire syllable), *Ns* for the beginning of the nucleus (or the end of the onset) and *Ne* for the end of the nucleus (and of the entire syllable).[4]

The rising *f0* movement in the stressed syllable was characterized by measuring the height (in Hz) and the position in time of its starting and ending points (L and H).[5] Hs were automatically located at *f0* maxima inside the stressed vowels, while the detection of Ls proved more challenging, as could be expected (Del Giudice et al. 2007; Petrone & D'Imperio 2009). A widely used automatic procedure is based on the detection of the local minima in the stressed syllable onset, but we found this method too sensitive to microprosodic perturbations at the consonant-vowel boundary. We determined that another strategy for the detection of Ls, the two-lines regression or Least Square Fitting algorithm, used for example in D'Imperio (2000: 92-93), was not suited for our goals either.

---

[4] See Figure 2.3: *Os*, *Ns* and *Ne* on x-axis.
[5] See Figure 2.3: *y(L)* and *y(H)* on y-axis for height (scaling), and *x(L)* and *x(H)* on x-axis for position (alignment).

2.2 Method

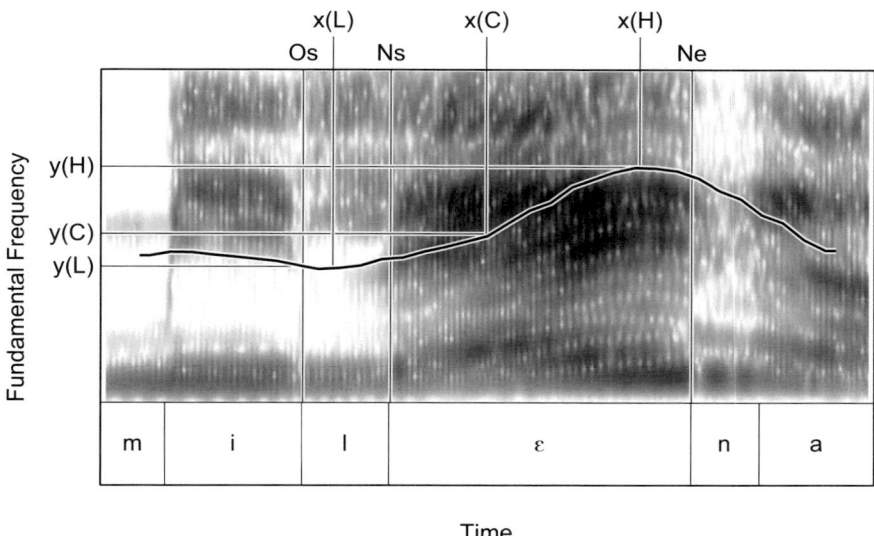

Figure 2.3: Example of acoustic measures.

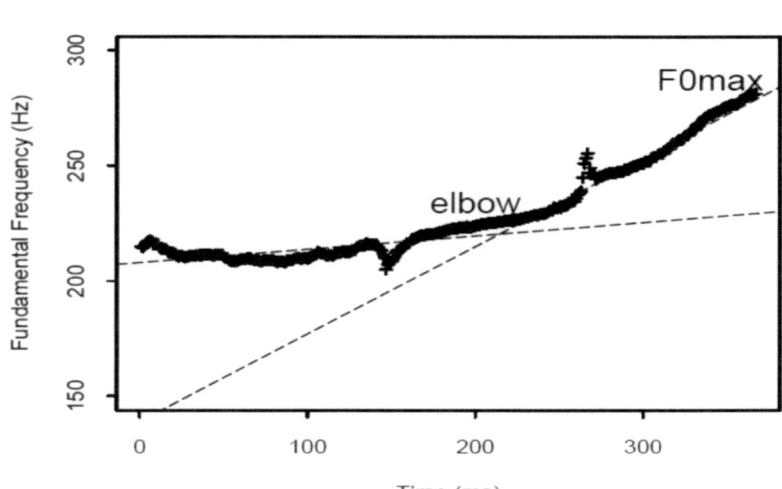

Figure 2.4: Two-line fitting (from D'Imperio 2000: 95).

2 Melodic detail in production

With this technique, the region in which the L must be found (in our case, the *f0* stretch from utterance start to H) is divided into steps. For each point, two straight lines are fitted with a linear regression to the contour on its left and on its right. The time of the L is chosen as the point associated with the pair of lines leading to the smallest modelling error. Since the differences between a concave and a convex rise have consequences on modelling and errors, the algorithm often locates Ls away from the point in which the *f0* curve visibly bends upwards (the *elbow*). Concave shapes tend to be associated to an L on the left of the elbow, and for convex ones the L is detected on its right. This means of course that we would still have an index to express our differences in interpolation, but in this case the information is conveyed in an implicit and indirect way: different shapes are translated into different position of a same tonal target. We decided to use a method which would ignore the specifically local features of the *f0* contour (such as microprosodic minima) and at the same time avoid the implicit encoding of the global proprieties we were trying to characterize explicitly (as in the case of the two lines regression). Trying to find a compromise between these two constraints, which ultimately means to find a compromise in the size of the analysis window, we decided to locate the elbows at the point of maximal acceleration of the curve. Through the elaboration of an automated procedure in *R* (R Development Core Team 2008), the L was located by inspecting the *f0* second derivative, looking for sufficiently wide local maxima.

Although the L detection procedure is innovative, height and position of tone targets remain traditional measures. Besides these, we also calculated the height of the mid-point in time between L and H (C).[6] This allowed us to calculate an index (based on Dombrowski & Niebuhr 2005) which could express the type of interpolation between the two targets in a simple and explicit way; see Section 2.2.3.

In conclusion, for every experimental item we measured the coordinates of L, C and H in the (time, *f0*) plane.

2.2.3 Indices

We used these coordinates to calculate various indices (see Table 2.1), which had to be compared as for their reliability in discriminating our two pragmatic contexts. In addition to the traditional indexes of scaling (height of L and H) and alignment (distance of L and H from both start and end of, respectively, stressed syllable onset and nucleus), we calculated a Curve Index (*Ci*), expressed as the

---

[6] See Figure 2.3: *y(C)* on y-axis.

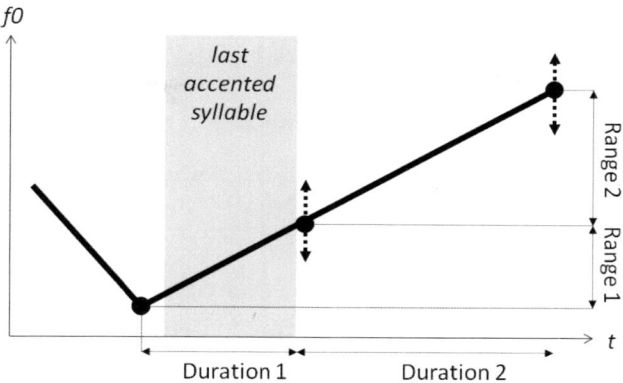

Figure 2.5: Range proportion (readapted from Dombrowski & Niebuhr (2005: Figure 3)).

ratio of the difference between the heights of the intermediate and the starting points, and the difference between the heights of the end and starting points of the rise:

$$Ci = \frac{y(C)-y(L)}{y(H)-y(L)}$$

This index is reminiscent of the Range Proportion (*Rp*), used by Dombrowski & Niebuhr (2005) to characterize phonetic variation of phrase-final rises in German task-oriented dialogues (see Figure 2.5 and Section 2.4.1).

Shape differences in these rises are calculated by dividing the extent of the rise within the stressed syllable by the extent of the rise up to the prosodic phrase boundary. In terms of the labels used in Figure 2.5, this means:

$$Rp = \frac{range1}{range1+range2}$$

The main difference between range proportion and curve index resides in the fact that the pivot used for the calculation of the curve index is constantly located at the midpoint in time between the Low and the High tone (Figure 2.3), while for the calculation of the range proportion the pivot can move to the left or to the right of the midpoint, according to the position of the stressed syllable right boundary (Figure 2.5). Given the nature of their semi-spontaneous corpus, in which the lexical material associated with the phrase-final rises is not controlled neither in quality (syllable structure) nor in quantity (of poststressed syllables), the choice of a moving pivot in Dombrowski and Niebuhr's study is justified.

2 Melodic detail in production

However, since in our read corpus the target words are strictly controlled, we considered that a tighter definition of pivot location could be easily enforced.

Table 2.1: Indices

Index	Description	Formula
sL	L scaling	$y(L)$
aLs	L alignment to start of stressed vowel onset	$x(L) - Os$
aLe	L alignment to end of stressed vowel onset	$Ns - x(L)$
sH	H scaling	$y(H)$
aHs	H alignment to start of stressed vowel nucleus	$x(H) - Ns$
aHe	H alignment to end of stressed vowel nucleus	$Ne - x(H)$
sC	C (intermediate point in time between L and H) scaling	$y(C)$
Ci	Curve index	$\frac{y(C)-y(L)}{y(H)-y(L)}$

2.3 Results

In this section we plot the distributions of the eight phonetic indices in the two pragmatic contexts for the two speakers. In Figures 2.6–2.8, columns report data for the two speakers (WP, female, and MB, male) and rows for the indices. The labels used for the indices (on the y-axis) correspond to those used in Table 2.1. Each individual plot shows the distribution of an individual index for an individual speaker, separating the two pragmatic contexts (QNF, narrow focus question, and SPT, partial topic statement).

Given the limited amount of data, for the calculation of statistical significance we restrain to two-sample Welch-Satterthwaite t-test. In the absence of inferable biases, the tests were two-tailed. Since data on *f0* height cannot be pooled across our speakers (a male and a female), for uniformity's sake we will split results for alignment as well. Results were pooled across the three sentences and the five repetition of each sentence. Each boxplot thus shows 15 observations.

2.3.1 Alignment

Figure 2.6 shows data on alignment of the High tone target relative to the vowel in the stressed syllable (e.g. [ɛ] in the case of *Milena*) and of the Low tone relative to its consonant (e.g. [l] in the same case). Since a preliminary exploration of the data showed that the two tonal targets co-occur with the relative segments, latencies were calculated either by subtracting the startpoint of the Segment (Ss) to the timepoint of the Tone (Tt) or by subtracting the timepoint of the Tone to the endpoint of the Segment (Se): $aTs = Tt - Ss$ and $aTe = Se - Tt$.

For both High and Low tones the alignment measures, either to the beginning or from the end of the relevant segment, failed to reliably differentiate between the two pragmatic contexts. As for Hs, the smallest p was above 0.1 (aHe for speaker MB), while for Ls it was above 0.15 (aLe for speaker WP). Data dispersion around the median appeared to be slightly more compact for questions in both speakers, but the effect was not statistically significant. Hence, tonal alignment does appear to differentiate between partial topic statements and narrow focus questions in NI.

2.3.2 Scaling

As for tone scaling (Figure 2.7), on the other hand, only one plot shows non significant results, namely Hs for speaker WP ($p>0.3$). The three other comparisons show a significant difference between the two pragmatic contexts ($p<0.01$). However, in one case (Ls for speaker MB) the difference was significant but very small: the mean L height is 92 Hz in questions and 97 Hz in statements. Moreover, this 5 Hz difference always fell inside a consonant, and usually very near to a segmental boundary, as the positive latencies for alignment in Figure 2.6 (two last left panels) show, thus allowing us to infer that its perceptual role is negligible (House 1990).

As for the two other statistically significant and perceptually relevant comparisons, statements show a higher H tone for speaker MB and a higher L tone for speaker WP. That is, tone scaling information is useful in indicating that both speakers use different $f0$ movements in the two pragmatic conditions, but does not yield a unified picture of how these $f0$ movements should be characterized.

2.3.3 Shape

The indices focussing on contour dynamics show a different picture (Figure 2.8). All comparisons were statistically highly significant (highest p is 0.033). Data on scaling, which is perceptually more easily interpretable, show that mean differences between midpoint height (sC) in questions and statement was above 40 Hz for speaker WP (female) and above 15 Hz for speaker MB (male). This latter difference can be considered as quite relevant, since speaker MB uses a very narrow pitch span: mean L to H excursion for this speaker is around 40 Hz (compare

2 Melodic detail in production

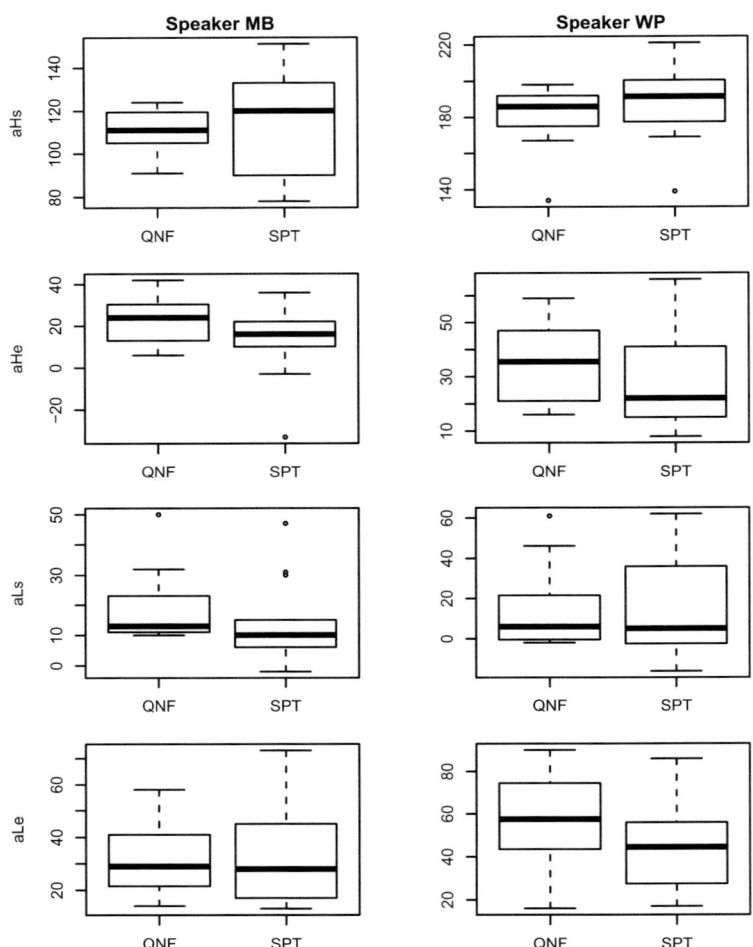

Figure 2.6: Latencies (ms) from H to vowel onset (first row) and offset (second row), and from L to consonant onset (third row) and offset (fourth row) in stressed syllable.

with a mean excursion of 135 Hz for speaker WP). In relative terms, the differences in C scaling among questions and statements was actually more salient in speaker MB.

Differences in the curve index (*Ci*) might be less straightforward to interpret in perceptual terms than differences in C scaling, but they have at least two advantages. First of all, being a ratio of differences, they do not need any further transformation in order to yield comparable data for speakers with very different pitch spans and ranges. Moreover, differences in curve index can be quite easily interpreted in geometrical terms: a value of 0.5 would indicate a linear interpolation, while values above or below 0.5 would indicate concave and convex rises, respectively. In our data, curve index differences are significant for both speakers. The *f0* rise between the L and the H composing the nuclear pitch accent is less concave in QNF contexts (mean *Ci*: 0.52 for MB, 0.35 for WP) and less convex in SPT contexts (mean *Ci*: 0.60 for MB, 0.52 for WP). Thus, even with some individual differences in level and span of curve index variation, we can conclude that speakers tend to show a convex interpolation in questions and to a concave interpolation in statements.

2.3.4 Summary of results

Among the four scenarios prospected in Section 2.1.2 our results support the third, namely that dynamic indices mirror the pragmatic contrast between narrow focus questions and partial topic statements, while the traditional indices of tone scaling and alignment do not.

No significant alignment differences could be found in our corpus, neither for High nor for Low tones, independent of the boundary (left or right) of the relevant segment in the stressed syllable (consonant for Ls, vowel for Hs). Tone scaling appears to be different in the two contexts, but differences are not consistent across speakers: partial topic statements are characterized by higher H tones for speaker MB and higher L tones for speaker WP. Thus, scaling does not qualify as a viable index to our pragmatic contrast. Dynamic indexes, on the other hand, proved robust: both speakers showed a statistically significant tendency to a concave interpolation in statements and to a convex interpolation in questions.

2 Melodic detail in production

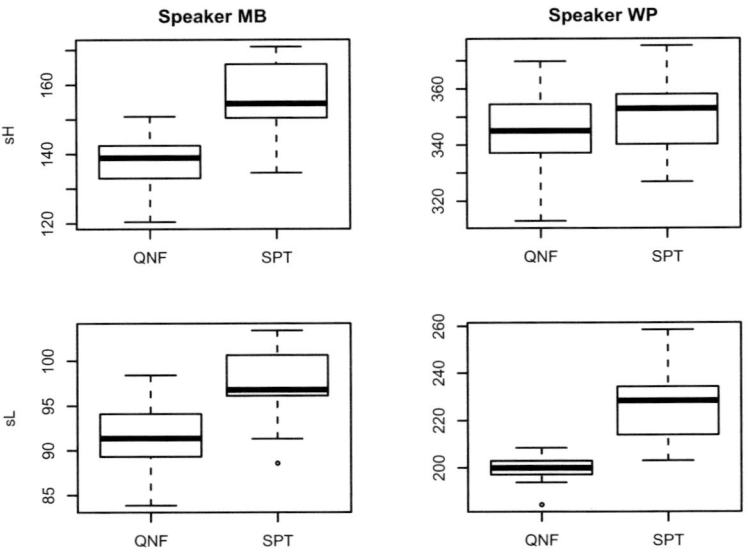

Figure 2.7: Height (Hz) of High (first row) and Low (second row) tonal target.

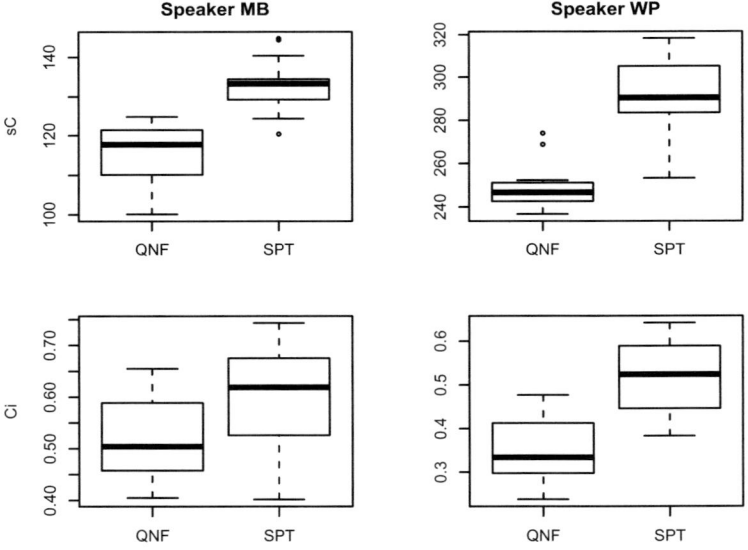

Figure 2.8: Height (Hz) of midpoint between L and H (first row) and curve index (second row).

2.4 Discussion

In our study, dynamic indices appear to be more consistent than scaling and alignment in mirroring the pragmatic contrast between partial topic statements and narrow focus questions. This finding underlines a potential loss of useful phonetic information in the abstraction procedure that maps signal onto discrete phonological categories in the AM framework. In this paragraph we will develop this line of thought, by discussing in some detail three other studies as they report previously unaccounted prosodic detail (Section 2.4.1) and prospect different avenues to the enrichment of phonological representations for intonation Section 2.4.2.

2.4.1 Contour shape in other contrasts

In order to decide whether shape information is a necessary enrichment to phonological representations of intonation, we must evaluate the scope of contrasts which can be expressed exclusively (or more robustly) by dynamic information.[7] In this experiment we focussed on only one pragmatic contrast, namely the one between narrow focus question and partial topic statement, but recent work on both Italian (D'Imperio 2000; Petrone & D'Imperio 2008) and German (Dombrowski & Niebuhr 2005; Petrone & Niebuhr 2014) shows that contour shape could be relevant for other contrasts as well. Interestingly, these studies focus on acoustic and functional differences in structural positions other than the nuclear pitch accents we analyzed in this chapter.

2.4.1.1 Turn management and utterance final rises in German

In their exploration of the dialogue section of the Kiel Corpus of Read and Spontaneous Speech (Institut für Phonetik und digitale Sprachverarbeitung 1994 and following), for example, Dombrowski & Niebuhr focus on phrase-final rises. They show that a given phonological entity, analyzed as an *early valley* in terms of the Kiel Intonation Model (henceforth *KIM*; see Kohler 1991), displays a consistent phonetic variation which is best analyzed in terms of dynamic proprieties (viz. convexity or concavity of the rise), and that those phonetic variants correlate with two opposite conversational functions (viz. activation or restriction of the

---

[7] This is not to say that the role of dynamic phonetic detail in $f0$ contours has to be reduced to phonological contrastiveness in itself. Recent studies are exploring the interspeaker variability in signalling phonological contrasts, showing that speakers might use different strategies which rely more or less strongly on dynamic cues; see Niebuhr et al. (2011).

2 Melodic detail in production

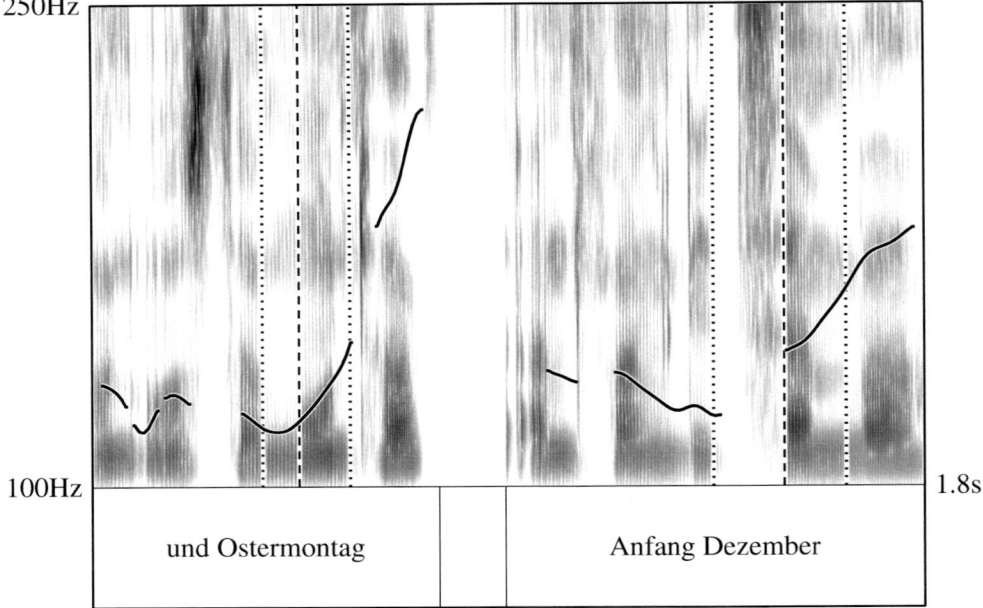

Figure 2.9: Activating (left) and restricting (right) final rises (readapted from Dombrowski & Niebuhr 2005: Figure 1). Dotted vertical lines delimit the accented syllables, dashed vertical lines indicate the accented-vowel onsets.

interlocutor). Their corpus consisted in task-oriented dialogues in which out of sight participants had to collaborate in scheduling meetings and events; the speakers had access to different sets of partial information and, crucially, they had to press (and hold) a button near to their individual microphones in order to activate their interlocutor's headphones. This permitted to avoid overlaps, since only one participant at a time was allowed to talk, but more importantly it served as an objectivation of speakers' intentions of turn-yielding (activation) or turn-holding (restriction of the interlocutor). Figure 2.9 shows an example of a convex rise in a turn-yielding condition (left panel) and a concave rise in a turn-holding condition (right panel).[8]

---

[8] Note that in the original paper, contrary to the common geometrical interpretation used in this book, the attributes of concavity and convexity are assigned to the half-plane *below* the curve.

2.4 Discussion

As we already pointed out (see Section 2.2.3), their phonetic analyses of contour shapes must have been made quite difficult by the lack of control of the number of poststressed syllables and of the syllable structure and, as Figure 2.9 shows, of voicing throughout the syllable. Figure 2.9 also shows that, in contrast with our results on Neapolitan Italian nuclear rises, the functional contrast could also be mirrored by alignment and scaling of both rise start- and endpoint, at least for this particular pair of utterances. However, a discriminant analysis showed that the highest correct classification results are achieved when the shape of the rise is the most important predictor.

2.4.1.2 Modality and prenuclear fall in Italian and German

Contour shape thus appears to be relevant in *nuclear rises*, both utterance internal (as we have seen in this chapter) and utterance final (as we have seen in the previous section), signalling different pragmatic or conversational contrasts, and in more than one language. In this section we review two studies focussing on the role of contour shape in *prenuclear falls*, respectively in Neapolitan Italian and in Northern Standard German.

Differences in the shape of postnuclear *f0* fall for Neapolitan Italian read speech are connected with sentence modality contrasts in Petrone & D'Imperio (2008). Figure 2.10 shows two utterances (as a statement, top panel and as a question, bottom panel) of the sentence in (11), both with narrow focus on the object.

(11) La   mamma vuole vedere la   Bina.
      the mother wants see   the Bina
      'Mom wants to meet Bina.'

The nuclear accent thus falls on the last stressed syllable ('bi.na), and is labelled as L+H* for the statement and as L*+H for the rise. The prenuclear accent, on the first stressed syllable ('mam.ma), is labelled in both cases as (L)H*, following Gili Fivela & D'Imperio (2003); Gili Fivela (2006). Its rising portion seems to have the same acoustic properties in both contexts; the fall, on the other hand, clearly follows different paths.

The first half of the tonal stretch between H_p and L_n can be characterized as convex in the statement and concave in the question. Statistical analyses based on different kinds of regression confirmed the significance of these differences. However, it should be noted that, as in the case of the German activating and restricting contours, alignment and scaling of the tones at both ends of the relevant *f0* stretch are also significantly different in the two contexts: for one of the

2 Melodic detail in production

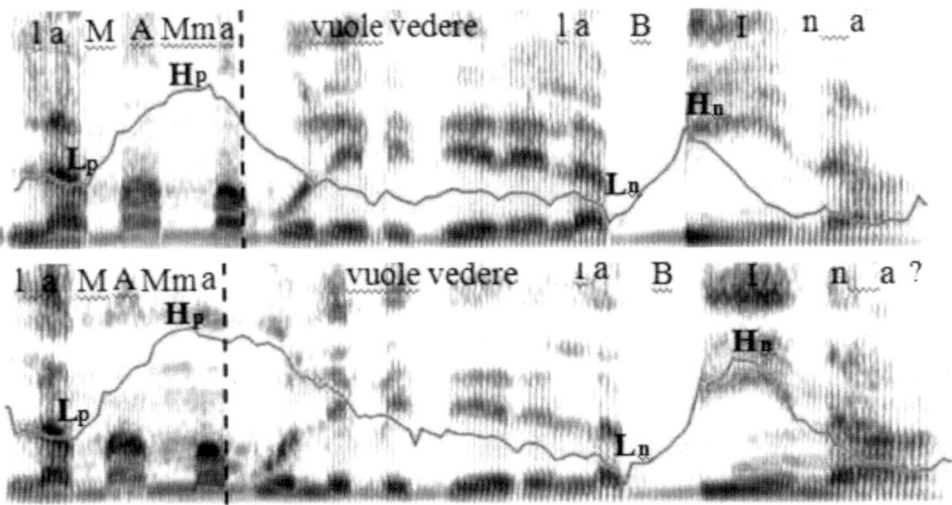

Figure 2.10: *f0* contours for (object) narrow focus statement (upper panel) and question (lower panel) utterances of a same sentence (from Petrone & D'Imperio 2008: Figure 1). Capital letters indicate the stressed syllables; tone targets for prenuclear and nuclear pitch accents are labelled with a subscript *p* and *n*, respectively.

two speakers, for example, the endpoint of the prenuclear rise (H_p) is aligned significantly later in questions.

Very similar results are presented as the starting point of a perception study on Northern Standard German by Petrone & Niebuhr (2014), which will be examined at length in Section 3. As in Neapolitan Italian, statements and questions with declarative syntax appear to be characterized by different shapes in the prenuclear fall (respectively, convex and concave). And as in the previous studies, these differences seem to qualify as a reinforcing cue, given that different properties for scaling and alignment are attested as well. Figure 2.11 shows three utterances of the sentence in (12), as a statement (a) and as a question (b-c).

(12)   Katherina sucht   'ne Wohnung.
       Katherina searches a flat
       'Katherina is looking for a flat.'

Apart from utterance (b), which shows a H-H% sequence at the end of the intonational phrase, the working hypothesis phonological transcription for all utterances is H* L*+H L-L%, following Grice & Baumann (2002). The fall of the

2.4 Discussion

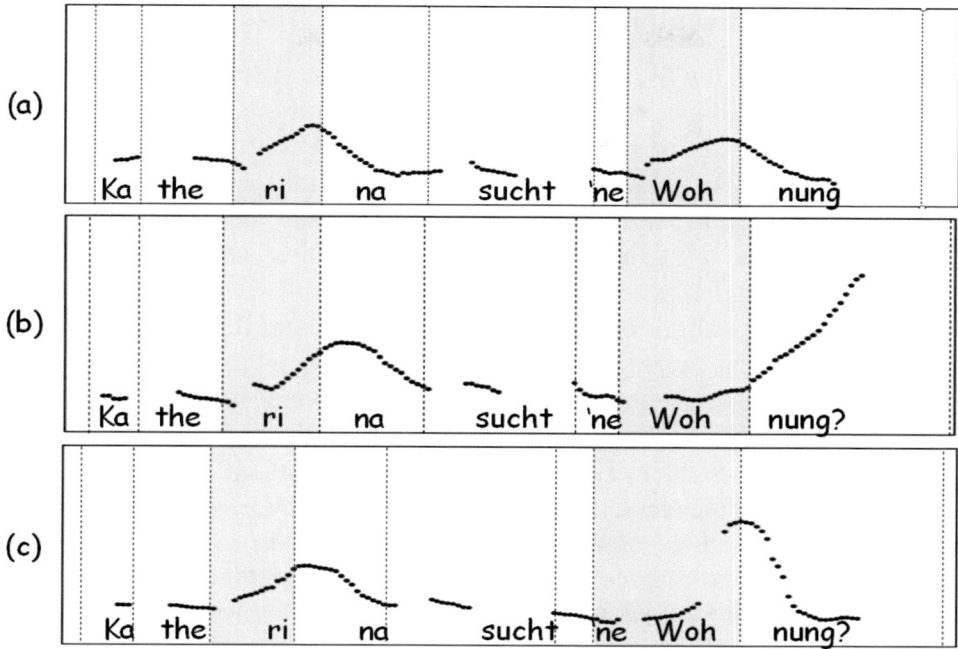

Figure 2.11: *f0* contours for statement (top) and question (mid and bottom) utterances of a same sentence with declarative syntax, *Katherina sucht 'ne Wohnung*. Grey boxes highlight accented syllables (*-ri-* and *Woh-*, respectively). Time range (x-axis) from 0 to 1.7s, f0 range (y-axis) from 70 to 350Hz. Readapted from Petrone and Niebuhr (2014), Figure 1.

prenuclear accent, located on the last syllable of the first word ([na] in *Katherina*), clearly has a different shape in the two contexts (statement vs questions), even if in questions it also starts from a later aligned and lower scaled High tone.

Thus, shape differences are attested both in other languages and in other structural positions. Moreover, they can be either the sole viable phonetic index to a given contrast, as in our data, or they can act in combination with other cues such as alignment and scaling, as in the studies reviewed in this section. In the next section, we will discuss how these phonetic facts can be accounted for in phonological modelling.

2.4.2 Enriching inventories or grammars?

Shape differences in the *f0* contour have been shown to match with various pragmatic and conversational contrasts. Now, phonetic differences matching with different functions can be organized in phonological contrasts. And if, as we said in the opening pages of this chapter, phonological accounts of intonation must deal with the intricate relations between grammar and inventories, it becomes clear that no refinement proposal can escape this issue. For example, if we believe shape differences to be a necessary enrichment of phonological representations of intonation, we must ask ourselves whether they should be coded by new entries in the inventory or as new instructions in the grammar.

Among the studies reviewed in the preceding section, the innovations proposed in the AM-based account of prenuclear falls and sentence modality in NI (Petrone & D'Imperio 2008) are a clear example of grammar enrichment. They mirror the general preference for *simple inventory and rich grammar* of the model they are framed in, thus somehow presenting themselves as "ecologically sustainable" innovations. Petrone & D'Imperio suggest that differences in the shape of the prenuclear fall should be accounted for by a different tone specification, namely a Low tone for statements (yielding a convex fall) and a High tone for questions (yielding a concave fall).[9] In an inventory enrichment perspective, this tone could have been specified as the trailing tone of the prenuclear pitch accent, yielding a new contrast between (L)H*+L for statements and (L)H*+H for questions. Instead, Petrone & D'Imperio propose to keep unmodified the inventory of prenuclear pitch accents, and to shift the contrast to the tonal specifications of the Accentual Phrase (AP), a prosodic domain smaller than the intermediate phrase and roughly corresponding to the phonological phrase (thus including a lexical head and all its complements on the non-recursive side). In this case, the phonological analysis would be (L)H* L_A L+H* L-L% for statements and (L)H* H_A L*+H L-L% for questions. It is important to stress out that this analysis emphasizes the phonological aspects of the association of the distinctive tone to the Accentual Phrase, since the phonetic differences between concave and convex falls are only visible in the portion that follows the end of the AP. However, some evidence for the AP has been collected for other languages as well (Jun 1993; Michelas 2011), and since the definition of phrasing levels in Italian is still

---

[9] This choice has also the advantage of being compatible with ethologically based accounts of the grammaticalization of the statement-question contrast, according to which questions are cross-linguistically more likely to be marked by a high tone somewhere in the utterance (Ohala 1983; Gussenhoven 2004). We will come back to this issue in the next chapters (see especially Section 4.5.1).

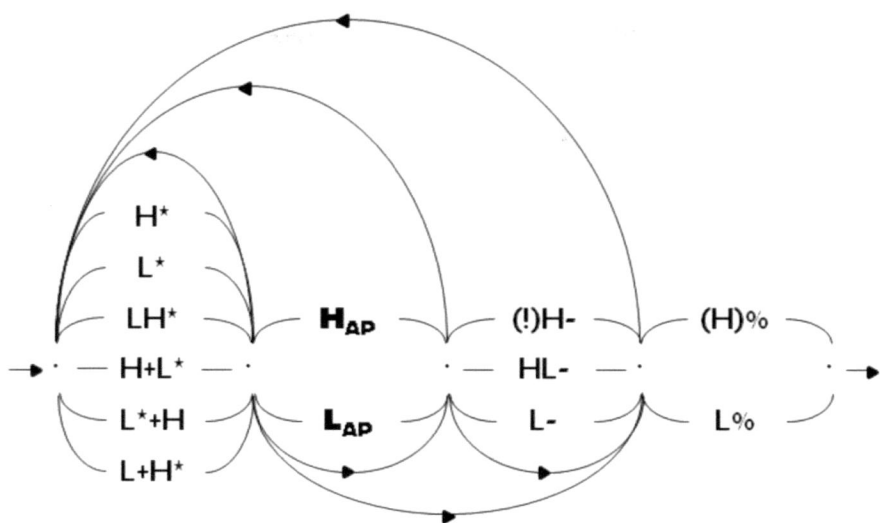

Figure 2.12: AM intonational grammar for NI expanded with the Accentual Phrase level.

controversial (D'Imperio & Gili Fivela 2003), the authors propose to associate the tone responsible for concave and convex prenuclear falls to the right edge of this constituent. As a result, the tonal inventory for both pitch accents and edge tones is unchanged, but the prosodic hierarchy in enriched with a new level (see Figure 2.12).

Less effort is devoted to the phonological modelling of activating and restricting phrase final rises in German (Dombrowski & Niebuhr 2005). The two phrase-final rises (concave and turn-holding, convex and turn-yielding) are treated as "sub-patterns" of the same "contour type", the early valley. The phonological inventory of the Kiel Intonation Model seems to be composed by a subset of the matrix created by two tonal movements (peaks and valleys) and three synchronization options (early, medial and late): as the authors put it, "There are early, medial, and late peaks; and there are early and late (i.e., non-early) valleys". It appears that the contrast between medial and late synchronizations options is neutralized when the tonal movement is a valley (see Figure 2.13 A). That is, the phonological inventory has an empty slot (i.e., medial valley) adjacent to the item (i.e., early valley) which displays the two sub-patterns (i.e., activating and restricting). Moreover, the activating and restricting sub-patterns of phrase-final early

2 Melodic detail in production

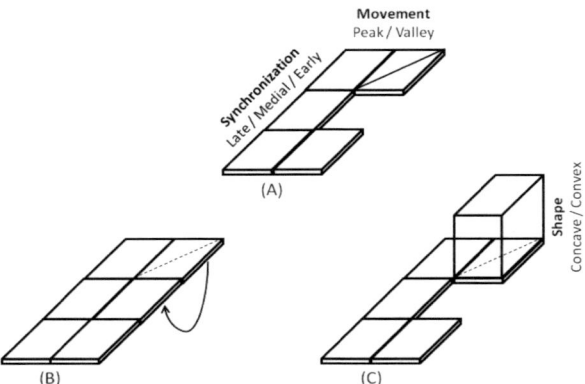

Figure 2.13: KIM inventory (A) expanded by using the empty slot of medial valleys (B) or by extruding the matrix with the shape dimension (C).

valleys are treated as "coherent gestalt-like shapes", as integral communicative gestures: the authors exclude the possibility of decomposing the rises in smaller unit, thus pointing to an inventory enrichment perspective. However, they do not take a clear position as for the restructuring of the inventory either. We could formulate two hypotheses here: in one case, we could distinguish between two sub-sub-types (concave and convex) in the sub-type (early) of the type (valley). This would entail the extrusion of another level (shape) in the already existing matrix (tonal movement x synchronization options), if only for one slot (see Figure 2.12 C). Alternatively, since (as we said earlier) medial valleys are not attested, the synchronization options could be broadened to account for shape differences as well, at least for non-early valleys (see Figure 2.12 B). These options of inventory enrichment are not explored in the original paper, but it appears that they would be less disruptive than a grammar enrichment anyway.

In the two studies cited above the issue of phonological modelling is either set and answered or not set at all: different prenuclear falls in Italian are due to a different Accentual Phrase tone, while phrase-final rises in German are two phonetic variants of the early valley. In the paper on prenuclear falls in German (Petrone & Niebuhr 2014) the question is set but left unanswered. The authors suggest to interpret the differences in the shape of the fall as the consequence of the implementation of a tonal contrast, leaving open the possibilities of a trailing tone and an edge tone. The latter hypothesis clearly echoes the grammar enrichment proposed for prenuclear falls in Italian, and postulates the existence of a prosodic constituent smaller than the intermediate phrase for German as well. The former hypothesis, on the other hand, would introduce a distinction in the inventory between a prenuclear accent in statements (to be labelled as H*+L) and one in questions (H*+H or, with a "crypto-phonetic" labelling in the terms of Atterer & Ladd 2004, H*+!H). It has to be noted that, when looking at Figure 2.11, alignment differences in the prenuclear accent are evident, even if they only relate to two individual productions. In KIM terms, we would be dealing with a medial peak (statement) and a late peak (questions): again, shape differences could be fairly easily subsumed in the broader, holistic difference between two established phonological entities. This view would be supported by the fact that, while in AM accounts of at least some languages the inventory of prenuclear pitch accents is somehow reduced, in KIM different synchronization options are still available for prenuclear peaks (Niebuhr & Ambrazaitis 2006). However, in the examples of Figure 2.11 the alignment differences are somehow smaller than usually reported for the H* vs L*+H contrast (40 ms, against the 80 ms reported in Niebuhr & Ambrazaitis 2006). And the results from the second perception experiment in Petrone & Niebuhr (2014) show that stimuli with later prenuclear peaks do not yield more question responses. This finding actually seems to contradict the idea that the two sentence modalities might be characterized by two different prenuclear accents (medial peak, H* with convex fall for statements and late peak, L*+H with concave fall for questions). Conversely, manipulations of fall shape seem to yield different responses (more convex, more statement), but only when the peak has been manipulated to an early position (and the slope of the fall is not too steep). However, the hypothesis of true differences in the phonological inventory of German cannot be too hastily dismissed: as the authors point out, the interplay between shape, slope and alignment in the two postnuclear falls still needs a thorough investigation. The exaggeration of alignment differences might have proven disruptive indeed: after all, shape differences become a stronger cue to sentence modality when the peak is early and the slope is shallow - that is, when the perceptibility of shape differences is maximized. In sum, given also that the creation of the manipulated stimuli did not rely on the modelling of a conspicuous set of production data, it is difficult to decide whether an enrichment of the grammar or of the inventory would provide the best account of sentence modality perception.

2.4.3 Segmental and suprasegmental phonology

But why would the issue of enriching inventories or grammars be so crucial in the refinement of phonological accounts of intonation? As we said in the

2 Melodic detail in production

opening pages of this chapter, it is a useful conceptual device to understand the relationships between the different phonological models of intonation. Moreover, it provides a link between models of intonation and of speech perception. But this issue is of central concern for another reason, namely the nature of the functions which can be expressed by intonational contrasts, as opposed to the functions played by phonemic contrasts. As Pierrehumbert & Hirschberg put it,

> In the segmental domain, linguistic categories are expected to relate both to differences in sounds and articulations and to differences in semantic interpretation. For example, we say that [p] is different from [b] because they are pronounced differently, and because [pit] means something different than [bit] does. (Pierrehumbert & Hirschberg 1990: 282)

In the suprasegmental domain, however, the establishment of phonological *forms* ("linguistic categories" in the quote) is less straightforward. First of all, intonational phonology is a very young field of study (especially if compared to segmental phonology) and no framework within it can be said to have reached the status of a stable system. For example, while the International Phonetic Alphabet has represented for years a valuable tool for research in segmental phonology, tonal transcription systems are still witnessing very partial consensus. But if it is true that intonational phonology is still very challenging because the first comprehensive modelling efforts only started some thirty years ago, the cause-effect relationship can also be flipped the other way round: intonation has eluded phonological modelling for a long time because of the many thorny issues it raises. A thorough examination of the reasons for the late inclusion of intonation in the core of linguistic studies is clearly beyond the scope of this chapter, so in the following we will only deal with the *functional* issues ("semantic interpretation" in the quote) which are immediately relevant to our discussion, but this reasoning could be very easily expanded to the difficulties raised by the *substantial* aspects ("sounds and articulations") of intonation.

2.4.3.1 Solidity of functional contrasts

In the quote, it is said that the establishment of phonological forms in the segmental domain ("[p] is different from [b]")[10] is guided by both substantial ("they are pronounced differently") and functional ("[pit] means something different than [bit] does") evidence. And, as the example in the quote shows, the functional evidence used in the establishment of forms in segmental (and tone) phonology is based on lexical semantic contrasts. These contrasts are characterized by

---

[10] Square brackets in the original text.

2.4 Discussion

a high degree of self-evidence, they are rooted in the epilinguistic knowledge of native speakers, and they do not require a theoretical systematization in order to be used as evidence for phonological contrasts. Of course, this is not to say that lexical semantic contrasts cannot be studied in their own right, but only that no semantic analysis is required when establishing a phonemic inventory. Pairs like the nouns *bug* ([bʌg], meaning 'insect') and *bun* ([bʌn], meaning 'small cake') allow for the individuation of the phonemes /g/ and /n/ irrespective of the fact that, as for their meanings, some semantic features are shared (e.g. [+organic]), some are not (e.g. [+animate]), and some could, depending on the context (e.g. [+edible]).

In the suprasegmental domain, on the other hand, functional evidence used in the determination of phonological form does not share the immediacy of lexical (semantic) contrasts. For instance, non-linguists are not necessarily aware of the mechanisms underlying post-lexical contrasts such as differences in focus placement and scope, and there is no consensus on how to model them among linguists either. Also, from a cross-linguistic point of view, the role of intonation in conveying sentence modality contrasts such as the difference between statements and questions can range from essential (e.g. Italian) to marginal (e.g. Mandarin Chinese, see Zeng et al. 2004). Combined with the difficulties of analysis at the substantial level (e.g. microprosodic perturbations, measuring issues), the unavailability of rock-solid functional evidence makes the establishment of phonological forms in the suprasegmental domain a very complicate enterprise. Researchers in intonational phonology must treat functional post-lexical contrasts as nothing more than working hypotheses whereas, in segmental phonology, functional lexical contrasts can be used as solid guidelines for the exploration of differences in phonetic substance and for the definition of phonological forms. This might be one of the reasons underlying the (relatively) untroubled definition of the phoneme as the atomic unit at the segmental level. That is, the opposition between *bug* and *bun*, both at the functional and substantial level, is framed in the terms of the contrast between /g/ and /n/, and not in terms of the features of place and manner of articulation. Having clearly defined the atomic level, the constitution of the inventory results simplified.

2.4.3.2 Implicit compositionality of intonational meaning

The *f0* contour shape differences discussed in this chapter are a good example of how the definition of phonological form in intonation can be problematic, and of how the interplay between inventory and grammar is indeed crucial. If the definition of the inventory relies on the individuation of what we called the atomic

2 Melodic detail in production

level, what role should shape differences play? If tones are the primitives, then shape differences can be accounted for as different tonal specifications for a new structural position: the inventory stays the same, the grammar is enriched (see Petrone & D'Imperio 2008). If, on the other hand, tonal configurations are seen as gestalt-like atomic wholes (see Dombrowski & Niebuhr 2005), the inventory has to be enriched by splitting a previously acknowledged slot (say KIM's early valley) into two novel forms, differentiated on the basis of the *feature* of convexity/concavity.

The issue of the atomic level in intonational phonology is also relevant on the functional side. This can be exemplified by looking at the pragmatic contrast we explored in this chapter (see Section 2.1.3), which we labelled as Partial Topic Statement (SPT) versus Narrow Focus Question (QNF). Is this functional contrast a viable starting point for the individuation of different phonological forms? The SPT vs QNF contrast is clearly multidimensional: sentence modality, focus placement, and topic contrastiveness all take different values in these two contexts. As we said in the preceding section, this is not an issue when dealing with functional contrasts on the segmental level, where the semantic features of the two items composing a minimal pair can safely be ignored, since the functional contrast is pre-theoretic and the atomic phonological level is clearly defined. But among the shifting sands of intonational phonology, where the interactions between inventory and grammar are still to be settled, the question has to be asked. To exemplify, no phonological account of the bug/bun contrast would suggest to relate the phonetic feature [+velar] with the semantic feature [+animate]. But in the discussion of phrase-final German rises, it appears that the phonetic feature [+convex] is related to the discourse feature [+activating]. And in the case of prenuclear Italian falls, the phonological option of a Low accentual phrase tone would relate the phonetic feature [+convex] with the sentence modality [+statement].

That is, given the provisional and theory-dependent nature of both post-lexical functions and atomic forms, it appears that theories of intonational meaning are prone to an implicit drift towards a compositional approach. A specific primitive might be seen as conveying different meaning on different dimension, depending on its role in the grammar: in the terms of Petrone & D'Imperio (2008); Grice et al. (2005b), an L tone would cue continuation on the discourse dimension if it is a prenuclear accent, and it would cue statement on the modality dimension if it is an accentual phrase accent. Or, given a single primitive, different features might relate to different meaning dimensions: in Dombrowski & Niebuhr (2005), within the general case of early valleys, it is the feature of concavity or convexity that relates to restriction or activation of the interlocutor. These accounts are implicitly compositional in the weak sense that at least some of the meaning of the whole can be associated with options pertaining to one of its parts, and that these parts are at least partially meaningful on their own. That is, with respect to meaning, units in intonational phonology have been treated more like morphemes than phonemes (Gussenhoven 1984). This is actually less surprising than expectable, since the arguments discussed in this section aimed to show that intonational phonology still hasn't located an atomic level comparable to the phoneme *with respect to form and substance as well.* And that a closer examination of the relationships between inventory and grammar could represent a necessary step to this end.

2.5 Conclusion

In this chapter we documented the production of melodic detail in read speech. Neapolitan Italian speakers produce nuclear rises with different shapes according to the pragmatic context of their utterances. Convex and concave rises are associated with narrow focus questions and partial topic statements, respectively. This phonetic information is a more reliable indicator of the QNF-SPT contrast than the traditional indices of tone scaling and alignment, but it is still unaccounted for in the autosegmental-metrical framework. That is, it is possible that phonological representations in the AM framework are too reductionists, and that they discard potentially useful prosodic detail.

We explored some of the avenues for enriching these representations, keeping in mind that phonetic information can be included in a phonological description either through an increase in the inventory or through a stratification of the grammar. The exploration of these two hypotheses, illustrated also by other studies on meaningful contour shape differences, allowed us to recognize that the articulation between inventory and grammar in intonational phonology suffers from a constitutional instability, mainly due to the nature of the function expressed by intonational contrasts. The post-lexical meaning vehiculated by intonation does not share the immediacy and the pre-theoretic character of the lexical semantic contrasts used in segmental phonology. And this might have led to some difficulties in individuating an atomic bundle of relationship between substance and function parallel to the phoneme at the segmental level. In turn, this situation could have generated a more or less implicit drift towards a morpheme-like interpretation of intonational units, which informed a more or less overt compositional approach to intonational meaning. This is not, in itself, a problem

2 Melodic detail in production

for intonational phonology. However, the limits of an *implicitly* compositional approach to meaning emerge when faced with the necessity of enriching phonological descriptions, because it is unclear whether the new features should be accounted for by an expansion of the inventory or a complexification of the grammar. In this sense, the accommodation of prosodic detail into an abstractionist model of intonation can prove challenging indeed.

The elaboration of such a frame for the enrichment of phonological representations in an abstractionist model, and a fortiori the exploration of a potential exemplar-based approach of intonation, are not the aim of this chapter, nor of this book altogether. Our investigation bears mainly on asking *whether* these enterprises are possible, useful or necessary. And as we said at the beginning of this chapter, in order to be considered as prosodic detail which must be included in a higher-order representation, phonetic variation must not only be regularly found in production, but also consistently used in perception. For this reason, in the next chapter we turn to an exploration of the perceptual role of differences in *f0* contour shape.

3 Perception of melodic detail

In the previous chapter we documented regularities in speakers' productions which are not accounted for by the Autosegmental-Metrical (AM) model of intonational phonology. Moreover, it appears that this previously unacknowledged phonetic information allows for the elaboration of metrics which are more effective than traditional AM indices in mirroring pragmatic contrasts. However, regularity in production and robust mirroring of pragmatic contrasts do not give sufficient reason to include phonetic information into phonological representations. The additional requirement that has to be met is actual use of this phonetic information in perception. If phonetic information is regularly produced but not perceived and parsed (or, more radically, not perceived at all), then it could be deemed a by-product of other contrasts, and its inclusion in a minimalist phonological representation would not be justified. As we saw in Section 2.4.2, enriching phonological representations is a complex operation. For this reason, before prospecting any modification in the inventory or in the grammar of the intonational phonology of Neapolitan Italian (NI), an evaluation of the perceptual role of the regularities found in production is in order.

3.1 Introduction

Even if the perception of intonation has witnessed a growing interest from the research community since the 1960s, studies which concentrate on the perception of phonologically salient dynamic proprieties of *f0* contours are rare. Such studies seem to bring together the two main threads which have characterized research on intonation perception, and which can also be (although very loosely) arranged diachronically. Early studies focussed on the psychoacoustics of pitch perception, attempting to define how listeners deal with fundamental frequency modulations over time (at least since Sergeant & Harris 1962). This research agenda, combined with the relative unavailability of stable procedures for speech resynthesis,[1] motivates, at least partially, the pervasive use of simple non-speech

---

[1] Linear Predictive Coding (*LPC*) based resynthesis was only available in 1970s, while Pitch-Synchronous OverLapp-Add (*PSOLA*) based methods are more recent.

3 Perception of melodic detail

signals as the basis for stimuli construction. However, it soon became evident that the pure tones used in early psychoacoustically-oriented research were but a first step towards the study of the specificities of the speech signal. The use of speech-like material in pitch perception investigations (Rossi 1971; Klatt 1973; 't Hart 1976; Schouten 1985) was instrumental in orienting research on the relationships between spectral content and $f0$ variation (House 1990, 1997), permitting a shift from psychoacoustic to proper linguistic research.

While the psychoacoustic approach was yielding its first mature fruits, research on the structure of intonational categories had gone its first steps. A new insight on intonation perception came from studies on categorical perception of segmental contrasts (see Section 1.2.1): the exploration of the viability of the categorical perception (Kohler 1987) for intonation as well started a line of studies in which intonational categories are central. Different paradigms for exploring the warping of perceptual space in intonation were proposed and tested, from classification and discrimination to imitation (Pierrehumbert & Steele 1989), semantic differential (from Osgood et al. 1957 through Uldall 1964 to Kirsner et al. 1994) and indirect identification (context matching, Nash & Mulac 1980), up to eye-tracking (Dahan et al. 2002). It seems that, unlike the one focussing on the pychoacoustics of pitch perception, this research thread on intonational categories still draws linguists' attention, as recent work questioning the viability of categorical perception for intonation (Gussenhoven 2006; Niebuhr 2007) shows.

Studies on the role of dynamic $f0$ contour cues in perception bring together these two lines of research, in that they rest at the same time on a deep understanding of how much detail in the signal is psychoacoustically perceptible and of how intonational categories can be identified.

In this section we will review two such studies, dealing with NI (Petrone & D'Imperio 2011) and with Northern Standard German (Petrone & Niebuhr 2014), respectively. Both studies analyze prenuclear falls and show that sentence modality contrasts are not exclusively cued by the intonational nucleus.

The first builds on production results of Petrone & D'Imperio (2008: see Section 2.4.1), in which the authors accounted for different shapes in prenuclear falls by suggesting a tonal contrast (H in questions and L in statements) for the tone associated to the right edge of the Accentual Phrase domain. A subsequent study (Petrone & D'Imperio 2011) performs two experiments on the perceptual role of the Accentual Phrase tone, establishing the hypothesis that listeners do not rely exclusively on nuclear pitch accent contrasts in order to classify questions and statements. The first experiment is based on an identification task using gated stimuli (see Figure 3.1). Utterances are cut after the prenuclear pitch accent

3.1 Introduction

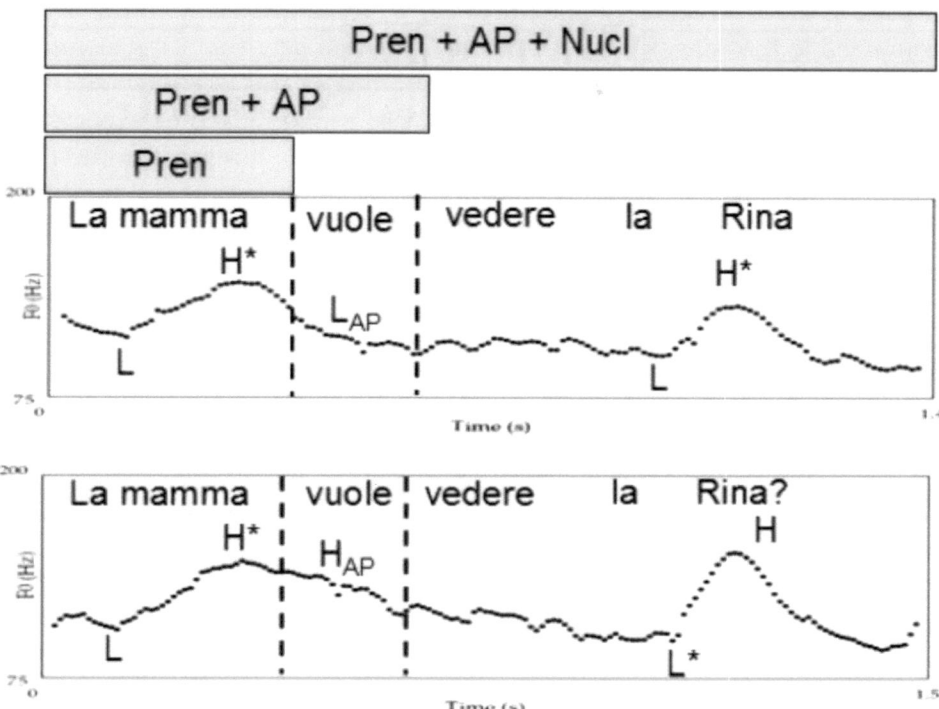

Figure 3.1: Schematized representation of the stimulus manipulation (three conditions: PREN, AP, NUCL) for the sentence *La mamma vuole vedere la Rina*, uttered as a narrow focus statement with late focus (top panel), and as a yes/no question (bottom panel). From Petrone (2008).

(PREN condition) and after the alleged Accentual Phrase tone (AP condition), and they were presented to listeners along with a control set of uncut stimuli (NUCL condition) for classification as either Statements or Questions.

Results show that the classification scores are already above chance level for the PREN condition, and that in the AP condition classification is even more robust for statements, but not for questions.[2] The authors suggest that the absence of a significant improvement in question identification from the PREN to the AP condition could be due to the fact that the *f0* contour stretching from the prenuc-

---

[2] This latter finding is the starting point for the second experiment, in which a semantic differential task is used to assess the nature of the meaning (attitudinal or pragmatic) conveyed by the AP tone.

lear peak to the H Accentual Phrase tone has a characteristically concave shape if compared to the convex shape of the interpolation between the peak and the L Accentual Phrase in statements. If listeners relied on this difference in *f0* contours to classify stimuli, the same performances would indeed be expected for PREN and AP condition. It is interesting to note that a difference in the shape of the fall, described with different tonal specifications for the AP right edge, actually seems to be perceived even in stimuli gated before the AP itself. In a radical perspective, this finding could be taken as evidence against the adequacy of a representation based on AP tones, and rather supporting the hypothesis that the shape of the interpolation between tonal targets is relevant in itself: in the concluding remarks, Petrone & D'Imperio themselves acknowledge the need for a closer examination of dynamic proprieties of the fall.

The perceptual role of prenuclear falls has been investigated for Northern Standard German as well (Petrone & Niebuhr 2014). In their first experiment, syntactically declarative Subject-Verb-Object sentences were uttered as questions or statements, using different nuclear configurations: statements all had a L- L% utterance-final fall combined with one of three different pitch accents (H+L*, H* and L*+H in AM terms or early, medial and late peak in KIM terms; see Section 2.4.2); questions had an L*+H pitch accent combined with either a final fall (L- L%) or rise (H- H%). The working-hypothesis transcription for the prenuclear fall was H*, but some phonetic differences between questions and statements can be spotted in the slope and the shape of the fall (see Figure 3.2).

Natural utterances were gated after the Subject and the Verb and presented (along with control uncut items) to listeners for a semantic differential task on three scales, namely 'astonished — not astonished', 'questioning — not questioning', 'uncertain — certain'. The esults show that phonetic information in prenuclear falls is used by listeners in order to classify questions and statements: sentences sound more astonished, uncertain and questioning when uttered as questions, even when gated right after the Subject, that is before the nuclear configuration. This is not to say that the nucleus itself plays no role at all: complete utterances yield stronger responses towards the astonished, uncertain and questioning pole of the semantic scales.[3] This finding leads the authors to claim that phonetic detail in *f0* contours can even be spotted in the nuclear pitch accent labelled as L*+H, which would have a more convex rise in statements and a more

---

[3] The increase is maximal when compared with stimuli gated after the Verb. For these cases, the authors suggest a Frequency Code based explanation for listeners' bias towards statement-like responses, given that *f0* on the Verb is a low plateau. However, a syntax based bias could also contribute to this result.

3.1 Introduction

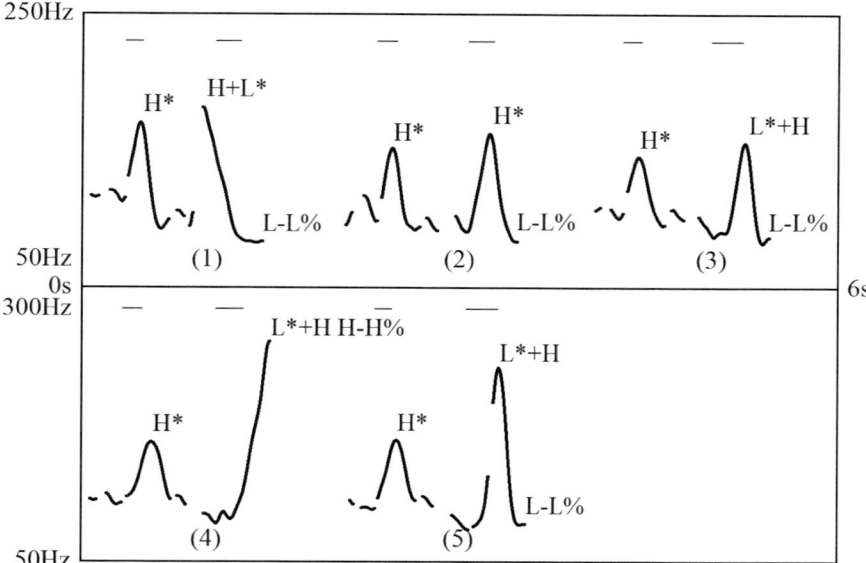

Figure 3.2: Phonological analyses and *f0* contours of the five naturally produced stimuli *Katherina sucht 'ne Wohnung*; (1)-(3) were produced as statements, (4)-(5) were produced as questions. The syllables -*ri*- and *Woh*- that showed the prenuclear and nuclear accents are delimited by horizontal lines. Readapted from Petrone and Niebuhr (2014), Fig. 2.

3 Perception of melodic detail

concave rise in questions. However, this evidence is not compelling, since the availability to the listener of a L*+H pitch accent seem to induce more question-like responses for original statements as well.

The second experiment aimed at precisely identifying which of the melodic properties in the prenuclear region are actually responsible for the shift in the listeners' perception. Stimuli with resynthesized peak alignment, fall slope and fall shape in the prenuclear region were used in a context matching task. The results show that alignment, slope and shape interact in cueing sentence modality: question classification, for example, is strongest with early aligned peak, shallow fall slopes and concave shapes. On the basis of this evidence and of similar findings reported by Petrone & D'Imperio (2011) for NI, Petrone & Niebuhr underline the necessity of accounting for *f0* dynamic information in phonological representations of prenuclear regions in German, through a different specification of either the prenuclear pitch accents (to be differentiated via trailing tones) or an alleged edge tone of a new prosodic domain (as in the NI analysis).

The two studies we reviewed in this section are both concerned with the prenuclear region, where shape differences can be attributed to either pitch accents or edge tones, as we have seen in the discussion of the German data. In the following section, we will report on two experiments on the perception of the nuclear rise shape differences documented in Section 2 (D'Imperio & Cangemi 2009). Focussing on nuclear rises has the advantage of discarding any account of shape differences based on additional edge tones, thus enabling a more straightforward phonological modelling of the data. Both experiments (henceforth E1 and E2) are based on a categorization task and use stimuli resynthesized from utterances contained in the *Tre Grazie* corpus (see Section 2.2.1).

3.2 Experiment 1

3.2.1 Background

The general aim of E1 was to test whether or not pitch accent classification is affected by dynamic intonational cues. Specifically, building on the regularities found in speakers' productions (see Section 2), we tested the perceptual role of rise shape in the contrast between nuclear accents of partial topic statements (SPT) and narrow focus questions (QNF). If rise shape differences are consistently produced by speakers and reliably used by listeners, then phonological representations of pitch accents should include this phonetic information: rise shape would qualify as prosodic detail in the sense of useful information not yet encoded in abstract accounts of intonation. In order to test this hypothesis, we devised a forced-choice categorization task in which we manipulated rise shape (from concave to convex), asking subjects to classify items as questions or statements. If listeners use rise shape information in classification, we expect more question responses for stimuli with a more convex rise and more statement responses for stimuli with a more concave rise.

In addition to rise shape, we decided to test the impact of another cue, namely the scaling of the elbow following the peak in the stressed syllable.[4] As we discussed in Section 2.4.1, Petrone & D'Imperio (2008) showed that productions of focus-final statements and questions in NI are characterized by postnuclear falls having different shapes, being more concave in questions and more convex in statements. They suggested that this contrast can be accounted for by a different tonal specification of a new prosodic domain, the Accentual Phrase, which would bear an H tone in questions (hence the concave fall) and an L tone in statements (hence the convex fall). Our corpus, on the other hand, focusses on shape differences in nuclear rises, and moreover on a different pragmatic contrast, namely the one between partial topic statements and narrow focus questions. However, through an examination of the *Tre Grazie* corpus, D'Imperio & Cangemi (2011) show that shape can also vary in postnuclear falls, with Partial Topics being characterized by an intermediate shape between concave questions and convex statements. In Petrone & D'Imperio's (2008) terms, SPT would also have an Accentual Phrase break, whose tonal specification could be transcribed as !H in order to account for the three way contrast with statements (L) and questions (H). Independent of the phonological analysis, it is true that, at least in some cases, postnuclear falls present different shapes in SPT and QNF, as Figure 2.1 shows. For this reason, along with the rise shape discussed above, the fall shape factor was included in the design of the perception experiment. In order to be able to tell apart the contribution of these two factors, we tested them both individually and jointly, thus creating three different manipulation sets (i.e. rise, fall, both rise and fall).

3.2.2 Hypotheses

E1 allows us to test two hypotheses concerning the classification as narrow focus questions or partial topic statements of trisyllabic stimuli bearing a nuclear accent:

---

[4] L1 alignment, in addition, was manipulated in order to test whether the entire rise is aligned later in questions; see D'Imperio (2003). Since this issue is not relevant here, we will not comment it any further.

H1: *identification is affected by rise shape.* The production experiment reported in Section 2 showed different interpolation forms between the tonal targets composing a rising accent. According to the null hypothesis, these differences are to be considered redundant phonetic information. The alternative hypothesis is that rise shape is perceptible and indeed used in classification.

H2: *identification is affected by fall shape.* Production data on prenuclear accents indicate that questions and statements are characterized by different fall shapes. According to the null hypothesis, these findings can not be extended to nuclear accents.

Given current limitations in our understanding of trading relationships between supposed phonetic details in different dimensions, we will restrain from explicitly formulating hypotheses on the joint manipulation of rise and fall.

Support for the alternative hypotheses will be evaluated by fitting subjects' responses to a Logit Mixed Model and by gauging the statistical significance of the factor *Stimulus step* (from allegedly SPT-like to QNF-like) for each of the two manipulation sets, namely rise shape (for H1) and fall shape (or scaling of the postaccentual elbow for H2). The significance level was set to < 0.05.

3.2.3 Method

The first forced-choice categorization task involved 22 native speakers of NI, mainly undergraduate science students with no training in linguistics. The experiment took place in a silent room, using a personal computer and a professional headphone set.[5] Subjects listened to audio stimuli and had to identify them as either Questions or Statements. They were asked to put their index fingers in resting position above one of the two designated computer keys, each bearing a coloured sticker label (blue on far left of the keyboard, red on the right). The colour code was reminded throughout the whole experiment by on-screen instructions which associated colours to the Italian labels *Domanda* 'Question' and *Risposta* 'Answer', and was counterbalanced across speakers. Stimulus presentation and response recording were managed by the software *Perceval* (André et al. 2003). The task lasted about 30 minutes and subjects were allowed to take a break between any of the five blocks.

---

[5] We would like to thank Franco Cutugno for allowing us to use the facilities at *DSFMN* (Dipartimento di Scienze Fisiche, Matematiche e Naturali), Naples University "Federico II", as well as Bogdan Ludusan for his assistance.

3.2 Experiment 1

Each block was composed of 28 experimental resynthesized items and 18 natural control items. We used 2 repetitions of the first word from 9 utterances recorded by a single speaker in the *Tre Grazie* corpus as control items. Two SPT and two QNF utterances of the two sentences *Valeria viene alle nove* and *Amelia dorme da nonna* were cut after the Subject, yielding 8 of the control items.[6] The ninth control item also served as the starting point for resynthesizing experimental items, and consisted in the first word of the sentence *Milena lo vuole amaro*, uttered as a SPT. The control items, along with the full utterances they were extracted from, were used in the training phase to make sure that subjects understood the task and the labels employed. This was particularly important, since SPT utterances are not as prototypical of the Statement category as QNF utterances are of the Question category (see Section 3.2.5). Control items were also used to determine a baseline for correct classification of resynthesized items (see Section 3.2.4).

Experimental stimuli were built by modifying the melodic properties of the base natural stimulus described above (*Milena* as SPT) using the *PSOLA* algorithm (Moulines & Charpentier 1990) embedded in *Praat* (Boersma & Weenink 2008). The first manipulation consisted in resynthesizing a base experimental stimulus with ambiguous *f0* features between those of a SPT and a QNF (see Figure 3.3, solid line). To achieve this, we calculated values for scaling and alignment with respect to the stressed vowel's boundaries of the *f0* peak (H) and the inflection points on its left (L1) and its right (L2) (see Figure 3.3, dotted line) for the base natural stimulus. Then we averaged these values with the ones extracted from a QNF utterance of the same speaker for the same sentence (see Figure 3.3, dashed line).

The resulting stimulus was used as the starting point for further *f0* manipulations. Four sets of stimuli were created by manipulating three dimensions and one of their combinations (see Figure 3.4 and Table 3.1). The three dimensions were L1 alignment, rise shape and L2 scaling, whereas the fourth set combined rise shape and L2 scaling manipulation. Each of the 4 sets was composed by 7 steps which were equally spaced in frequency as expressed in Hz.[7] Values of the ambiguous base stimulus were assigned to the central step (n. 4); values of the original stimuli were assigned to penultimate steps in the two directions (i.e. SPT = 2 and QNF = 6). This allowed us to create 4 sets which, for each parameter, went from an overtly SPT characterized stimulus (n. 1) to an overt QNF (n. 7).

---

[6] See Section 2.2.1 for more details on the test sentences (6-8) and the pragmatic contexts (9-10).
[7] In the first set (which we will not discuss any further; see Footnote 4) we manipulated L1 alignment, so steps were rather equally spaced in time.

3 Perception of melodic detail

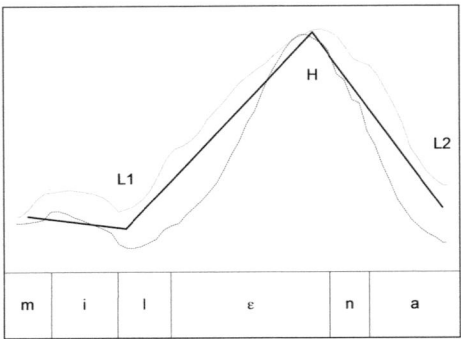

Figure 3.3: Base stimulus averaging.

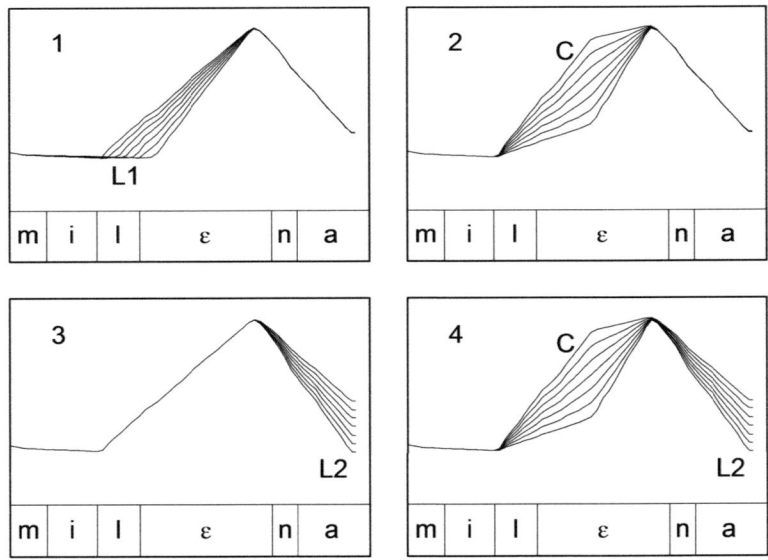

Figure 3.4: Sketches of the 4 manipulation sets (1: L1 alignment; 2: rise shape; 3: L2 scaling; 4: rise shape and L2 scaling), aligned with the name *Milena*.

3.2 Experiment 1

Table 3.1: Summary of manipulations

Set	Feature(s)	Steps
1	L1 alignment	15 ms
2	Rise midpoint	15 Hz
3	L2 scaling	10 Hz
4	Rise midpoint and L2 scaling	15 and 10 Hz

All in all, 3080 responses were gathered for experimental items (22 subjects x 5 blocks x 4 sets x 7 steps) and 1980 for control items (22 subjects x 5 blocks x 2 repetitions x 9 stimuli).

3.2.4 Results

Responses to control stimuli show that listeners found the task very difficult. During the training phase, no subject experienced difficulties in classifying the uncut stimuli. However, during the test phase, subjects had to classify 90 (5 blocks x 9 items x 2 repetitions) natural stimuli cut after the first word. Results show that only 5 out of 22 listeners managed to make a reliable distinction (above 60% of correct classification) between unresynthesized SPTs and QNFs.

Figure 3.5 (left panel) plots the frequency of Statement responses (y-axis) against the seven manipulation steps (x-axis) for the three individual sets (rise curvature, L2 scaling, rise curvature and L2 scaling), pooled across all subjects. The results do not show the expected trend to higher Statement responses for the first (1-3) manipulation steps.

Given the results of the control items classification, we decided to plot separately the responses to experimental stimuli for the five subjects with the highest control performance, in order to ascertain whether the degree of sensitivity to resynthesis was different across subjects. However, as Figure 3.5 (right panel) shows, no trends are discernible for this subgroup either. Statistical analyses are omitted, since the visual inspection of the results clearly indicates no effect of any of the experimental treatments on subjects' responses, for both groups of subjects. The inspection of the two panels in Figure 3.5, however, shows that the five "reliable" subjects had a slight bias towards the Statement response, irrespective of the dimension, the direction and the intensity of the manipulation (see Section 3.3 for discussion).

3 Perception of melodic detail

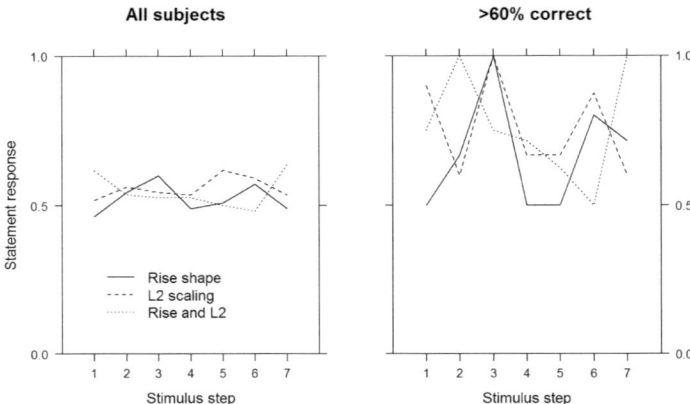

Figure 3.5: Experiment I. Frequency of Statement responses for the three relevant manipulations sets (2-4 in Table 3.1). Data for all subjects (left panel) and for the 5 subjects with best performance on control items (right panel).

3.2.5 Discussion

Results show that subjects do not use L1 alignment, rise shape or L2 scaling as cues for the classification of trisyllabic stimuli as narrow focus questions or partial topic statements. The interpretation of negative results being an epistemologically complex operation, in the following we will concentrate on some hypotheses accounting for this outcome, and on further testing needed in order to validate them.

First of all, it is possible that our manipulations did not involve phonetic information actually used in classification. In this case, the differences in rise shape we found to be consistent in production (see Section 2) could be deemed perceptually irrelevant by-products of other paradigmatic options, as the tonal specification of the accentual phrase (Petrone & D'Imperio 2008) or the compression of postnuclear register (D'Imperio & Cangemi 2011). This perspective would constitute evidence for the appropriateness of a strongly abstractionist approach to intonation, in which some of the phonetic information contained in the signal, even if consistently present, is actually discarded in the mapping phase.

Going a step further, we could also hypothesize that our manipulations are not only unused in classification, but are also not perceptible at all. In this case, rise shape differences could absolutely not qualify as prosodic detail, but only as side effects of phonetic implementation. This hypothesis could be readily tested with a discrimination task; however, informal testing by three NI native speakers suggested that different steps along the manipulated dimensions are indeed discriminable. For this reason, we cannot rule out without further testing the option that task-related issues affected the validation of the research hypothesis.

One of the issues which might have played this role is the difficulty of the task itself. The poor performances in correct classification of natural control stimuli seem to strengthen this view. If only 5 out of 22 subjects managed to make a somewhat reliable (above 60%) classification of natural stimuli, we can not expect high performances on experimental items either. It is true, after all, that no subject experienced any difficulties in correctly classifying the uncut utterances from which the stimuli were excerpted. Test items, however, consisted in a single trisyllabic word, and control items consisted in one of two trisyllabic words as well. Each subject had to listen to 230 short and similar items. Moreover, 150 out of these 230 items consisted in various forms of the same one proper name used for the experimental stimuli (namely *Milena*). During informal post-experiment interviews, nine subjects stated that one of the names in the test was very frequent, and almost all of them reported to have found the test frustrating and boring for this very reason.

However, as anticipated in the Method section (see Section 3.2.3), additional difficulties might have arisen from the interaction between the category labels used for classification (namely *Question* and *Answer*) and the particular pragmatic contrast under examination (i.e. question narrow focus vs statement partial topic). Even if we made sure that subjects could make a reliable association between stimuli and labels during the training phase, it is nonetheless true that QNF and SPT differ in how strongly they can represent questions and statements respectively. SPT, in particular, can be thought of as partial answer — that is a statement, but one calling for an integration. QNF, on the contrary, can be seen as more prototypically representing the question category.

In retrospect, the negative results presented in this section could have been determined by a variety of more or less controllable experimental factors. For this reason we devised and ran a second experiment, before dismissing the hypothesis of the perceptual relevance of rise shape in pitch accent categorization altogether.

3.3 Experiment 2

3.3.1 Background

E2 was meant to reduce the impact of all the task-related factors which could have hindered the appreciation of the perceptual relevance of rise shape in E1. As

3 Perception of melodic detail

discussed in the preceding section, the task might have been made more difficult by the excessive presence of the test word in each block. This was due to the fact that four (sets of) cues were manipulated, each in seven steps. For E2 then, we decided to test the most relevant feature alone, namely rise curvature.

More importantly, the task might have suffered by the association of SPT and QNF with the labels *Answer* and *Question*, since partial topics are characterized by openness and non-conclusiveness, thus not qualifying as prototypical statements. Instead of modifying the labels, since issues in compositionality of pragmatic meaning could still have affected classification choices (see Section 2.4.3), we decided to use a more clear-cut contrast on the meaning side. Narrow focus questions were contrasted to Narrow Focus Statements (*SNF*), thus permitting a more straightforward association with our two labels. It is true that nuclear pitch accents in SNF are characterized by an earlier peak alignment than both QNFs and SPTs, and that shape proprieties in SNF have not been directly contrasted with those from QNF. However, an informal examination of the *Tre Grazie* corpus showed that SNF exhibit a concave rise, as in the case of SPT (see also examples from D'Imperio et al. 2008).[8] Moreover, in the perspective of research on prosodic detail, the fact that SNF and QNF have different peak alignment could actually represent an asset. Since the role of peak alignment in question-statement classification has been shown to be crucial (D'Imperio 2002, among others), it is reasonable to hypothesize that if rise shape is also a cue to sentence modality, its role will be ancillary to stronger cues such as peak alignment. By creating stimuli with ambiguous timing of the peak and by manipulating rise shape, we have the opportunity to test if listeners rely on prosodic detail in the very condition in which they are supposed to do so, namely when other stronger and already acknowledged cues are not available. E2 will then test the hypothesis that classification of utterances as narrow focus question or statement will be influenced by the scaling of the midpoint of the rise when peak timing is ambiguous.

For E2, a last improvement was devised. Results from E1 showed that subjects with higher correct classification rate of control stimuli had a consistent bias towards more *Answer* responses for experimental stimuli (see Section 3.2.4).[9] Recall

---

[8] SPTs appear to share features of QNF and SNF in both substance and meaning: on the phonetic side, they are characterized by QNF peak alignment and SNF rise shape, while on the pragmatic side they share SNF sentence modality and QNF openness. An utterly compositional approach to intonational meaning could suggest a direct link between the two sets. Given the arguments exposed in Section 2.4.3, we will not pursue this hypothesis here.

[9] Bias towards statement responses is not infrequent in various percceptual tasks: see Petrone & Niebuhr (2014) for a discussion of the possible statistical or cognitive (Pandelaere & Dewitte 2006) reasons behind the phenomenon.

that experimental items were created by manipulating an original SPT stimulus, which we tried to de-characterize by averaging out some of its melodic proprieties with those extracted from a QNF stimulus. However, listeners might also have paid attention to other features in the original stimulus, for example details along other prosodic cues, such as intensity, duration, or even voice quality or segmental proprieties. This hypothesis can be tested by using two stimuli (extracted from sentences uttered in different pragmatic contexts) instead of one as a basis for further manipulations. Support to this hypothesis would disclose the possibility of investigating prosodic detail not only within intonation contours, but also along other prosodic dimensions, with potentially severe implications on phonological modelling.

3.3.2 Hypotheses

E2 thus allows us to test two hypotheses concerning the classification as questions or statements of trisyllabic stimuli with ambiguous peak alignment of the nuclear accent:

H1: *identification is affected by rise shape.* The production experiment reported in Section 2 showed different interpolation paths between the tonal targets composing a rising accent. According to the null hypothesis, the negative findings of E1 in Section 3.2 suggest that these differences are to be considered redundant phonetic information. The alternative hypothesis is that rise shape is perceptible and indeed used in classification, and that the negative findings of E1 are due to a number of confounding factors in the administered task.

H2: *identification is affected by non-melodic cues.* The responses of the most reliable listeners in E1 had a bias towards the category of the stimulus used as a source for resynthesis. Since $f0$ was made ambiguous between the two tested categories, phonetic information other than $f0$ must be recoverable and indeed used for classification. According to the null hypothesis, intonational cues alone are at work in pitch accent categorization.

Support for the alternative hypotheses will be evaluated by fitting subjects' responses to a Logit Mixed Model and by gauging the statistical significance of the factors *Stimulus step* (that is, degrees of concavity or convexity in rise shape manipulation) and *Base stimulus* (for stimuli resynthesized starting from either a Question or a Statement), for H1 and H2 respectively. Significance level was set to < 0.05.

3.3.3 Method

15 Neapolitan Italian native speakers took part in the second forced-choice categorization task. They were mainly undergraduate students from various faculties of Naples' University, and none had training in prosody and intonation. They performed the task using their own computers and headphones, after downloading 5 soundfiles (one for each block) and 1 textfile (the answer sheet) from a website. Subjects had to listen to the soundfiles and write their answer on the textfile; they were asked not to pause during blocks, but no restrictions were given as for pauses between blocks. In each block, stimuli were separated by 5 seconds of silence, during which subjects were supposed to write down their answer. No subject reported problems in performing this operation within the time they were given. Each of the 5 blocks was 5 minutes long, so the entire experiment lasted approximately 30 minutes.

As mentioned above, E2 differs from E1 in (1) the use of Narrow Focus instead of Partial Topic, (2) the manipulation of two base stimuli instead of one and (3) the manipulation of a single dimension (namely rise shape) instead of four. However, as for E1, stimuli consisted in utterances recorded for the *Tre Grazie* corpus.[10]

Using SNF instead of SPT affected the creation of the ambiguous stimuli to be used as the basis for further manipulations. Unlike SPTs, SNF have a peak aligned earlier than QNF, a phonetic property mirrored in the different analyses and transcriptions of Narrow Focus accents in questions (L*+H, see Section 2.1.3) and statements (L+H*). Averaging the peak alignment required a 2 ms manipulation for E1 and a 15 ms manipulation for E2. However, informal testing from three NI native speakers confirmed that the resulting stimuli sounded both ambiguous and natural, thus qualifying as viable bases for further manipulations.

The use of two base stimuli instead of one did not lead to an increase in the number of experimental stimuli because instead of manipulating four (sets of) cues we only manipulated one. For E2 there were 14 test items (2 base stimuli x 1 dimension x 7 steps), i.e. half of those used in E1 (1 base stimulus x 4 dimensions x 7 steps). This allowed us to increase from 18 to 34 the number of control natural items. Control items were composed by the two unresynthesized base stimuli and by two repetitions of 16 trisyllabic Subjects extracted from the *Tre Grazie* corpus. This time, we excerpted the names from 4 utterances of 2 different sentences in the 2 pragmatic contexts. Again, the first names used for control items were

---

[10] See Section 3.2.3 and especially Section 2.2.1 for details on the elicitation procedure. SNF utterances were preceded by a contextualizing question suggesting a wrong instantiation for the Subject position, as in "Is it Mary the one who arrives at 9?" preceding the target sentence *Valeria viene alle nove*.

different from the one used for test items, but in this case the percentage of the three first names was perfectly balanced.[11], whereas the test name was almost four times as frequent as each of the other two in E1.[12] Subjects participating to E1 spontaneously reported a certain degree of sensitivity to the relative frequency of the test items' name (see Section 3.2.5). Thus, for E2 stimuli we rescaled the relative frequencies of the three names. Moreover, after the test we asked subjects whether they considered one of the three names to be frequent than the others, but none reported any noticeable skew.

As for the experimental items, we modified the curve index by shifting the height of rise midpoint in 7 steps, identical to the procedure for the second set of E1, using the *PSOLA* algorithm (Moulines & Charpentier 1990) embedded in *Praat* (Boersma & Weenink 2008). This was done for both ambiguous base stimuli. The central step (n. 4) was assigned a value that corresponded to a linear interpolation between L1 and H; steps from 3 to 1 had progressively higher height values, corresponding to a progressively increasing concave interpolation, and steps from 5 to 7 had progressively lower height values, corresponding to a more and more convex interpolation (see Figure 3.6). Step size was 15 Hz, as determined through the use of actual values of rise midpoint in the two base stimuli (used as penultimate in both direction) and the number of steps.

We gathered responses for 1050 experimental items (15 subjects x 5 blocks x 7 steps x 2 base stimuli) and 2550 control items (15 subjects x 5 blocks, each composed by 2 base stimuli and 2 repetitions of 16 natural stimuli).

3.3.4 Results

Responses to control stimuli show that listeners found this task far easier than the preceding one. We had 170 control stimuli for each subject (5 blocks x (2 base stimuli + 2 repetitions x 16 natural stimuli)), and this time only one speaker out of 15 did not reach the 60% correct response threshold (17 out of 22 in E1).

The top panel of Figure 3.7 shows the observed responses to experimental stimuli. Percent of question responses is plotted on the y-axis and step in manipulation on the x-axis (1 being the most concave and 7 the most convex). Results for items created from the two base stimuli are plotted separately (solid line: question, dashed line: statement). Results show a trend to more question responses

---

[11] 7 steps x 1 set x 2 ambiguous bases + 2 natural bases = **16** *Valeria* as experimental items, and 4 utterances x 2 contexts x 2 repetitions = **16** for both *Amelia* and *Milena* as control items.

[12] 7 steps x 4 sets x 1 ambiguous base + 2 repetitions x 1 natural base = **30** *Milena* as experimental items, and 2 utterances x 2 contexts x 2 repetitions = **8** for both *Amelia* and *Valeria* as control items.

3 Perception of melodic detail

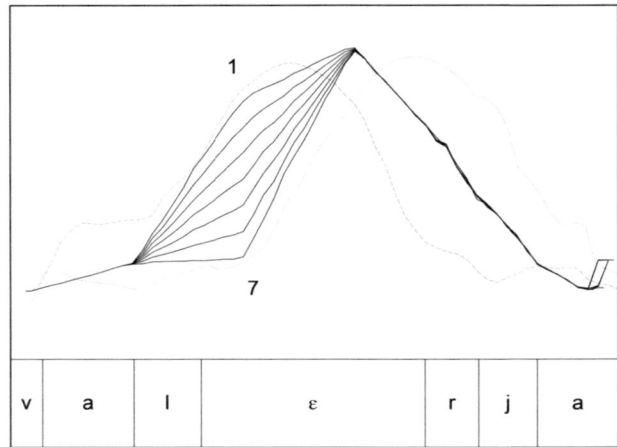

Figure 3.6: *f0* contours and averaged phone segmentation for original stimuli (dashed: statement; dotted: question) and resynthezied items (numbers indicate continuum's ends).

for more convex rises. Observed responses to experimental stimuli were fitted to a Logit Mixed Model, in which *Stimulus step* (1 to 7) and *Base stimulus* (Statement or Question) were chosen as fixed factors, while *Subjects* was assigned random status (with variable slope and intercept). Results of the model are shown in Figure 3.7, bottom panel.

Stimulus step and *Base stimulus* proved to be highly significant (respectively, beta= 0.252, z=3.1, p < 0.002 and beta= -1.196, z=-3.3, p < 0.001), while the interaction between the two factors was not significant (z= -0.018, p= 0.98), indicating that the slopes relative to the two base stimuli are not significantly different.

This means that, although a Stimulus step effect can be recovered for both continua, items obtain consistently different scores according to the base stimulus from which they are resynthetized. As Figure 3.7 (right panel) shows, the Question-based stimuli always elicited more Question responses than the respective Statement-based stimuli. Moreover, if for S-based stimuli there is an actual shift in perception,[13] Q-based stimuli only display a strengthening of Q-responses.[14]

---

[13] From less than 40% Q-responses for step 1 to more than 60% Q-responses for step 7, through about 50% Q-responses for the intermediate step 4.
[14] From more than 60% for step 1 to more than 90% for step 7.

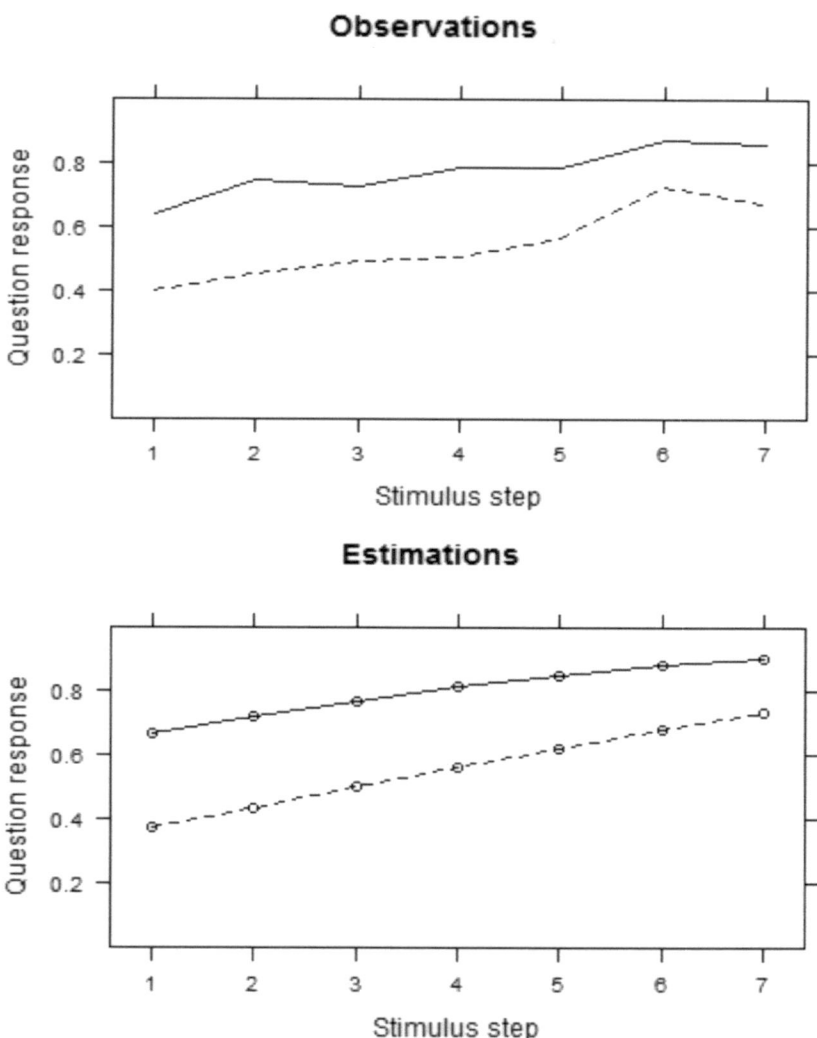

Figure 3.7: Experiment II. Observed (top panel) and estimated (bottom panel) question response frequency (y-axis) as a function of manipulation step (x-axis, 1 being very concave and 7 being very convex) and grouped according to base stimulus (solid line: question; dashed line: statement).

3.3.5 Discussion

Results from E2 suggest that NI listeners do use rise shape information in order to classify stimuli with ambiguous peak alignment as either questions or statements. Lower rise midpoints (i.e. convex rises) cue more question responses while higher rise midpoints (i.e. concave rises) cue more statement responses, independently of the nature of the stimulus used as starting point for the resynthesis.

As the results for control items show, subjects found the task involving QNF and SNF far easier than the one involving QNF and SPT. 14 subjects out of 15 had a correct classification rate on control stimuli of above 60%, indicating that judgements on trisyllabic stimuli are reliable. This shows that the low performances recorded for E1 are indeed due to the specific pragmatic contrast under examination rather than to the task itself (see Section 3.2.5), even if it is reasonable to assume that the rescaling of first name proportions also had a positive effect on the listeners' attention (see Section 3.3.3).

Performance rates on control stimuli show that task results are reliable, but the magnitude of the shift in the subjects' responses to experimental stimuli indicate that rise shape is not a primary cue. While resynthesis of peak alignment can yield up to a 90% shift in subjects' responses to a question-statement classification task (D'Imperio 2000: §3, among others), in our experiment the shift is only around 30%. This is consistent with the role of shape information as prosodic detail: in normal conditions, listeners would rely on peak alignment information. When this information is removed (through averaging in resynthesis), subsidiary information from rise shape can partially surrogate the disambiguation load.

Our results also show that the nature of the base stimulus has a significant effect on subjects' responses. Items resynthesized from a question or statement base always elicited more question or statement responses, respectively. We could speculate that the procedure employed to de-characterize base stimuli (see Section 3.2.3) did not really produce ambiguous items, as it only involved averaging out tone scaling and peak alignment. In more general terms, the procedure only involved $f0$ manipulations, but we cannot exclude that modality contrasts could also be signalled by cues other than $f0$, such as spectral or rhythmic cues (Niebuhr & Pfitzinger 2010; D'Imperio 2000: §5, among others). With regard to the issue of prosodic detail, this finding is particularly interesting: phonological representations of intonation could be underspecified not only with respect to details of phonetic information relative to the fundamental frequency, but also with respect to other prosodic cues.

3.4 General discussion

The two experiments reported in this chapter aimed at evaluating the perceptual role of shape differences in rising nuclear accents, in order to determine whether the phonological representation of pitch accents must be enriched with dynamic *f0* information. In summary, we could say that E1 and E2 bring mixed evidence to our research question, but they also point towards its broadening.

In the first experiment we asked our listeners to classify short manipulated stimuli as QNF or SPT. Manipulations were carried out according to the production evidence found in Section 2 (where rises were more convex in Questions and more concave in Statements), under the hypothesis that regularities in production are exploited in perception. The results show that classification is not affected by rise shape manipulation, thus invalidating our research hypothesis. However, the results could have been affected by a number of factors linked to the nature of the task itself, rather than actually mirroring a total lack of significant effects. We devised a follow-up experiment (E2) in order to reduce the impact of some of these possibly confounding factors. From an epistemological point of view, the evaluation of negative results is a very complex operation, which requires the exploration of several repair strategies. In the following, we discuss three improvements we did not apply to E2 (Section 3.4.1; see Section 3.3.3 for a discussion of the adopted ones). Then we turn to the main finding of E2, namely the influence of base stimulus category on subjects' responses, and discuss how it reshapes the research question we tackled so far (Section 3.4.2).

3.4.1 Possible task improvements

To begin with, a first remark is that shape differences cannot be used in classification if they are not perceived at all. That is, if negative results to the classification task proposed in E1 had been complemented by negative results for a parallel discrimination task, dismissing the hypothesis of the perceptual relevance of shape differences would have been easier. We thus proceeded to an informal evaluation of the discriminability of pitch accents with different rise shapes. Given the limited pool of available subjects for this additional task and the encouraging results of the informal exploration (in which three out of three listeners reported to "hear a difference" between concave and convex rises), we decided to concentrate our efforts in devising a second classification task. The epistemological assumption behind this choice was that positive results to a second task could have allowed us for a clearer interpretation of the negative results to the first.

Another possible improvement could have been the use of a different task.

3 Perception of melodic detail

We have seen in the introduction that identification is not the only task available to the researcher: indeed, semantic differential and context matching both have already been used for the exploration of the perceptual role of prosodic detail. When discussing the results from E1, we stated that one of the possible confounding factor was the use of the labels *Question* and *Answer* for the classification of narrow focus questions and partial topic statements. Given the particularly open pragmatic value of SPT, it is possible that the two labels would not represent equally well the two categories. In E2, we overrode this issue by using narrow focus statements instead of SPT, thus resetting the symmetry between categories and labels. However, it could be noted that the use of a context matching task would have eluded the categories and label issue from its very roots. Upon listening to the excerpted short stimuli, subjects could have been asked to either choose the most appropriate completion between the ones typed on screen, or to rate the appropriateness of one single completion. We could also have avoided the use of possibly misleading labels through the use of a semantic differential task. However, which semantic scales would have allowed us for a clear characterization of QNF and SPT? As we said above, SPT share with Q(NF) a certain degree of openness, in that they qualify as both giving information and suggesting that more information is needed. This feature could have complicated the positioning of SPT on the other hand of QNF on any given semantic scale. For these reasons, we decided to drop the SPT context altogether, in favour of a more straightforward pragmatic contrast. This obviously introduced an asymmetry between the exploration of production and perception data on two different contrasts (production of SPT vs QNF in Section 2; perception of SNF vs QNF in Section 3, E2). However, this choice also had the advantage of situating our experiment in the broader frame of other studies on phonetic detail along contrasts in sentence modality, as the work on prenuclear falls in both NI and Northern Standard German we discussed in the introduction (Section 3.1).

One last possible improvement to the task was the use of stimuli modified in order to maximize the listeners' attention to the possibly relevant cues under investigation. The use of degraded stimuli, for example, has proven useful in the exploration of the role of phonetic detail in speaker recognition (Sheffert et al. 2002). However, as responses to control items in E1 show, no further complexification of task or stimuli was possible, since the subjects already reported serious difficulties in performing the original task, even with simply excerpted (and thus not resynthesized) stimuli.

While the choice of not using degraded stimuli or a semantic differential task was motivated by the reasons we exposed above, the options of a discrimination task or of a context matching had no clear drawbacks, and were discarded only out of the relative unavailability of NI native speakers at the Université de Provence.

3.4.2 A broader research question

The perceptual evaluation of shape differences in nuclear rises was instrumental in deciding whether phonological representations of pitch accents should be enriched with dynamic melodic information. The experiments reported in this chapter bring mixed evidence to this research question. On the one hand, the shape differences attested in the SPT vs QNF contrast in production were not found to be used in perception. On the other hand, we documented an effect of rise shape on classification in the SNF vs QNF contrast, a contrast for which we had not documented shape differences in production yet. Perhaps the most linear way to complement our positive perception results was to verify the presence of rise shape differences in production for SNF vs QNF as well. However, we felt that E2 yielded evidence for a phenomenon which could reshape our initial research question altogether: if listeners responses are biased by the nature of the base stimulus even when $f0$ contours are made the same (see the offset between the two curves in Figure 3.7), then phonological categories could need an enrichment not only with respect to melodic information, but also to phonetic information along different dimensions, such as intensity, duration, voice quality or spectral composition.

Research on intonational phonology has long acknowledged that cues other than $f0$ could play a role in the signalling of post-lexical meaning (Hirschberg & Ward 1992): base-related effects have been reported in perceptual experiments since D'Imperio (2000), and have recently made the object of direct investigation (Niebuhr & Pfitzinger 2010). If other phonetic cues are involved in coding and decoding prosodic categories, the question of whether phonological representations of pitch accents should include dynamic $f0$ detail could be generalized and reshaped as to ask whether phonological approaches to intonation should include non-$f0$ information. That is, investigating prosodic detail would mean not only to concentrate on unacknowledged features (such as shape) for acknowledged dimension ($f0$), but to unacknowledged features themselves. Throughout the remeinder of this book we will verify the potential importance of one of these dimensions, namely tempo. Therefore, a discussion as to whether or not the shape differences explored in this chapter should be accommodated into phonological descriptions of intonation needs to be postponed. If duration or intensity variations have to be included in the representation of pitch accents,

3 Perception of melodic detail

the restructuring will be deeper than if only new features for already existing dimensions had to be added. For this reason, before suggesting any account of if and how shape differences should be included in phonological representations of pitch accents, we will turn to the potential role of other prosodic cues as prosodic detail.

3.5 Conclusion

In this chapter we evaluated the perceptual role of rise shape as documented for production in Section 2. Two experiments based on identification tasks showed that listeners perceive the difference between concave and convex nuclear rises, and that they exploit it for classification purposes. While the first experiment failed to show that classification of Partial Topic Statements and Narrow Focus Questions is affected by rise shape, evidence from the second experiment shows that these negative results might be due to task-related issues. This is because, as soon as stimuli are made ambiguous with respect to the main cue of peak alignment, listeners do use rise shape information in order to classify them as Narrow Focus Questions or Statements.

While not being explicitly tested, a strong effect of the nature of the stimulus used as base for *f0* manipulations was also found in both experiments. In the first experiment, where we only used stimuli resynthesized from a (Partial Topic) Statement base, the listeners who showed the best performance on control stimuli showed a consistent Statement bias for test items. In the second experiment we decided to resynthesize test stimuli from both (Narrow Focus) Question and Statements. Responses from all subjects displayed a strong base effect: for a given step on the continuum in the manipulation of shape proprieties, stimuli resynthesized from a base question always elicited more question responses. That is, while looking for evidence for phonetic detail within a single prosodic dimension (rise shape within *f0* contours), we found reason to believe that other entire prosodic dimensions (duration, intensity, voice quality, spectral proprieties) could represent a source for phonetic detail as well.

Given the possibility of a radical restructuring of phonological representations for pitch accents due to the inclusion of new prosodic dimensions in intonational phonology, our investigation of the role of dynamic melodic detail risks to qualify as minimalist and inconclusive. For these reasons, before returning to the issue of the enrichment of phonological categories, in the next experimental chapters we turn to the evaluation of the role of one of these possible additional dimension, namely tempo, both from a production (Section 4) and a perception (Section 5) viewpoint.

4 Temporal detail in production

The experiments reported in the previous chapters document consistently produced (Section 2) and perceived (Section 3) phonetic information which is not included in phonological representations of intonation. Specifically, in the Autosegmental-Metrical approach (AM), phonological representations are essentially based on a discretization of melodic information. In the two latter chapters we questioned the degree of discretization that can be performed without losing useful information, whereas in the two next chapters we will explore whether or not restricting to melodic information alone (independent of the degree of discretization) already entails potential losses.

The research question of whether phonological contrasts in intonation should be specified on other prosodic dimensions than melody alone stems from the findings of an experiment on the identification of sentence modality contrasts in Neapolitan Italian (NI; see Section 3.4). Prior to the Manipulation phase, in which rise shape was modified along a continuum of values, sentences which were originally uttered as (narrow focus) Questions and Statements (respectively, QNF and SNF) were resynthesized such as to have an ambiguous $f0$ contour (Preparation phase). However, identification results showed a consistent base effect: independent of rise shape manipulation, stimuli which were resynthesized from a Statement base always elicited more Statement responses. If we assume that the creation of the ambiguous $f0$ contour was successful, one of the possible motivations for this base effect is that the original stimuli contain other non-$f0$ cues to sentence modality. Such cues, which were not averaged out and made ambiguous in the Preparation phase, could have biased listeners' responses.

But are there not any other phonetic cues that could also be relevant in the signalling of sentence modality contrasts in NI? A reasonable starting point would be the investigation of the prosodic dimensions involved in the question/statement contrast in other languages. Annie Rialland, for example, found that tempo and voice quality are involved in sentence modality contrasts in various African languages, either in addition to or in replacement of the melodic cues (Rialland 2007). Specifically, statements are characterized by shorter and abruptly ending final vowels in Moba, a four-tone Gur language of Togo (Rialland 1984). Other Gur

4 *Temporal detail in production*

languages, such as Ncam (Podi 1995), associate breathy terminations with other question markers, such as a falling tone. Low tones function as question markers in about half of the languages surveyed by Rialland, but High or Rising tones are attested as well: the same end of a given prosodic dimension is associated with opposite functions in the various languages. This is also true for lengthening phenomena: longer final vowels are a cue to question modality, either on their own (as in Nateni, a Gur language, and Wobé, a Kru language: see Neukom 1995 and Marchese 1978, respectively) or more often in conjunction with other cues (see Ncam, again). In contrast, questions show a suppression of penultimate lengthening in some Bantu languages (such as Zulu, see Taljaard & Bosch 1988). In sum, and despite the different patterns attested in the various languages, these findings point to the possible relevance of tempo and voice quality in the signalling of sentence modality contrasts. Could these dimension then be relevant in NI as well? Could they be responsible, for example, of the base effect documented in Section 3? This issue is crucial for our broader research interest in prosodic detail: whereas in the previous chapters we looked for detail in *f0* contours, namely inside the prosodic dimension traditionally acknowledged to be relevant for intonation, we now move to an investigation of other prosodic dimensions altogether.

In the following chapters, we will explore the role of non-*f0* detail in sentence modality contrasts, from both a production (Section 4) and perception (Section 5) perspective. Our investigations will bear more specifically on the temporal dimension since, in comparison with voice quality, its effect on post-lexical meaning has been more widely studied (see Section 4.1) and it can be investigated more reliably using acoustic data alone. Before reporting on the two studies which constitute the core of this chapter, and elaborating on previously published results (Cangemi & D'Imperio 2011a,b, forthcoming), we will clarify the terminological choices made here (see Section 1.4.2). In this book, reviving a proposal by Ilse Lehiste, the term *tempo* makes reference to the formal dimension bridging patterns in segmental durations on the substantive side with post-lexical meaning on the functional side (Lehiste 1970). In this respect, it can be contrasted along a single dimension with both *quantity*, which deals with lexical meaning on the functional side, and *intonation*, which deals with patterns in fundamental frequency on the substantive side. Tempo can also be contrasted along both dimensions with *tone*, which bridges patterns in fundamental frequency with lexical meaning. The existence of the phonological dimension of tempo, and thus of different *temporal patterns* comparable to tunes on the intonational level, is taken as a research hypothesis (see Section 4.5.2): when referring to actual and measurable phonetic differences in the signal, we rather use *duration* for single segments and *durational pattern* when referring to larger structures.

4.1 Introduction

The increasing number of studies on the temporal structure of speech has led to a better understanding of the various prosodic cues and of their roles. Whereas post-lexical meaning has almost been studied exclusively in relation with fundamental frequency data (viz. on the intonation dimension) for a long time, recent studies show the importance of other cues, such as duration (along with articulation rate and similar metrics, viz. on the tempo dimension), intensity or voice quality.

Speech rate, for example, has long been acknowledged as an important factor to control for in studies on phone durations (see Turk et al. 2006). Studies on paralinguistic and extralinguistic meaning recognize speech rate as a predictor, as in the cases of emotional speech (Williams & Stevens 1972) and in applications of speaker recognition (van Heerden & Barnard 2007). Recognition of proper linguistic functions for speech rate probably began with investigations on its role as a resource for turn management (Duncan 1972). The role of temporal variations in connection with discretely structured post-lexical meaning, on the other hand, has been less explored, though notable exceptions exist (e.g. Eefting 1991 on given/new and accented/unaccented contrasts). Even if the picture we can draw from the literature on this topic is far from coherent (see Section 4.3.2), sentence modality contrasts represent perhaps the most studied case of relationships between post-lexical meaning and temporal patterns.

Work on the role of tempo in the question-statement contrasts is affected by various difficulties. First of all, many among the studies discussing the effect of sentence modality on temporal patterns are primarily concerned with the analysis of *f0* and intonation (Maturi 1988; Ryalls et al. 1994; Smith 2002; Rialland 2007; Petrone 2008): results on duration and tempo are, in this case, almost a by-product of analyses centred on other issues. As a natural consequence, in many cases the speech material is not perfectly suited for the analysis of duration, either because of a lack of segmentally controlled material (e.g. presence of geminates, diphthongs) or because of problems in the control of other possibly confounding factors, such as focus patterns (see Gubian et al. 2011). Comparisons between the results are also complicated by the fact that, apart from several studies on Dutch (van Heuven & Haan 2000, 2002; van Heuven & van Zanten 2005), the languages investigated in the literature are typologically quite different, ranging from Manado Malay (van Heuven & van Zanten 2005) to various African languages (Rialland 2007) and different varieties of English (van Heuven & van Zanten 2005 on Orkney English), French (Ryalls et al. 1994 on Canadian French; Smith 2002 on Hexagonal French), Italian (Maturi 1988; Petrone 2008 on Neapolitan Italian; De Dominicis 2010 on Bomarzo's dialect) and Spanish (Henriksen 2012 on Manchego Peninsular Spanish). Moreover, the studies cited above use various metrics for the assessment of temporal patterns, ranging from individual phone durations to a single speech rate value for the entire utterance. We will provide a synopsis of these studies in Section 4.3.2.

In what follows, we will illustrate the results of a production study on the effect of sentence modality on tempo in read NI speech. We devised two experiments, based on the use of the same corpora, which will thus be presented in a separate section (Section 4.2.1), along with a segmentation tool developed on purpose for this study (Section 4.2.2). These corpora, unlike the materials used in most of the previous studies, were explicitly designed for the analysis of tempo, allowing for both an easy segmentation and a thorough control of focus patterns. The first experiment (E1, see Section 4.3) uses a discrete metric, namely phone durations, in order to provide data as comparable as possible with studies from the literature, and to enrich them through the use of more controlled material. The role of focus will be taken up in the second experiment (E2, see Section 4.4), which is based on the use of a continuous metric (viz. local phone rate).

4.2 Material

Both the discrete and continuous analyses were conducted on two corpora of read speech explicitly designed for the investigation of temporal phenomena. The corpora were also optimized for the automated extraction of phone durations with *ASSI* (Cangemi et al. 2011), a forced alignment tool for Italian developed for the purposes of this study. Since the corpora are used in both analyses, and since some of the *ASSI* features oriented the corpora design, we will present them before turning to the two analyses.

4.2.1 Corpora

As we said above, many of the studies reporting data on durational patterns across sentence modality used corpora originally designed for the analysis of intonation. As a consequence, these materials are often difficult to measure because of the presence of diphthongs, geminate consonants and other design features which are compatible with the analysis of intonation, but troublesome in the analysis of tempo. The two corpora used in our study, then, are designed to exert a strict control on various, possibly confounding factors, though at different degrees.

4.2.1.1 Orlando

Control is strictly enforced in the first corpus. Since test sentences had to be compatible with both levels (Question and Statement) of the *Modality* factor, we opted for a simple syntactic structure, namely Subject-Verb-Object. This allowed us to create an orthogonal factor of *Focus placement* with three levels (Subject, Verb and Object). The six interpretations deriving from the combination of the two factors were induced by pairing the test sentence with a contextualization paragraph, which was meant to be silently read before uttering the test sentence. In order to control for confounds induced by lexical frequency effects, we used fantasy names for Subjects and Objects and switched their role across sentences, with the consequence of restraining Verbs to forms of the third person singular. The morphological constraint was reinforced by allowing present tenses only. Each of the syntactic positions was instantiated by a single paroxytone word, composed by a fixed number of syllables (three for Subjects and Objects, two for Verbs) all of which had a Consonant-Vowel structure, yielding a $[CV.'CV.CV]_S$ $['CV.CV]_V$ $[CV.'CV.CV]_O$ template. Additional restrictions were placed at the phonetic level, by allowing only voiced consonants and monophthongs in order to further reduce predictable durational differences. A side effect of this constraint is that the present corpus is also especially suited for the study of read speech intonation. Since we used a tool to automatically align phone boundaries (*ASSI*, see Section 4.2.2) in order to minimize the arbitrariness of the segmentation procedure, we also decided to avoid phones which were not highly frequent in the training dataset, i.e. with less than 4000 occurrences.

In order to maintain a thematic coherence among the sentences we chose fantasy names and actual verbs which were compatible with a heroic poem setting (hence the corpus' name, which is the Italian translation for Hruodland). Here is an example of a test trial, composed of the context (1a) to be read silently, and the test item (1b), to be read aloud. In this example, the context was intended to elicit focus placement on the subject in a statement interpretation of the test item (in italics):

4 Temporal detail in production

(1) a. The knights are wandering in the maze, each struggling to come first to the chamber. Despite their oath of honour, the prize is so important that they don't refrain from attacking each other. In this situation, being able to see the enemy before he spots you is a very important factor. Now, for example, is it Gramante who noticed the arrival of Ladona?
b. No, *Ralego vede Ladona.*
c. 'Ralego sees Ladona.'

4.2.1.2 Danser

The use of constraints on so many levels (pragmatics, syntax, lexicon, morphology, phonology, phonetics and automatic analysis) inevitably results in a reduction of the communicative plausibility of the test sentences. For this reason, a smaller set of sentences (less tightly controlled and more plausible) was designed in order to verify the generalizability of results from the *Orlando* corpus. Target sentences in the *Danser* corpus weakened the constraints on lexical frequency and on total voicing. This allowed for the use of phones which are more frequent in *ASSI* training set (from a minimum of 4000 to 6000 occurrences), Prepositional Phrases as verb arguments, and real first names as Subjects. The two subjects' names used in sentences (2a) and (2c) motivate the choice of the name of the corpus.

(2) a. *Danilo vola da Roma.*
b. 'Danilo flies from Rome.'
c. *Serena vive da Lara.*
d. 'Serena lives at Lara's.'

4.2.1.3 Recordings

Recordings of both corpora were made in the sound-treated booth.[1] Speakers were recruited among 20-25 year old students from the School of Humanities. They were all native speakers of the Neapolitan variety of Italian. The trials were prompted on a computer screen using *Perceval* (André et al. 2003), while the recordings were made using an AKG MicroMic C520 head-mounted microphone

---

[1] We would like to thank Elio Marciano for allowing us to use the facilities at *CIRASS* (Centro Interdipartimentale di Ricerca per l'Analisi e la Sintesi dei Segnali), Naples University "Federico II", and Giovanni Abete for his assistance.

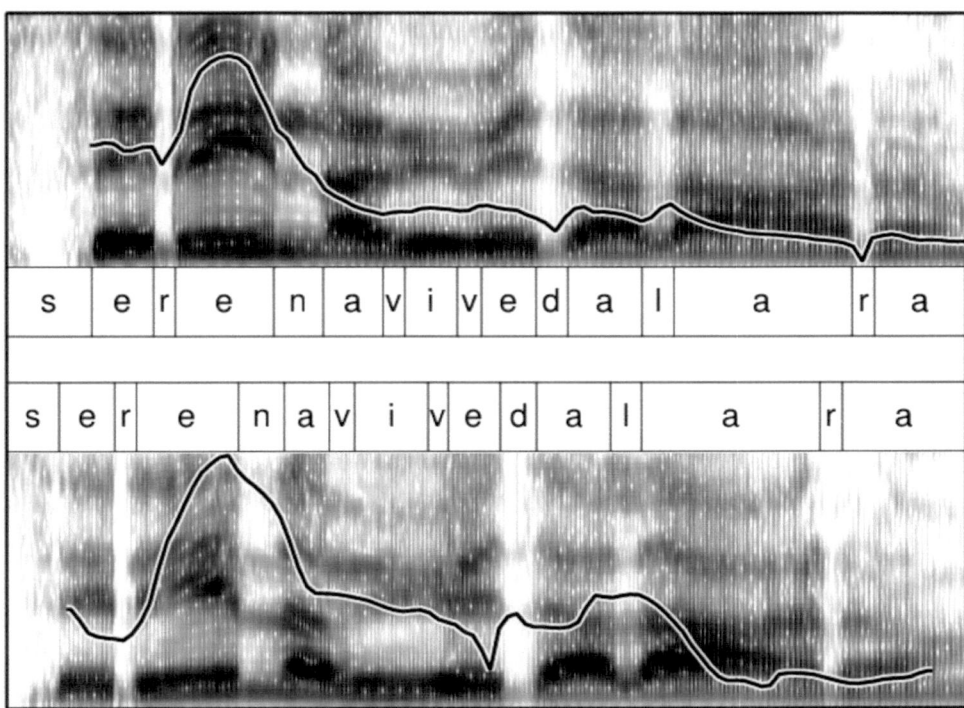

Figure 4.1: Spectrogram, *f0* track and phone segmentation for the sentence *Serena vive da Lara* uttered with subject narrow focus, as a statement (top panel) and as a question (bottom panel).

4 Temporal detail in production

linked through a Shure X2u adapter to a personal computer running *Audacity* (Audacity Development Team 2006).

For the *Orlando* corpus, 30 speakers read 3 repetitions of the 6 interpretations for each of the 3 test sentences, resulting in a total of 1620 items. For the *Danser* corpus, 21 speakers read 3 repetitions of the 6 interpretations for each of the 2 test sentences, resultin in a total of 756 utterances. Each experimental item was isolated from the recording blocks and opportunely coded using a scripted procedure in *Praat* (Boersma & Weenink 2008). A small amount (ca. 3%) of the recorded utterances contained disfluencies or prosodic breaks after the focussed constituent, and were thus excluded from the analysis.

4.2.2 Forced alignment

The 2376 utterances from the two corpora were segmented to phones. Since every sentence was composed of eight CV syllables, phone segmentation would have required the placement of more than 35000 segmental boundaries, making manual segmentation extremely costly. We opted for an automated segmentation procedure, based on forced alignment. In the absence of free forced alignment tools for Italian (but now see Bigi & Hirst 2012), we decided to create our own tool, *ASSI* (Automatic Speech Segmentation for Italian; see Cangemi et al. 2011). The tool requires the input of (1) sound files, (2) orthographic transcriptions and (3) lexicon with pronunciation variants, and yields as output a *Praat*-compatible segmentation file. Data from our corpora are especially suited for use with *ASSI*: by providing an orthographic transcription of 5 sentences and a phonological transcription of 12 words, we obtained segmentation for 2376 utterances in 38016 phones. In order to maximize performances, test sentences were designed so as to avoid the use of phonemes which were scarcely represented in the corpus used to train the acoustic models (viz. the *CLIPS* corpus, Savy & Cutugno 2009).

The quality of the output was scrupulously tested (see Cangemi et al. 2011 for details). This testing involved comparisons with manual expert segmentation of both boundary placement and of metrics extracted from the segmentations. As for the boundary placement, 94% of the markers placed by *ASSI* are within 20 ms from the manual reference in both a subset of the *Orlando* corpus (405 boundaries) and of the *APASCI* corpus (17474 boundaries; see Angelini et al. 1993). If the error from the reference is extended to 30 ms, *ASSI* performances reach 97% with *APASCI* and 99% with the *Orlando* corpus. More importantly for our purposes, *ASSI* and manual segmentations for 27 utterances with three different focus patterns in the Orlando corpus were used to calculate Local Phone Rate curves (see Section 4.4.3). The obtained functions were compared pairwise for focus condition using a two sample F-test for equal variances, and no significant difference was found.

4.3 Experiment 1

4.3.1 Background

As we saw in the introduction of this chapter, tempo has been related to sentence modality contrasts in recent studies only. Durational differences in question/statement contrast have been reported for various languages, on the basis of material drawn from differently designed corpora and measured at different degrees of precision. Two working hypotheses seem to have informed, more or less implicitly, the studies on this topic: first, that there are durational differences across statements and questions, and second, that these differences are localized in specific portions of the utterance. E1 was devised in order to test an explicitly operationalized version of these two hypothesis (Section 4.3.2) by capitalizing on the mixed results available from the literature that we review in this section.

In order to illustrate the issues which arise when comparing studies from the literature, we group the available results in Table 4.1. For each study (column 1) we indicated the investigated language(s) (column 2) and which modality is associated with longer durations (or slower speech rates) at the *Utt*erance level (column 3).[2]

As Table 4.1 shows, questions and statements *do* display different global durations at the utterance level for a variety of languages. However, no universal trend can be extracted from the data: questions are longer in some languages and shorter in others, thus the effect of sentence modality on tempo is language-specific. More interestingly, as the comparison from data on NI shows, the available studies report opposite results even for the same regional variety of a given language. According to Maturi (1988: table 6), sentences are slightly shorter when uttered as a question, but the reverse is true for Petrone (2008: 163).[3]

However, a closer examination of the test items shows that other factors should be taken into account when comparing these results, such as syntax and information structure (see columns 6 and 7 respectively). Whereas Petrone only used

---

[2] We use *S* for statements, *Q* for questions and = for statistically non-significant differences. Cells are left empty if no relevant results are available.
[3] Approximatively, the magnitude of the effect is 30 ms for 1-second long utterances for Maturi and 70 ms for 1.4-second long utterances for Petrone.

4 Temporal detail in production

Table 4.1: Synopsis of findings in the literature on tempo and sentence modality.

Reference	Language	Utt	Beg	End	Syntax	Focus	Domain
Maturi (1988)	Neapolitan Italian	S			(S)V(O)	?	Utterance
Ryalls et al. (1994)	Canadian French	S		Q			Final syllable
Smith (2002)	Hexagonal French			=			Final vowel
Rialland (2007)	Various African	Q		Q			Final vowel
van Heuven & van Zanten (2005)	Manado Malay	S		S			Foot
	Dutch	S	=	=	SOV		Interstress stretch
Petrone (2008)	Neapolitan Italian	Q	S/Q	Q/?	SVO	O	Phonological word
De Dominicis (2010)	Bomarzo (Italy)	Q					Foot

SVO sentences with narrow focus on the Object, the sentences used by Maturi are syntactically different (SV, VO and SVO, with no indication of information structure). Tempo variations are not only language-specific, but they also seem to depend on other factors than sentence modality alone.

An additional layer of variability is represented by speaker-specific behaviour, which can turn into an interpretative problem given the usually low number of subjects (mostly between two and ten). For instance, the two NI speakers in Petrone's corpus have opposite patterns for the first phonological word of the utterances (column 4). This brings us to another source of complexity in the results: other studies have tried to individuate more specifically the domain of durational differences across sentence modalities as well, but the global picture is even more difficult to seize since the domains are of different size (column 8).[4] Specifically, Smith (2002) focusses on the last vowel, Ryalls et al. (1994) on the last syllable, van Heuven & van Zanten (2005) on the last foot (Manado Malay), Petrone (2008) on the first and last phonological word, and van Heuven & van Zanten (2005) on "the stretch between the stressed syllable on the subject and that on the object" (Dutch).

---

[4] For this reason, columns 4 and 5 only broadly refer to "Utterance *beg*inning" and "utterance *End*".

In sum, we can draw three main conclusions on the methodological level from the literature synopsis. First, it is clear that tight control of the test material is needed. Since syntactic and information structure can affect the results (as data on NI shows), the experimental design must be tailored accordingly. For this reason, in our corpora we only used SVO sentences and we varied orthogonally the position of focus.[5] Second, data from Petrone also shows the possibility of strong inter-speaker variability. Therefore, our corpora include recordings from more than fifty speakers altogether. Third, accurate comparisons for the precise localization of durational differences are made impossible by the use of different metrics across the various studies. Measuring the entire utterance duration alone, for example, would reduce the possibility of comparing specific results at the syllable level. For this reason, even if a thorough comparison with the other studies is not our priority, we measured the duration of individual segments, thus permitting their grouping in higher level structures of all sizes.

4.3.2 Hypotheses

The literature synopsis also enables an explicit elaboration of the research hypotheses which implicitly underlie previous work. In general terms, it appears that sentence modality has a *global* effect on tempo, namely at the utterance level, though in opposite ways across languages (questions are shorter in Manado Malay, Orkney English and Dutch, but longer in various African languages, in Bomarzo's dialect and in NI). Morerover, sentence modality also seems to have a *local* effect on tempo, in that durational differences are more intense on some specific portions of the utterance (though with conspicuous differences across studies and languages, e.g. from the first phonological word to the last vowel). Given the mixed results in the literature, the two hypotheses are operationalized in the most general terms possible:

H1 *sentences have a different duration when uttered as questions or statements*, independent of the direction of the effect. Utterance length (U) is different for questions (Q) and statements (S):
$U_Q \neq U_S$.

H2 *durational differences are localized in some specific portions of the utterance*, independent of their position and their size. Duration of the various (from 1 to *n*) segments (P) in a question (Q) is not a linear transformation or uniform stretching/compression (a) of duration in the respective statement

---
[5] Focus will be treated as a *factor* in E2.

(S):
$P\{1,n\}_Q \neq aP\{1,n\}_S$.

Note that the validation of H1 is not a necessary prerequisite for the existence of different durational patterns across the utterance. This is because we cannot exclude a priori the possibility of generating the same utterance duration from two different (but counter-balanced) durational patterns at the segment level. Thus, H1 and H2 can be combined to test whether sentence modality affects tempo at a global (utterance) or at a local (segment) level (see Table 4.2).

Table 4.2: Summary of hypotheses.

		H2	
		No	Yes
H1	No	NO	LOCAL
	Yes	GLOBAL	GLOBAL+LOCAL

Should H1 and H2 be disconfirmed, we will have evidence of a total absence of sentence modality effect on tempo patterns (H0). If H1 is confirmed and H2 is disconfirmed, we will be able to conclude that modality affects utterance duration as a whole. In case H1 is disconfirmed and H2 confirmed, we will have evidence of local tempo variations which do not affect total utterance duration (i.e. they would be counterbalanced). Should both H1 and H2 be confirmed, we will be able to conclude that modality in the first place affects some specific portions of the utterance, and that this effect is visible in terms of total utterance duration as well.

4.3.3 Method

We evaluated these two hypotheses using data from both corpora and extracted with scripted procedures in *Praat*. For the validation of H1, no measurement other than utterance duration was needed. As for H2, we extracted individual phone durations and coded them using the ordinal number of the parent syllable preceded by an identifier for consonant or vowel (e.g. segment [i] in sentence (3) was coded as phone position V2; see Figure 4.2). Phone durations were normalized on parent utterance duration in order to account for idiolectal variations in speech rate. This normalization has the effect of blurring eventual global differences among sentences uttered as questions or statements as well. However, since H1 and H2 are evaluated independently, no confound is possible. It indeed permits an immediate qualitative evaluation of H2 given a plot of relative duration against phone position: for any given value of *a* (see Section 4.3.2), H2 is validated by completely overlapping polylines.

Statistical tests will be described separately for the two hypotheses in the next section, with respect to data from the *Danser* corpus.

4.3.4 Results

H1 was tested with a linear mixed model which predicted the dependent variable *Utterance Duration* by using the fixed factors *Modality* (question or statement), *Focus* (on NP, VP or PP) and *Sentence* (two levels, see (3) and (4)), adding a random intercept for the 21 Speakers. Both the factor *Modality* and its interactions with the factor *Focus* did not reach significance ($t < 2$), leading to the rejection of H1. A Likelihood Ratio Test comparing the model with the fixed factors *Focus* and *Sentence* (and their interaction) with a model including *Modality* as well showed no significant differences ($\chi^2 = 9.9, df = 6, p = 0.13$).

For the sake of completeness, we report that the factor *Focus* on its own did reach significance ($|t| > 3$), indicating that, compared to NP-focussed utterances, VP-focussed utterances are longer while PP-focussed utterances are shorter (mean difference of about ±30 ms on a mean duration of 1.15 s).

We then tested H2 by running a linear mixed model predicting *Phone Duration* from three fixed factors: *Focus* (three levels: NP, VP and PP), *Sentence* (two levels) and the *Combination* of Phone position (from C1 to V8) and Modality (Question or Statement). A successive difference contrast was associated with the 32 levels of the factor *Combination* in order to verify which phone position yielded significantly different durational values across modality. 11376 phone durations were analyzed, and a random intercept was added to account for variability across the 21 Speakers. A Likelihood Ratio Test showed that, compared with the model including three-way interactions, a two-way interaction model had a slightly (and significantly) smaller likelihood, but better AIC and BIC. Therefore, in what follows we will only refer to the more economical model.

Our model showed a number of significant contrasts, but since their combined size effect was less than 10 ms (see Lehiste 1970 for a discussion of difference limina in the perception of duration for speech signals), they will not be further commented one here. Apart from that, three significant interaction coefficients between *Combination* and *Focus* were found, indicating (together with the non-interacting contrasts) that the stressed vowel of a focussed phrase is significantly longer (~10 ms) in Statements. Most importantly, independently of other factors,

4 Temporal detail in production

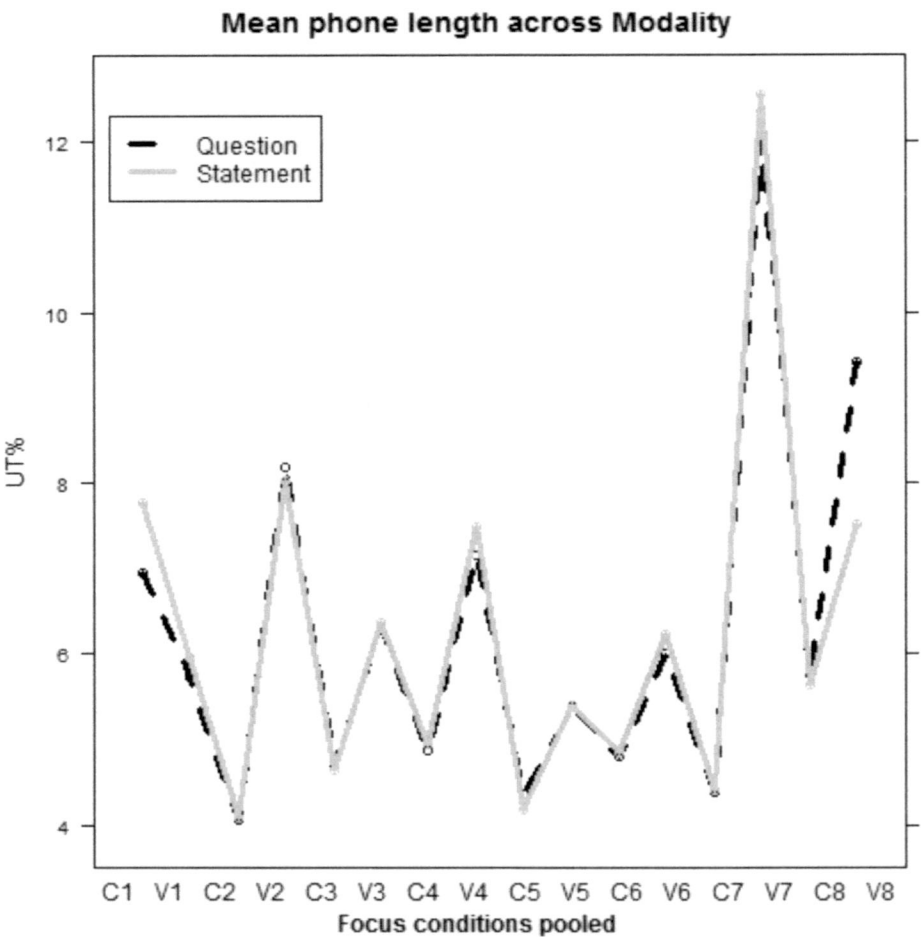

Figure 4.2: Phone duration against position (E1, H2).

the two most highly significant contrasts ($pMCMC < 0.001$) indicated that the first segment (C1) is longer (~12 ms) in Statements and the last segment (V8) is longer (~20 ms) in Questions.

A more readable account of these results can be provided by plotting, for every phone, its *Position* in the utterance (x-axis) against its *Duration* (normalized on utterance length, y-axis) for the two levels of the factor *Modality* (question: dashed black line, and statement: continuous grey line; see Figure 4.2). If *Modality* were not significant, we would expect two exactly overlapping polylines, but the plot does show localized differences (mainly on C1 and V8), thus confirming H2.

4.3.5 Discussion

Our results show that sentence modality does not affect the duration of the entire utterance, which disconfirms H1, but that it affects individual phone durations, thus confirming H2. As a result, E1 found support for the existence of a *local* effect of sentence modality on tempo (see Table 4.2). Specifically, the first segment is longer in statements and the last is longer in questions, but total utterance duration is not significantly different. These findings do not seem compatible with results available from the literature on first sight. In this section, we provide some reasons which could account for the difficulties in drawing a coherent picture from former studies on this topic.

The first unexpected finding is the absence of any durational differences at the utterance level for the two modalities. Indeed, speculating on the results available at the time, van Heuven & van Zanten (2005) even suggested that questions might have been universally linked to a faster speech rate (and thus to shorter durations). We will come back to this issue in greater detail in Section 4.5.1: for the moment it suffices to say that, together with other studies, our data is rather consistent with a language-specific nature of the eventual temporal encoding of sentence modalities. This is perhaps the main factor accounting for the great variance in results in the literature.

Nonetheless, our results are in line with former research in showing that durational differences might be concentrated at specific portions of the utterance. However, because of the choice of different levels of analysis and measurement among the various studies, a direct comparison is not possible. Nonetheless, it is striking that durational differences seem more robust at both utterance ends in almost all studies which reported a localized effect. Our results seem to confirm this trend, showing that the first segment is longer in statements and the last segment is longer in questions. Since phone duration is inversely correlated with speech rate, we can reformulate this finding by saying that sentences are faster in their initial portion when uttered as questions and faster in their final portion when uttered as statements. That is, if we take speech rate to be variable in time, we might expect it to accelerate in statements and decelerate in questions. We will try to use such a dynamic metric in E2. For the sake of our present discussion, the main finding to focus on is that the use of excessively synthetic metrics (such as total utterance duration alone, as in the case of Maturi 1988) could hinder the evaluation of localized effects.

Our last observation concerns the role of syntactic and information structure. Previous studies based on reading tasks featured no balancing of focus placement, and in some cases different syntactic structures as well. In our study, each sentence had the same syntactic structure made of three positions, and was uttered in all three possible narrow focus patterns. Our results show that shifting focus placement can indeed affect both utterance and phone durations. A closer investigation of focus placement as a factor will be provided in E2, but for the purposes of our present discussion we can at least state that differences in syntactic and information structure can be regarded as the third element accounting for the mixed results in the literature on tempo and modality.

4.4 Experiment 2

4.4.1 Background

In E1 we gathered evidence for a localized effect of sentence modality and information structure on tempo, pointing to the need for (1) accurate metrics in measuring durational differences and (2) control for focus. E2 elaborates on these two points by providing an alternative visualization of durational data based on a continuous metric and by testing the effect of focus on temporal patterns.

As for the first point, we have seen that temporal differences across questions and statements are localized within the utterance, yet they counterbalance each other at a global level. This means that our data is best represented using a metric which computes and displays durational patterns in an inherently relational way. In the discussion of the data on phone durations (see Section 4.3.5) we have already suggested that differences in the duration of the segments at both utterance ends could be seen as the result of speech rate variations in time. Instead of calculating a single value for the speech rate of the entire utterance, we could calculate several values using a sliding window on the segmented signal, thus obtaining a continuous representation of speech rate variations. This way, the differences between questions (which have shorter initial segments and longer final segments) and statements (which have longer initial segments and shorter final segments) could be seen, more synthetically, as a difference between globally decelerating and accelerating speech rates across the utterance. A single property would thus be responsible of both local differences in phone durations and global equality of utterance duration. The details of the algorithm for the calculation of continuous speech rate data will be presented in Section 4.4.3.

The other main finding of E1 was that information structure must be controlled for in order to gather reliable data on temporal patterns. The sentences used in E1 were designed to be elicited in a variety of focus placement conditions, and focus placement was controlled (and balanced) under the assumption that it has an effect on temporal patterns. This assumption is motivated by the fact that, in Italian, focalization entails accenting and thus lengthening (Farnetani & Kori 1991). E2, however, turns this assumption into an hypothesis, thus transforming focalization from a controlled (E1) to an independently manipulated (E2) factor. Taking into account the intricate findings in former studies, our interest lies in the possibility that sentence modality and focus structure interact in such a way that surface differences in temporal patterns could be blurred.

4.4.2 Hypotheses

We know that the temporal structure is affected both by focus placement (through accenting and consequent lengthening phenomena) and sentence modality, but do these two factors operate in a completely independent way? We operationalized this hypothesis by predicting that, if focus and modality were independent, the overall modality-induced differences (faster utterance beginning and slower utterance ending for questions) should be found regardless of focus condition.

Unlike the other experiments in this book, the evaluation of this particular hypothesis will be based on qualitative observations. This choice is not only motivated by the relative rareness of statistical analyses of continuous data in linguistics (but see recent work on Functional Data Analysis, e.g. Gubian et al. 2010), but also by the necessity of evaluating the visual impact of the proposed metric.

4.4.3 Method

Using the ASSI phone segmentation as input, we extracted a continuous representation of speech rate variations by using a slightly modified version of the Local Phone Rate (henceforth *LPR*) function proposed by Pfitzinger (2001). As indicated by its name, LPR is calculated for a given point in time by counting the number of phone boundaries falling inside a window centred around the point itself. If LPR is calculated for multiple points and plotted against time, the result will be a graphical display of variations in speech rate as a function of time. Obviously, the calculation relies on a number of parameters which have to be adapted to the characteristics of the speech material under examination. In particular, the size of the analysis window and of the steps must be short enough to capture variations of the desired magnitude. In our case, we decided to use a 0.2s window and 0.01s steps.

We also modified the original formula in two respects. First, we calculated no values when the window exceeded the signal boundary. That is, given an analysis window of 0.2s, we calculated no LPR values for $t < 0.1$ and $t > T - 0.1$ (T being total utterance duration). Also, the original formula was meant to deal with speech material containing pauses as well. Since utterances with pauses and disfluencies were excluded from our corpora, we could simplify the original formula in this respect. As a result, LPR was calculated using the formula in (5), through the use of an automated procedure in R (R Development Core Team 2008):

(5) $$LPR_i = \frac{\frac{t_{(l+1)} - (i - \frac{w}{2})}{t_{(l+1)} - t_l} + \frac{(i + \frac{w}{2}) - t_r}{t_{(r+1)} - t_r} + r - l - 1}{w}$$

In the formula, w stands for the analysis window length and i for the analysis point in normalized time, ranging in its actual values from $w/2$ to $T - w/2$. The number of phones entirely encompassed before the right and left window boundary are indicated with r an l, respectively. Given the phone x, the following phone is indicated as $x + 1$. The point in time where the boundary for phone x falls is indicated with t_x. Figure 4.3 shows two examples of LPR calculation.

In short, for each point in the normalized time of the utterance, we calculated the Local Phone Rate as the number of phones falling inside a window centred on the time point, weighting accordingly the phones partially included in the window, and dividing the total by the size of the window. LPRs extracted for individual utterances were averaged across speakers and utterance repetition within modality and focalization conditions, and plotted against normalized time.

4.4.4 Results

Since none of the previous studies featured Verb-focussed test items, and since the discrete analysis found durational differences at the edges of utterances (while verbs occupy their medial position), in what follows we will concentrate on Subject- and Object-focussed utterances.

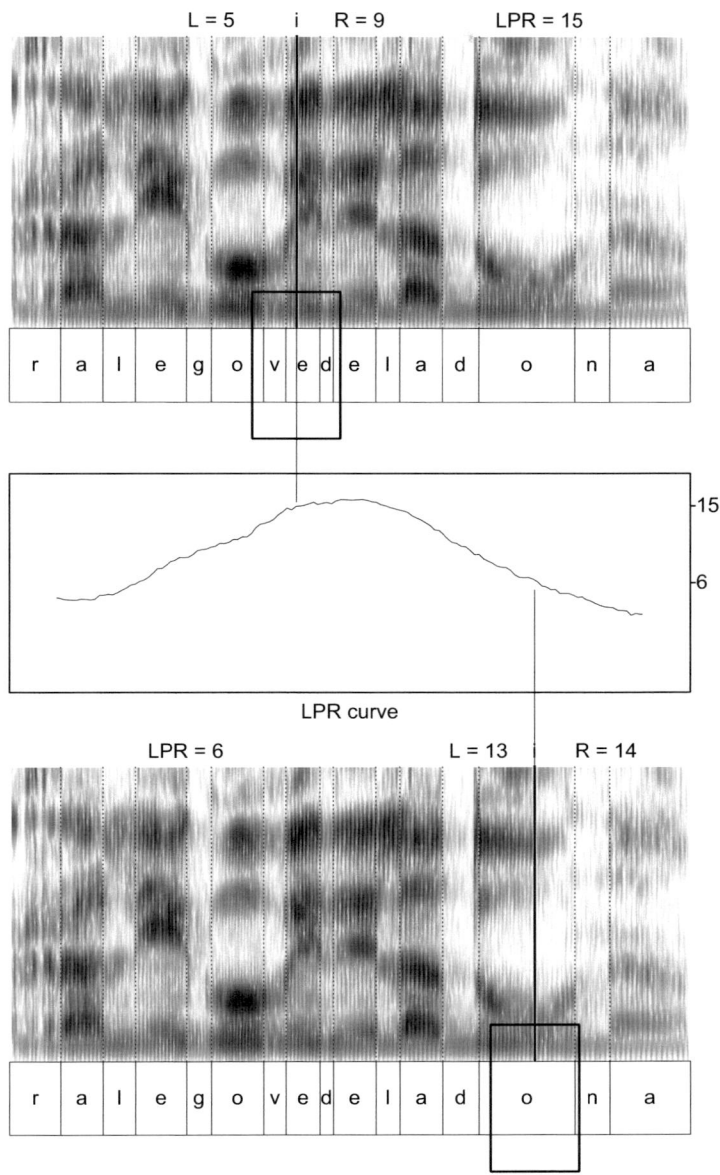

Figure 4.3: LPR calculation for the sentence *Ralego vede Ladona* uttered as an object-focus question.

4 Temporal detail in production

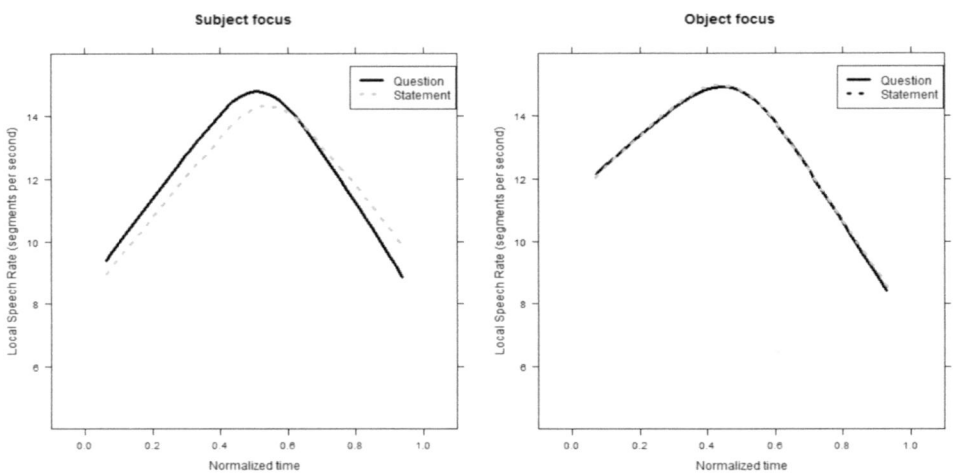

Figure 4.4: Local phone rate against normalized time (E2).

Data from the *Orlando* corpus shows that LPR curves for S-focussed utterances conform to results from the discrete analysis (see Section 4.3.4) and provide a readable display of modality induced effects: questions are characterized by a faster speech rate at the beginning and a slower speech rate at the end, while the opposite is true for statements, which accelerate through the utterance (see Figure 4.4, left panel). The results for O-focussed utterances show indistinguishable LPR curves for question and statements (see Figure 4.4, right panel).

4.4.5 Discussion

A visual inspection of the LPR curve sets provides a qualitative validation of our research hypothesis on the interaction between Modality and Focus. The null hypothesis of equal differences between questions and statements independent of focalization was not verified. The finding of exactly matching LPR curves for O-focussed utterance, however, is particularly interesting, and demands further elaboration.

4.4.5.1 Post-hoc analysis

A possible explanation for this result lies in one of the minor findings of E1. The discrete analysis found significant interactions between Modality and Focus, indicating that the stressed vowel of a focussed phrase is significantly longer (~10 ms) in Statements (see Section 4.3.4). This means that if the focussed phrase is at

4.4 Experiment 2

the beginning of the utterance (where Statements have slower speech rate), the difference will be even more salient. But if the focussed phrase is at the end of the utterance, where Questions have slower speech rate, the result could be the blurring of effects induced by modality (see next section).

Another explanation for the different results from S- and O-focussed items comes from a possible flaw in the corpus design. As we said above (see Section 4.2.1), Statement interpretations were elicited by presenting the test items along with a context paragraph requiring correction from speakers. In Statement condition, test items were recorded along with a *No* which introduced the correction. The negation was then excised from the final test item. In a striking majority of cases, the negation and the test item were uttered as two separate intonational phrases, with a strong phrase break and a silent pause between the two. However, in some cases negation and test item were uttered as a single intonational phrase, a fact which could affect segmental durations. Crucially, utterances with a single intonation phrase were more frequent for O-focussed interpretations. We then decided to plot separately utterances with one and two intonational phrases from the *Danser* corpus. Utterances were assigned to one of the two classes not only by accurate listening, but also by visual inspection of intensity profiles, under the conservative assumption that while prosodic breaks do not necessarily entail silences, silences do cue prosodic breaks. Figure 4.5 shows a plot of intensity profiles in a window centred around the end of the negation, for all statement utterances from a given speaker. Dips in the intensity contour were taken as a cue to separate phrasing; for this particular speaker, thus, only two utterances (RS1B3 and RS3A1) had no phrase break after the negation.

If we exclude single phrased utterances from comparison with questions, durational differences between questions and statements for S-focussed items are even more visible (compare dashed grey line with dot-dashed black line in Figure 4.6, left panel). Again, statements are slower in the beginning and questions are slower towards the end. As for O-focussed items, we see that statements are comparable to questions in the end portion of the utterance, yet they are slower in the beginning.

4.4.5.2 Interpretation of the results

To summarize, the analysis of LPR curves on comparably phrased utterances in the Danser corpus showed that sentence modality and focus interact in determining speech rate patterns. Specifically, S-focus utterances begin faster in questions while ending faster in statements. As for O-focussed utterances, questions have faster beginnings. Our results can be neatly accommodated in a superpositional

4 Temporal detail in production

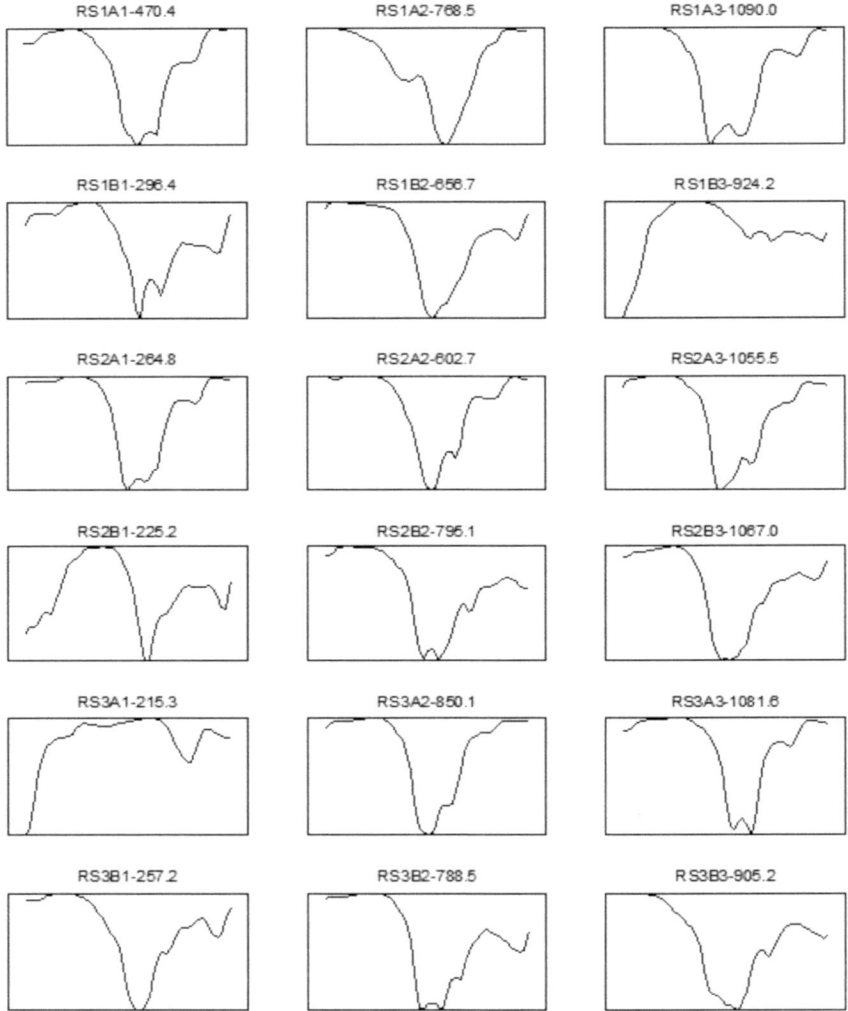

Figure 4.5: Intensity contours centered around stimulus onset.

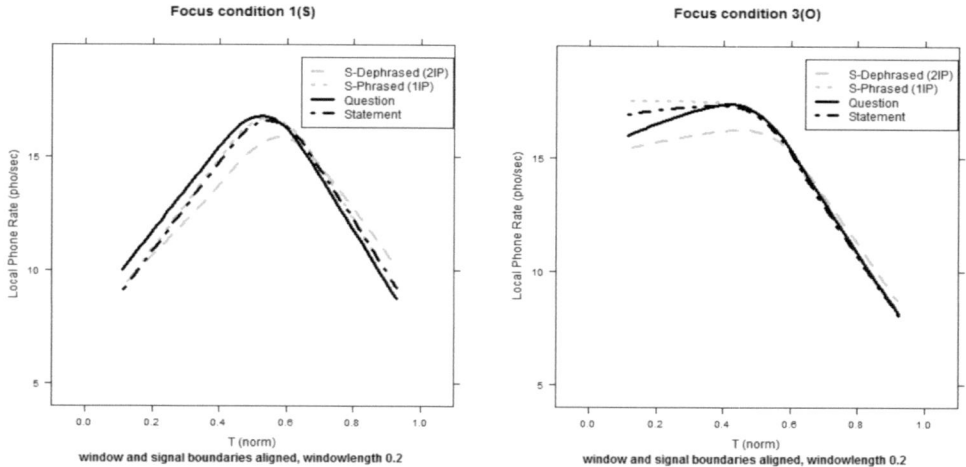

Figure 4.6: Local phone rate for stimuli with different phrasing.

account of speech rate determination, according to which variations in speech rate patterns are determined by modality, by focus, and by their interactions.[6]

First of all, both Figure 4.4 and 4.6 show that, despite the particular details, Focus has a direct effect on speech rate in that speech rate is slower on focussed constituents. For example, given SVO sentences, the first part of the utterance is faster if S bears no focal accent: see higher LPR values for O-focussed utterances in the first third of the curves.[7] Figure 4.6 also shows that speech rate in statements is lower at the beginning of the utterance for both S- and O-focussed items. This could be ascribed to the effect of modality, slowing down statements in their beginning, as discussed in the presentation of results from the discrete analysis (see Section 4.3.5). The discrete analysis also showed that questions tend to be slower towards the end of the utterance. This is confirmed by our continuous

---

[6] An exhaustive model of tempo management is clearly beyond the scope of this chapter. The account we present in this section is merely meant to provide a first structuring of the available data, and no claims are made on the mechanisms which shape speech rate patterns. Even the "generative vibe" of this account, evoking underlying patterns which are modified by intervening factors down to a final output, is only meant to be an expository device. See Section 4.5 for discussion on the possible linguistic reality of the interaction between Focus and Modality.

[7] The effect does not seem to be symmetrical, in that we do not find the same difference between focussed and unfocussed Objects, indicating that speech rate at utterance edges might be affected by other factors (such as preboundary lengthening, for example). Our corpora were not designed to test this claim, so results from sentences with syntactic structures other than SVO are needed in order to settle this issue.

4 Temporal detail in production

display for S-focussed utterances only. O-focussed utterances have a comparable speech rate at the edges of the utterance in both sentence modalities. However, this is where the Focus-Modality interaction might play its role. As we said above (Section 4.3.4), stressed vowels are longer in focussed constituents than in non-focussed constituents, but they are yet longer in focussed constituents in statements. This interaction between focus and modality could be responsible for enhancing speech rate differences in the first portion of S-focussed utterances (where statements are yet slower than questions) and by counteracting them in the last portion of O-focussed utterances (yielding comparable speech rate values).

Table 4.3 shows which portion of the utterance (*S*, Subject at utterance beginning, and *O*, Object at utterance end) is expected to be lengthened (+) according to Focus induced effects, Modality induced effects, and to their interaction (first column) in the two modalities (second row). This is done separately for utterances focussed on the Subject or the Object (first row).

Table 4.3: Overlay model

	Subject-focus				Object-focus			
	Statement		Question		Statement		Question	
	S	O	S	O	S	O	S	O
Focus	+		+			+		+
Modality	+			+	+			+
Interaction	+					+		
	+++		+	+	+	++		++

According to the table, we expect statements to be slower at the beginning and questions to be slower at the end of the utterance in the S-focus condition, whereas we expect statements to be slower at the beginning but no difference at the end of the utterance in the O-focus condition. A comparison of these expectations with actual data (see Figure 4.6) yields a very good match.

4.5 General discussion

Evidence from E1 and E2 shows that sentences have different durational patterns when uttered as questions or statements. However, sentence modality does not affect utterance duration as a whole, but rather particular portions of the utterance. Specifically, statements are faster (shorter phone durations) at the beginning and slower (longer phone durations) towards the end when compared to questions. Moreover, differences in durational patterns across questions and statements are not independent of focal accent placement, up to the point that speech rate differences can be reduced or blurred in some circumstances (as in Object-focussed SVO sentences).

These findings account for the difficulty in drawing a clear picture from the various studies in the literature, which analyze durational patterns for different languages at different degrees of finesse, and do not always control for focus placement or syntactic structure. They also enable an examination of the allegedly universal character of the link between questions and fast speech rate (see Section 4.5.1). And, more importantly for the general purposes of our thesis, they question the degree of phonetic information that can or must be included in prosodic abstract categories (see Section 4.5.2).

4.5.1 Universality and specificity

The finding of no global effect of sentence modality on utterance duration, together with those emerging from the literature on the topic, argue in favour of language-specific relationships between tempo and sentence modality. An alternative view is embraced by van Heuven & van Zanten (2005). Cautiously speculating on their results on Dutch, English and Manado Malay, they suggested that the higher speech rate found in questions could be interpreted as a (trend to a) prosodic universal, based on both ethological, perceptual and production mechanisms.

According to their account, faster speech rate could be taken as the temporal counterpart of high pitch values. From an ethological perspective, grammaticalization of high pitch as cue to question modality would be mediated by submissiveness (Ohala 1984; Gussenhoven 2004). Given that "small (harmless) creatures have higher pitches, and make faster movements, than large (dangerous) creatures" (van Heuven & van Zanten 2005: 97), faster speech rate could cue submissiveness as well. The link between higher pitch and faster speech rate would be testified by speech perception research as well: Rietveld & Gussenhoven (1987) found that temporally unchanged utterances were judged by listeners to be faster when their pitch was artificially raised. As for production mechanisms, van Heuven and van Zanten build on Bolinger's (1964; 1989) proposal that "statements and questions are characterized universally by a dichotomy between relaxation (low, falling pitch) and tension (high, rising pitch), respectively" (van Heuven & van Zanten 2005: *ibid.*). If we take slower and higher speech rate to be correlates of relaxation

4 Temporal detail in production

and tension, we see how questions could be characterized by shorter durations.

However, as pointed out by van Heuven & van Zanten themselves, the association between question on one hand and fast rate and high pitch on the other must be considered as ultimately arbitrary and conventional in the light of Rialland's findings on "lax question prosody" in some of the languages she surveyed (see the opening pages of this chapter for a more detailed review). Our results from E1 strongly support this arbitrary and language-specific account, since questions in our data do not seem to relate straightforwardly to a faster speech rate. Temporal patterns seem to rather interact in complicated ways with other linguistic dimensions, such as syntactic and information structure, mediated through accent placement.

4.5.2 Tempo (and intonation)

The interplay between modality and focus in shaping durational patterns is perhaps the major finding of E2. We suggested that differences in speech rate patterns between questions and statements across focus conditions can be framed in an overlay model, where modality-induced effects are cumulated with focus-induced effects, and with their interactions as well. The modality-focus interaction also proved statistically significant and perceptually relevant in the analysis of discrete phone durations (see Section 4.3.4), which showed that the stressed vowel of a focussed phrase is longer in statements than in questions.

In the perspective of research on prosodic detail, these differences are not interesting in themselves, as a simple quantitative account of phonetic facts. The main interest of the quantitative modality-focus interaction lies in the exploration of what we could call its linguistic reality. Can we really claim that speakers actually control individual segmental durations according to modality and focus options? More importantly, such a question relies on the implicit and unverified assumption that temporal aspects are *independently* handled by speakers. In this view, tempo is indeed the formal dimension bridging post-lexical meaning with durational patterns (as we defined it in the opening pages of this chapter), and it constitutes along with intonation an orthogonal phonological axis to be included in the representation of prosody. To exemplify, in a rule-based text-to-speech system informed by this view, we would expect to find, along with a low-level module responsible for the intrinsic pitch and duration adjustments, a prosodic module including both an intonational component (responsible for the generation of *f0* contours) and a temporal component (responsible for the generation of durational patterns).

This view, however, is no more than a working hypothesis.[8] The evidence we gathered in this chapter is actually rather consistent with the alternative view of a strong interplay between tempo and intonation. What we called the modality-focus interaction in the quantitative account of the data is compatible with the view according to which prosodic categories are specified with respect to both the melodic and temporal dimensions. In AM terms, for example, we could imagine that a single paradigmatic option on the phonological level (e.g. a pitch accent) affects both the phonetic dimensions of fundamental frequency and duration. That is, the finding that stressed vowels in focussed phrases are longer in statements than in questions could be seen as due to the choice of different pitch accents. In other words, pitch accents for narrow focus statements could be characterized not only by earlier peak alignment, but also by longer vowel durations.[9]

The exploration of this specific claim is beyond the scope of this chapter. What is crucial to the present discussion is that sentence modality does have an effect on segmental durations, independently of whether tempo should be regarded as orthogonal to intonational contrasts or embedded into those.

4.6 Conclusion

In this chapter we documented the existence of produced temporal detail in read speech. Segmental durations in NI are affected not only by focus placement, but also by sentence modality. Specifically, while total utterance duration is not different across modalities, speech rate is faster at the beginning of the utterance for questions and at its end for statements. However, since stressed vowels of focussed constituents are longer in statements, modality-induced effects on durations can be blurred under some circumstances. These findings are not compatible with claims of a universal trend to faster speech rate in questions, and are instead consistent with language-specific behaviours.

Differences in phone durations (or in speech rate) are not considered as cues to modality in the AM framework. As in the case of the consistently produced dynamic melodic detail we explored in Section 2, it is possible that the current phonological categories accounting for sentence modality contrasts are phonetically underspecified. And, as in the case of the perception of dynamic melodic

---

[8] This will be indeed questioned in the following chapter by exploring the perception of the durational differences we just reported on.
[9] Informal tests based on the *ShAli* corpus (Niebuhr et al. 2011) yields results which are consistent with this claim.

4 Temporal detail in production

detail we explored in Section 3, perceptual validation will be instrumental in deciding whether these durational differences qualify as prosodic detail. The next chapter will thus focus on speech rate changes across utterances and the perception of sentence modality.

To conclude, the analysis of durational patterns across sentence modalities required the development and the fine-tuning of new and existing tools. The treatment of a great amount of data (more than 38000 phone durations) was made possible by the development of *ASSI*, a tool which performs forced alignment of Italian speech (see Section 4.2.2) and which has been made publicly available.[10] While being specifically developed for the purposes of this study, these tools could also prove useful for research on other topics, and present an additional practical outcome of this work along with our multiparametric resynthesis procedure (see Section 5.2.2).

---

[10] See http://www.esat.kuleuven.be/psi/spraak/demo/Italian/align.php . The scripts used for the calculation of Local Phone Rate curves are also available upon request.

5 Perception of temporal detail

In the previous chapter we documented the existence of regularly produced temporal detail which is not captured by the AM framework. Questions and statements in NI are phonetically characterized not only by different $f0$ contours, but also by different durational patterns. The AM framework already provides a phonological account of $f0$ contours (i.e. tunes), but for durational patterns there is no equivalent phonological counterpart yet. We used in the previous chapter the label *temporal patterns* to refer to such phonological entities, which were assumed to bridge between durational differences (on the substantive side) and post-lexical meaning (on the functional side). As such, temporal patterns would represent for tempo what tunes represent for intonation. However, while the phonological relevance of intonation in the signalling of post-lexical meaning is nowadays undisputed, the very existence of tempo as a legitimate phonological dimension is no more than a working hypothesis. As a result, whereas tunes have made the object of extensive research on their internal structure (at least since the so-called "level vs configurations" debate, see Ladd 2008: among others), at this stage we are unable to propose any internal structuring of temporal patterns. The aim of this chapter is not, of course, to bridge this gap. We rather ask whether tempo, such as we conceive it,[1] must be considered as a necessary dimension in phonological accounts of prosody. That is, we ask whether further research on relationships between durational differences and post-lexical meaning is dispensable, useful or necessary. The question is best asked in advance since research on tempo, being a relatively recent enterprise, is still very time consuming. For example, we had to tweak or develop our own tools to analyse production data (see Sections 4.2.2 and 4.4.3) and to resynthesize stimuli for perception experiments (see Section 5.2.2). More importantly, since we have seen that enriching with melodic detail the intonational dimension already present in our phonological representations is a delicate operation (see Section 2.4.2), we can easily imagine how adding to our representations a new dimension altogether, namely the temporal one, could be the object of an entire research pro-

---

[1] Again, in our understanding tempo is the formal dimension bridging variations in duration with post-lexical meaning (see Sections 1.4.2, 4 and 5.1.1).

5 Perception of temporal detail

gram (see Section 3.4.2). However, the evidence presented in Section 4 showed that variations in durational patterns in NI consistently mirror sentence modality contrasts. If these variations are also exploited in perception, we would have a strong argument in favour of an enrichment with temporal information of phonological representations, pointing to the necessity of a deep revision of the relationships between tempo, intonation and prosody. For this reason, as Section 3 provided a perceptual evaluation of the melodic detail that Section 2 attested in production, in the present chapter we report on a study (Cangemi & D'Imperio 2013) which provides a perceptual evaluation of the temporal detail discovered in Section 4.

5.1 Introduction

Research in phonetics and phonology has long acknowledged the relevance of phenomena concerning the temporal dimension. Speech unfolds in time as the result of coordinated movements of the articulators, thus making the temporal dimension an essential aspect of speech production. Its acoustic manifestation is perhaps the most easily measurable propriety of the speech signal, and the perceptual salience of durational differences is already attested by the earliest writing systems. As for linguistic typology, time is a crucial dimension in the patterning of strong and weak positions which constitute rhythm. And phonology has relied from its very first steps on the notion of quantity to provide a description and an explanation of an immense amount of linguistic phenomena. When it comes to prosody, however, the status of tempo appears less uncontroversial. This is not surprising, since our current understanding of prosody itself is not uncontroversial either, which in turn makes the definition of tempo a highly theory-dependent operation. According a given place to tempo implicitly means to suggest a particular structure for prosody altogether. A detailed account of the various notions and definitions of tempo in the prosodic literature falls outside the scope of this chapter; however, we can exemplify this state of affairs by looking at what is called tempo in two different approaches.

5.1.1 Two views of tempo

In her pioneering work on prosodic or suprasegmental features, Ilse Lehiste suggested that three axes are relevant to the study of prosody, namely quantity, tonal and stress features. For each of these three dimensions, the study of "all inherent constraints and conditioned variations" is the first step towards its evaluation as an "independent variable" (Lehiste 1970: 3). That is, phonetic knowledge (both articulatory, acoustic and perceptual) is a necessary requisite for the exploration of linguistic function (on both word and sentence level) and ultimately, we might add, of phonology. To exemplify, given the tonal dimension, phonetic knowledge on phonation (articulation), fundamental frequency (acoustics) and pitch (perception) allows the exploration of tone (word level) and intonation (sentence level). Thus, for example, intonation refers to sentence level functions of tonal features. In her account, tempo represents for the quantity dimension what intonation represents on the tonal dimension, namely sentence level functions of quantity features (see Table 5.1). An alternative view of intonation is provided by Bob Ladd in his account of the AM framework. According to Ladd, intonation "refers to the use of *suprasegmental* phonetic features to convey 'postlexical' or *sentence-level* pragmatic meanings in a *linguistically structured way*" (Ladd 2008: 4; original emphasis). In agreement with Lehiste's definition, the functions of intonation are restricted to the sentence level. However, in the AM framework the phonetic features relevant to intonation are not limited to tonal features, but include all suprasegmentals, namely "features of fundamental frequency, intensity and duration" (Ladd 2008: ibid.). As a result, the notion of intonation according to Ladd encompasses the wider spectrum of all phonetic features relevant to Lehiste's prosody. However, intonation in the AM framework is also characterized by linguistic structuring: intonational features "exclude 'paralinguistic' features in which continuously variable physical parameters (e.g. tempo and loudness) directly signal continuously variable states of the speaker (e.g. degree of involvement or arousal)" (Ladd 2008: 6). This last quote clearly exemplifies the terminological clashes which pervade the literature on tempo. Tempo is taken as a physical parameter for Ladd and as a phonological dimension for Lehiste.[2] However, in both cases it is seen as mainly related to paralinguistic meaning: for Lehiste as well, "changes of the relative durations of linguistic units within a sentence do not change the meanings of individual words; however, they do convey something about the mood of the speaker or about the circumstances under which the utterance was made" (Lehiste 1970: §2.5.3).

---

[2] As a comparison with Table 5.1 shows, the notion of *loudness* as well is different in the two cases: whereas for Lehiste it relates to perception, Ladd treats it as a physical parameter.

5 Perception of temporal detail

Table 5.1: Suprasegmentals (Table 1.1 from Lehiste 1970)

Suprasegmental	Physiological	Acoustic Manifestation	Perception	Phonetic Characteristics	Linguistic Function	
					Word Level	Sentence Level
Quantity features	2.1. Timing of articulatory sequences	2.2. Time dimensional of the acoustic signal	2.3. Perception of duration	2.4.1. Intrinsic duration of vowels 2.4.2. Segmental conditioning 2.4.3. Intrinsic duration of consonants 2.4.4. Quantity and phonetic quality 2.4.5. Magnitude of relevant differences 2.4.6. Suprasegmental conditioning factors 2.4.7. Position within higher-level phonological unit as conditioning factor	2.5. Quantity	2.5. Tempo
Tonal features	3.1. Phonation	3.2. Fundamental frequency	3.3. Perception of pitch	3.4.1. Intrinsic pitch 3.4.2. Segmental conditioning 3.4.3. Dependence of tone upon phonation 3.4.4. Phonetic quality 3.4.5. Magnitude and kind of relevant differences 3.4.6. Suprasegmental conditioning factors	3.5. Tone	3.5. Intonation
Stress features	4.1. Physiological mechanism	4.2. Intensity and amplitude	4.3. Perception of loudness and perception of stress	4.4.1. Intrinsic intensity 4.4.2. Role of fundamental frequency, intensity and duration 4.4.3. Suprasegmental correlates of stress 4.4.4. Segmental cues	4.5. Word stress	4.5. Sentence-level stress

This last fact points to an asymmetry in the kind of function that Lehiste attributes to suprasegmentals at the sentence level: whereas stress features and intonation map on both linguistic and attitudinal meaning, tempo would map on attitudinal meaning alone. The literature we reviewed in Section 4.3 and the general findings of Section 4, on the other hand, show that durational patterns might cue sentence modality contrasts. That is, meaning which is not lexical, yet non paralinguistic either. This kind of evidence could be accommodated in Lehiste's account of prosody by investing tempo with a non exclusively paralinguistic function. Indeed, this would restore symmetry in the kind of functions exerted by the various suprasegmental features. However, a link between durational patterns and sentence modality could also be accommodated in the AM framework. In this case, tempo would not cue linguistic functions in itself, but durational features could enrich phonological representations of intonation. In principle, such an enrichment would not be disruptive either, since in AM all suprasegmental phonetic features are potentially relevant to intonation (see Ladd's definition above). Both perspectives, however, rely on the assumption that the different durational patterns we found in the production of sentence modality contrasts (see Section 4) are perceptible and actually used by listeners. In this respect, the discussion above on the place of tempo within prosody joins ends with our investigation on prosodic detail. For this reason, we now move to a perceptual evaluation of temporal detail.

5.1.2 Hypotheses

In the previous chapter we saw that, in NI, SVO sentences composed of the same lexical material are uttered with a different temporal pattern when read as questions or statements, despite presenting the same intonational properties (accent placement and prosodic breaks). Specifically, questions display shorter phone durations at the beginning of the utterance, while statements are characterized by shorter phone durations at utterance end, independent of focus placement. These results are compatible with the hypothesis that questions and statements, in addition to bearing different intonational specifications (viz. by different tunes), are also phonologically contrasting along the dimension of tempo, namely through different temporal patterns. In this view, which is compatible with Lehiste's account of prosody, tempo and intonation are *orthogonal* (H1). However, if intonational contrasts are taken to be cued by all suprasegmental features, as in Ladd's account of the AM framework, differences in phone durations could also be included in intonational representations. In this view, tempo is *nested* within intonation (H2). Different durational patterns could arise as

5 Perception of temporal detail

a by-product of the use of different pitch accents (see Section 4.5.2): we have already seen that, as for narrow focussed constituents, AM analyses of NI posit an L*+H pitch accent in questions and an L+H* pitch accent in statements (see Section 3.3.3). In this case, durational differences would be due to the phonetic implementation of intonational contrasts, and there would be no need to posit an orthogonal dimension for tempo. Both hypotheses, however, crucially rely on the assumption that the durational differences reported in the production study are also relevant for perception, and that they interact with $f0$ movements in cueing sentence modality contrasts. That is, only if tempo qualifies as prosodic detail we might ask whether it should be considered as orthogonal to (H1) or nested within (H2) intonation. This assumption must be questioned through the evaluation of the null hypothesis stating that durational differences do not cue sentence modality contrasts (H0). In very general terms:

H0 *Null hypothesis*: durational differences do not cue sentence modality contrasts.

H1 *Orthogonality hypothesis*: durational differences cue sentence modality contrasts and should be organized on the phonological dimension of tempo, which constitutes one of the prosodic axes, along with intonation.

H2 *Nesting hypothesis*: durational differences cue sentence modality contrasts as part of the phonetic specification of contrasts on the phonological dimension of intonation.

The null hypothesis is challenged by the acoustic evidence presented in Section 4, but it is consistent both with claims on the paralinguistic nature of tempo-related contrasts and, especially, with the long term priority accorded to fundamental frequency and intonation in research on post-lexical meaning. This obviously relates to the different power acknowledged for fundamental frequency and durational patterns in cueing post-lexical meaning: as in the case of segmental contrasts, not all phonetic cues are of equal importance (see e.g. Lisker 1986 on voicing). Even if little is known about the integration of multiple prosodic cues in accessing post-lexical meaning, this insight can still be used for a first step towards a testable version of our general hypotheses.[3] If tempo can be evaluated independently from intonation (H1), one would expect different responses

---

[3] Testing will rely on a forced-choice identification task similar to the one used to investigate perception of melodic detail (see Section 3.3). Since the resynthesis procedure of temporal and melodic detail over the span of an entire utterance requires the development of specific algorithms (which will be presented in Section 5.2.2), we will describe the task itself (Section 5.2.1) before providing full operationalization for H1. As for H2, on the other hand, we

to stimuli with different temporal patterns but same intonation contour. In particular, if temporal cues are ancillary to melodic ones, one would expect the magnitude of differences in responses to temporally manipulated stimuli to be lower than that of melodically manipulated stimuli. Moreover, one could predict that the effect of temporal manipulation would increase if melodic information is made ambiguous or unavailable. If, on the other hand, phonetic temporal information is only nested within phonological intonational categories (H2), one can expect that stimuli resynthesized such as to have mismatching cues would require longer processing, but still yield responses consistent with melodic information. And if durational differences are not used in perception at all, one would expect absence of effect of temporal manipulation on both responses and response times.

5.2 Method

26 NI subjects participated in a forced-choice categorization task under *Perceval* (André et al. 2003), using a two-button response box to code audio stimuli as either questions or statements. The experimental items consisted of 18 resynthesized stimuli, which were created by using as base stimuli two utterances of a same sentence from the *Danser* corpus (see Section 4.2.1.2). Base stimuli were the question and statement version (coded as *bQ* and *bS*) of Subject-focussed sentence *Danilo vola da Roma* ('Danilo flies from Rome'). Using a resynthesis procedure which will be detailed at Section 5.2.2, we extracted the *f0* contours (*fQ, fS*) and the durational patterns (*dQ, dS*) of the two base stimuli. Then we calculated arithmetically ambiguous *f0* contour (*fA*) and durational pattern (*dA*). We resynthesized each of the two base stimuli with the nine combinations between the two factors (*f* and *d*) and their three levels (*Q, S* and *A*), thus obtaining 18 experimental items.[4] These were block randomized and interspersed with twice as much filler stimuli; each block was presented three times to each of the 26 subjects. For each experimental trial, we recorded both subjects' responses and their reaction times from stimulus offset, yielding a total of 2808 observations.

---

will only provide partial (qualitative) operationalization, since its evaluation relies on response times to stimuli with different durations and with diffuse cues (see Section 5.4.1 for discussion).

[4] Items were coded by concatenating information about the base stimulus (*bQ* or *bS*), the *f0* contour (*fQ, fS* or *fA*) and the durational pattern (*dQ, dS* or *dA*). For example, the item resynthesized from a question base by keeping its original question contour but by switching to statement durational pattern was coded as *bQfQdS*. In the following, we will use X as an indicator of pooling: for example, *bXfQdS* indicates stimuli with question *f0* contour (*fQ*) and statement durational pattern (*dS*), resynthesized *from either base* (*bX*). In the graphs, indication of the base stimulus is dropped altogether.

5 Perception of temporal detail

5.2.1 Operationalization

If durational differences are a cue to phonological temporal contrasts, we would expect to find significantly different responses for stimuli with different durational patterns (*bXfQdQ* vs *bXfQdA* vs *bXfQdS* and *bXfSdQ* vs *bXfSdA* vs *bXfSdS*: see black histogram triplets in Figure 5.1). Moreover, if duration was a secondary (compared to *f0* contour) prosodic cue to sentence modality contrasts, we would expect a stronger effect of tempo manipulation when intonation is ambiguous (*bXfAdQ* vs *bXfAdA* vs *bXfAdS*: see gray histogram triplet in Figure 5.1). These hypothesized results could be taken as support for H1. H2, on the other hand, could be supported even in the absence of significant differences in subjects' responses, and namely by different reaction times. Specifically, we would expect shorter reaction times for stimuli with consistent intonational and temporal cues (*bXfQdQ* and *bXfSdS*) compared with stimuli with incongruous information (*bXfQdS* and *bXfSdQ*). Absence of a significant effect of temporal manipulations on both subject's responses and reaction times would yield instead support for H0. H1 and H2 will be tested using generalized Mixed Logit and Linear Mixed models, respectively. For a discussion of the issues in full operationalization of H2, see Section 5.4.1.

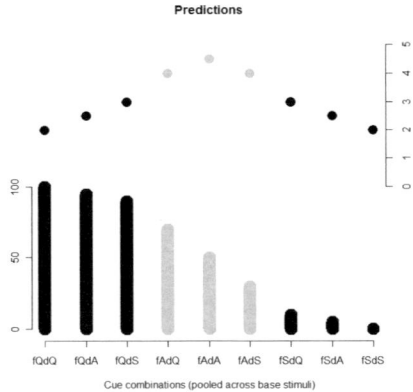

Figure 5.1: Predicted question responses percent (bar plot) and reaction times (points) for the 9 resynthesis conditions: *f* and *d* indicate *f0* contours and durational patterns, *Q*, *A* and *S* indicate question-like, ambiguous and statement-like patterns. See Cangemi and D'Imperio (2013).

5.2.2 Material

We used a resynthesis procedure partially based on work by Gubian et al. (2010, 2011) and implemented through a set of scripts in *R* (R Development Core Team 2008) and *Praat* (Boersma & Weenink 2008). We extracted the segmentally aligned *f0* contours of the two base stimuli (*fQ, fS*) and turned them into continuous functions through b-spline smoothing. That is, the *f0* curve was not discretized as is usually done in perceptual studies involving resynthesis. No top-down knowledge was fed into the resynthesis procedure, apart from anchoring the *f0* contours to the segmental boundaries. Moreover, by using continuous phonetic representations instead of a sequence of turning points, we avoid losing potentially useful melodic information. Minimalist top-down based assumptions were also made in the extraction of the durational patterns of the two base stimuli (*dQ, dS*), for which we stored the duration of each phone as annotated by manual segmentation. Then we calculated an acoustically ambiguous durational pattern (*dA*), by averaging phone durations, and an acoustically ambiguous *f0* contour (*fA*), by averaging functions with respect to the segmental landmarks. Function averaging was accomplished by extracting a transform function which turned a given contour into the opposite, and by applying it with a weight of 0.5. We resynthesized each of the two base stimuli with the nine combinations between the two factors (*f* and *d*) and their three levels (*Q, S* and *A*), thus obtaining 18 experimental items.

5.3 Results

A plot of the raw data shows that melodic cues alone are relevant in sentence modality contrasts perception. As for identification results (Figure 5.2), the strong effect of melodic manipulations is attested by the drop in question identification rates between stimuli with question intonation (*bXfQdX*), with ambiguous intonation (*bXfAdX*)[5] and with statement intonation (*bXfSdX*). Temporal manipulations, on the other hand, do not seem to affect subjects' responses: none of the triplets above show an internal drop in question identification (e.g. given the triplet QX, same rates for QQ, QA and QS).

Reaction times also show no effect of temporal manipulations (Figure 5.3). In particular, responses are not faster when stimuli have congruous (white) rather than incongruous (black) temporal and intonational cues. On the other hand, stimuli with ambiguous intonation elicited longer reaction times.

---

[5] For a discussion of the consistent bias toward question response in stimuli with ambiguous intonation, see Section 5.4.1.

5 Perception of temporal detail

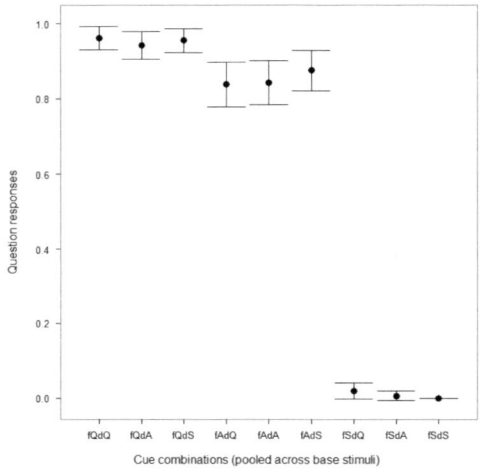

Figure 5.2: Hypothesis 1. Observed question responses (mean and error bars) for the 9 resynthesis conditions. See Cangemi and D'Imperio (2013).

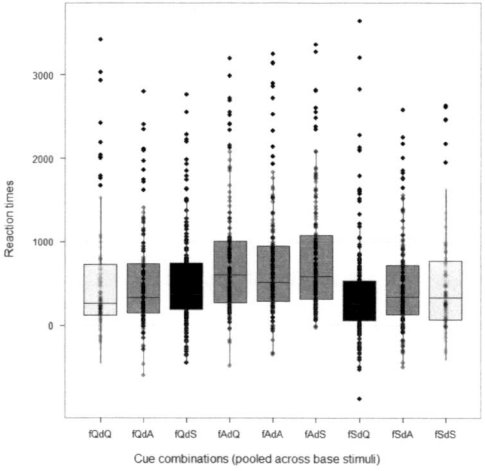

Figure 5.3: Hypothesis 2. Observed reaction times (boxplot and observations) for the 9 resynthesis conditions. Congruous conditions in white, incongruous conditions in black (non relevant conditions in grey). See Cangemi and D'Imperio (2013).

5.3 Results

5.3.1 Orthogonality hypothesis

In order to test H1 we ran a series of generalized mixed logit models, aimed at evaluating the effect of temporal manipulations on subjects' identification responses. The most comprehensive model included the three fixed factors *Intonation* (three levels: question, ambiguous and statement), *Tempo* (question, ambiguous and statement), and *Base* stimulus (question and statement), as well as their interaction, together with a random intercept for our 26 *Subjects*. The model was then pruned, excluding three-way interactions first, then two-way interactions, and ultimately non-significant factors. As a result, the comparison between the most comprehensive model and the one containing the fixed factor *Intonation* alone shows no significant Likelihood difference ($\chi^2 = 16.7, df = 15, p = 0.33$), thus leading to the rejection of H1. *A fortiori*, the corollary of a stronger effect of temporal manipulations for stimuli with ambiguous intonation is not validated either. The corollary would have been validated by significant interactions between *Intonation* and *Tempo*. However, as can be inferred from the comparison between the model including *Intonation*, *Tempo*, *Base* and their interaction with the model containing *Intonation* alone, no difference in Likelihood is attested when comparing the model containing *Intonation*, *Tempo* and their interactions with the model containing *Intonation* and *Tempo* alone ($\chi^2 = 5.6, df = 4, p = 0.23$).

5.3.2 Nesting hypothesis

As for H2, we ran a series of generalized linear mixed models evaluating the effect of temporal manipulations on subjects' reaction times. Prior to modelling, latencies were made positive and log-transformed.[6] The most comprehensive model included the three fixed factors *Intonation* (three levels: question, ambiguous and statement), *Tempo* (question, ambiguous and statement), and *Base* stimulus (question and statement), as well as their interaction, together with a random intercept for our 26 *Subjects*. A Likelihood Ratio Test between this model and the one without the *Base* factor showed no significant difference ($\chi^2 = 14.32, df = 9, p = 0.11$), so in the following we will only refer to the more economical model. In our model, differences between response times to stimuli with congruous (bXfQdQ and bXfSdS) and incongruous (bXfSdQ and bXfQdS) sets of intonational and temporal cues are estimated by the interactions between intonation

---

[6] Since reaction times were calculated with respect to stimulus offset, a negative value for latency indicates that response to trial has been provided before the end of the stimulus itself. See Section 5.4.1 for discussion.

and tempo.[7] A comparison between the model including *Intonation*, *Tempo* as well as their interactions with the model including *Intonation* and *Tempo* alone shows no significant Likelihood difference ($\chi^2 = 2.66, df = 4, p = 0.61$),[8] thus leading to the rejection of H2.

5.4 Discussion

Our results suggest that listeners do not use durational patterns as a cue for the identification of resynthesized stimuli as either questions or statements. Listeners' responses were not affected by resynthesis of temporal patterns, not even when intonational cues were made ambiguous. This finding speaks against a model of prosody in which tempo is seen as an orthogonal dimension to intonation, contra H1. Moreover, identification of sentence modality does not seem to be hindered by a mismatch between melodic and temporal cues: reaction times were similar in responses to stimuli with either conflicting (i.e. *bXfQdS* and *bXfStQ*) or cooperating (i.e. *bXfQdQ* and *bXfSdS*) cues. In these cases as well, listeners only seemed to rely on intonation. This finding is not consistent with the hypothesis that temporal information is part of representations for intonational categories, contra H2 as well. Response times are only slightly higher when intonation is made ambiguous, a fact which can be seen as additional evidence for the exclusive role of intonational cues. In sum, it seems that temporal detail is not a cue to the perception of sentence modality contrasts.

5.4.1 Design-related issues

Before discussing the epistemological issues which limit the scope of our findings (Section 5.4.2) and concluding on their possible relevance in the broader frame

---

[7] Specifically, if one takes latencies for *bXfQdQ* as a reference (i, intercept), one must estimate the coefficient for temporal manipulation from Question to Statement (*tempoS*) in the case of *bXfQdS*, the coefficient for intonational manipulation from Question to Statement (*intonS*) in the case of *bXfSdQ*, and the two previously mentioned coefficients along with the interaction between temporal and durational manipulations from Questions to Statement (*tempoSintonS*) in the case of *bXfSdS*. Grouping the four stimuli in the two congruous and incongruous conditions, we obtain that different latencies among the two groups require a significant coefficient for *tempoSintonS*:

$$(bXfQdQ + bXfSdS) - (bXfSdQ + bXfQdS) =$$
$$= (i + i + intonS + tempoS + tempoSintonS) - (i + intonS + i + tempoS) =$$
$$= tempoSintonS$$

[8] Specifically, the coefficient for *tempoSintonS* is non significant ($t = 0.11$).

of research on prosodic detail (Section 5.5), we now turn to an examination of some issues in the experimental design which could have affected our results, and report on a small-scale spin-off experiment which addressed part of them.

5.4.1.1 Resynthesis

Experimental stimuli were created with an innovative resynthesis procedure, which combines modifications of *f0* contours and of temporal patterns (see Section 5.2.2). Since the procedure was elaborated for the purposes of this study, no independent testing of its performance was available. However, in addition to being used for the evaluation of our research hypotheses on tempo, the data collected for our experiment can also be used to provide a first evaluation of the continuous resynthesis of *f0* contours. Subjects' responses show that cross-modality manipulation was extremely successful. Identification responses were not affected by the nature of the stimulus used as base for the resynthesis: question identification for natural questions (*bQfQdX*) and for natural statements resynthesized with question intonation (*bSfQdX*) is not significantly different, and the same holds for question to statement resynthesis.[9] On the other hand, the resynthesis procedure could not produce a truly *perceptually ambiguous f0* contour between questions and statements. Stimuli intended to be intonationally ambiguous (*bXfAtX*) were identified as question well above chance level (see Figure 5.2). This finding is not surprising. As we said above (see Section 5.2.2), ambiguous contours were obtained by setting to 0.5 the transformation coefficient c or, in other words, by calculating the arithmetic mean of the two time-warped *f0* contours. In order to achieve truly ambiguous stimuli with a procedure of this kind, the perceptual space between questions and statements should be linear. However, the non-linear warping of perceptual space has been long acknowledged for contrasts at the segmental level, which makes the assumption of a linear perceptual space for utterance-wide intonational contrasts even more untenable (Gubian et al. 2010). By allowing a fine-grained control of separate acoustic dimensions, our resynthesis procedure is indeed especially suited for the exploration of the perceptual space of intonational contrasts, which would ultimately

---

[9] In the Generalized Mixed Logit model predicting subjects' responses from *Intonation* and *Base* as fixed factors, together with their interactions and adding a random intercept for *Subjects*, no base-related coefficient reaches the significance level. Excluding the *Base:Intonation* interaction for stimuli with ambiguous intonation (which are not relevant for the present discussion, and in any case non significant as well: $\beta = 0.98, z = 1.70, p = 0.09$), Base ($\beta = -0.45, z = -0.93, p = 0.35$) and *Base:Intonation* interaction ($\beta = 0.45, z = 0.35, p = 0.72$) fail to reach significance.

5 Perception of temporal detail

provide the necessary insights for the creation of truly perceptually ambiguous stimuli. In the absence of this preparatory work, for the purposes of our current study we consciously restrained to the simplistic choice of using *acoustically ambiguous* stimuli. It has to be noted, however, that the use of acoustically rather than perceptually ambiguous stimuli potentially hinders the complete evaluation of H1 (*orthogonality* hypothesis). As we said above, in the hypothesis of an independent processing of temporal and melodic cues, we made the corollary prediction that the effect of temporal manipulations is stronger if melodic information is made ambiguous or unavailable. The fact that our resynthesis procedure only yielded stimuli with acoustically (and not perceptually) ambiguous melodic information does not allow us to draw definitive conclusions on this prediction. However, discarding the main hypothesis of significant temporal-related effects across all stimuli entails discarding the corollary prediction of stronger temporal-related effects when no intonational cues are available. This does not mean that proper resynthesis of perceptually ambiguous intonation is unnecessary in the evaluation of temporal effects. We could also formulate a separate hypothesis, stating that temporal-related effects are significant *only* when no intonational cues are available. In this case, our data on exclusively acoustically ambiguous stimuli would not be conclusive.

5.4.1.2 Reaction times

As we said above (see Section 5.1.2), the evaluation of H2 as well needs particular caution. We suggested that the relevance of temporal information in the phonological representations of intonational contrasts (*nesting* hypothesis) could have been indicated by different reaction times between stimuli with congruous (*bXfQdQ* and *bXfSdS*) and incongruous (*bXfSdQ* and *bXfSdQ*) information on the melodic and temporal levels. However, the quantitative evaluation of significant differences in reaction times is affected by two kinds of issues. On a lower level, a first problem is represented by the fact that total stimulus duration was not fixed. The production experiments in Section 4 showed that global utterance duration is not significantly different across questions and statements. However, this does not mean that differences in the duration of individual items are unattested. Specifically, the durations of the utterances used as bases for the resynthesis procedure were 1.2 sec for the statement version (*bXfXdS*) and 1.3 sec for the question (*bXfXdQ*). Since resynthesis of ambiguous durational patterns was based on arithmetical averaging (see discussion in the subsection above), duration of temporally ambiguous stimuli was 1.25 sec (*bXfXdA*). Given that *Perceval* calculates reaction times with reference to stimulus onset, stimulus duration was subtracted from latencies in order to obtain results which can be interpreted as reaction times from the end of the stimulus. However, given the nature of our stimuli, can we really consider reaction times as a reliable measure for the validation of H2? Response latencies from stimulus offset would be an indicator of ease of processing only if listeners delayed the evaluation of (mis)match between melodic and temporal information until the end of stimulus. This, however, is only a simplifying assumption, made in the absence of relevant knowledge on the integration of suprasegmental cues in perception of post-lexical meaning. Indeed, there is reason to believe that, since temporal and melodic cues unfold in time, their integration could be best captured by on-line tasks or by the monitoring of multiple references for reaction times. Specifically, as for intonation, the very idea of analyzing phonetic data ($f0$ contours) as a succession of phonological events (pitch accents and edge tones) entails the existence of multiple points in time where bundles of perceptually relevant material is made available. If we chose to measure reaction times from utterance end, it is because the experiments of Section 4 showed that durational patterns are best characterized as variations of speech rate across the utterance. However, future studies on the interplay between temporal and melodic cues should definitely take into account the possibility of evaluating cue integration as time unfolds. As for the more restricted purposes of our study, the use of response latencies relative to utterance end is a factor which could have limited the conclusiveness of H2 validation. In particular, in the case of attested statistically significant difference between reaction times to congruous and incongruous stimuli, the evaluation of its perceptual meaningfulness would have required further research. However, since our data show that no significant differences are attested, H2 can be safely rejected.

5.4.1.3 Spin-off

As we said above, if we assume that tempo is a secondary cue to sentence modality, a corollary of the orthogonality hypothesis (H1) is that differences in durational patterns are best perceived when intonational cues are not available. That is, we expect a greater difference between responses to stimuli with question-like and statement-like durational patterns for items with ambiguous $f0$ contours than for items with either question-like or statement-like $f0$ contour. This motivates the steeper fall in the hypothesized rate of question responses for the grey triplet in Figure 5.1, compared to the black triplets. That is, maximal difference in subjects' responses is expected between the pairs *bXfAdQ* and *bXfAdS*. Our results did not support the orthogonality hypothesis (see Section 5.3). Moreover, resynthesis of ambiguous $f0$ contours was not entirely satisfactory. However, given the set of stimuli used in the task, we cannot rule out the possibility of ceiling effects in subjects' responses due to the availability of intonationally unambiguous stimuli. That is, listeners' attention might have been diverted from subtle temporal cues because of the presence of striking intonational differences. For this reason, we devised a short spin-off experiment to be ran after the main test. Subjects were asked to identify as question or statements stimuli in the *bXfAdQ* and *bXfAdS* conditions alone; no fillers or intonationally clear stimuli were presented. We hypothesized that, if durational differences are perceptible and used in sentence modality categorization, presenting intonationally ambiguous stimuli *alone* would have maximised the visibility of the effect of tempo on perception. We gathered responses from 26 subjects for the 2 conditions resynthesized from 2 bases, presented 4 times in each of 2 independently randomized blocks, for a total of 832 items. Subjects' *Responses* were predicted using a generalized linear mixed model with *Tempo* as a fixed factor and *Subject* as a random factor. The coefficient for Tempo, however, did not prove significant ($\beta = -0.03, z = -0.199, p = 0.843$). This shows that, even when stimuli are presented such as to maximize listeners' attention to temporal manipulations, durational differences are not a cue to sentence modality contrasts.

5.4.2 Epistemological issues

The main limitation to the use of our results in drawing clear-cut conclusions on the role of tempo as a prosodic detail, however, comes from a different source. Our experiment aimed at evaluating whether the acoustic differences in durational patterns we documented with our production study (see Sections 4.3 and 4.4) are used as a cue in the perception of sentence modality contrasts. A positive answer to this research question would have implied that tempo has to be somehow included in phonological representations of intonation (H2) or prosody (H1). The negative evidence (H0) we gathered through our experiment, on the other hand, does not allow us to draw the opposite conclusion, namely that tempo should *not* be included in phonological representations. The scope of generalization for negative findings must be accurately determined. We can only state that perception of *sentence modality* contrasts in NI clean read speech is not affected by durational differences, but we cannot rule out that durational differences play a role in the perception of other linguistically structured contrasts or in other communicative contexts. To be more specific, the scope of our results can be further narrowed down to the conclusion that perception of sentence modality contrasts is not affected by durational differences *as we modelled them* in Section 4, and namely as related to variations in phone durations (rather

5.4 Discussion

than lower or higher level units). We cannot exclude that, had we modelled production differences in a different way, perceptual evaluation could have yielded positive results. The production study presented in Section 4.3 might have been, at the same time, a starting point and a bottleneck to our perceptual validation. Before definitively dismissing the hypothesis of a perceptual relevance for temporal detail, further explorations of its acoustic manifestation could be necessary. Pushing this line of reasoning to its extremes, the scope of our testing cannot actually be stretched beyond the role of phone durations in cueing sentence modality contrasts for our *two base stimuli*. The input for our resynthesis procedure consisted in *f0* contours and durational patterns extracted from two individual utterances, which were (transformed and) combined to yield nine test stimuli. Thus, in a radical perspective, we cannot exclude that choosing a different pair of base stimuli could have affected our results as well. On the other hand, in the view of our discussion above on production modelling as a bottleneck to perceptual validation, the use of a data-driven resynthesis procedure based on the properties of individual stimuli (rather than on an explicit rule-based modelling of the allegedly relevant dimensions) could also prove an effective choice. In a data-driven approach to resynthesis, in fact, there is less room for top-down fed information, and thus the downfalls of an incorrect modelling of production data are strongly limited. For example, our intonational resynthesis gave excellent results (see Section 5.4.1) by simply warping time-aligned *f0* contours. In other words, all previous knowledge from the literature on the phonetics and phonology of intonation was condensed and limited to "alignment of *f0* contours with segmental boundaries is relevant". For cross-modality resynthesis of utterances with the same segmental content, this top-down information alone caused a 94% shift[10] in subjects' identification responses. For temporal resynthesis, we limited our assumptions to "variations in segmental durations are relevant", as the most general formulation of the findings from our production study.[11] That is, as in the case of intonation above, we did not feed the procedure with specific information from our own account of temporal differences across sentence modality. Our interpretation of the role of the edge segments in the utterance (see Section 4.3.5) or of the interaction between modality and focus (see Section 4.4.5)

---

[10] This is the absolute value of the estimated coefficient of question to statement manipulation in a linear mixed model predicting subjects' *Response* (coded as a continuous variable) from *Intonation* as a fixed factor and *Subject* as a random factor. The coefficient was highly significant ($t = 62.53$).

[11] The segmental level was preferred over smaller (i.e. subsegmental phases) or bigger (e.g. syllables) domains, as a reasonable compromise between a fine-grained temporal analysis and the degree of precision allowed by our forced alignment tool (see Section 4.2.2).

5 Perception of temporal detail

does not inform the resynthesis procedure we used in this chapter: rejection of our account of produced temporal detail (Section 4) does not entail rejection of the perceptual validation we provided here. In sum, as in the case of every study in which the alternative hypotheses are not supported, no definitive statement can be inferred from our results. We have to limit the scope of our conclusions according to the features of our study, and restrain from claiming that temporal detail is irrelevant in cueing post-lexical meaning. We can nonetheless conclude that its effects are hard to track in sentence modality contrasts in read speech, that its exploration is unlikely to reveal the need for an enrichment of the phonological structure of prosody, and that its perceptual evaluation is ultimately a sorely unrewarding enterprise.

5.5 Conclusion

In this chapter we tested the perceptual role of different durational patterns in sentence modality contrasts. The experiments in Section 4 showed that production of questions and statements in Neapolitan Italian is characterized by subtle but consistent differences in segmental durations. However, these acoustic differences do not seem to be used as perceptual cues: listeners' responses in a forced choice identification task are not affected by the manipulation of durational patterns. Moreover, no difference was found in response times to stimuli with congruous and incongruous information on the temporal and on the melodic levels. These findings are consistent with an abstractionist view of perception of post-lexical contrasts, in which some of the available information on regularly produced contrasts is indeed discarded. However, both methodological and epistemological issues prevent us from considering the evidence gathered in this chapter as truly conclusive. On the one side, the multiparametric resynthesis procedure used in the creation of the experimental stimuli should be refined, especially as far as the creation of intonationally ambiguous stimuli is concerned. Our procedure performs nonetheless very well in cross-modal resynthesis of intonation, and could represent a useful tool in the exploration of perceptual space at the utterance level. On the epistemological side, since the experiment was designed to test the perceptual importance of temporal detail, we only found evidence supporting the null hypothesis, a fact which limits the scope on the generalizability of our findings. With these caveat in mind, we can still conclude that, inside the limited scope of our investigations, temporal detail in NI does not appear to be as salient as the melodic detail we explored in Sections 2–3. The findings of Section 4, while tapping into relationships between phonetic cues which are potentially interesting in the study of production mechanisms, cannot be stretched to constitute evidence for the existence of meaningful prosodic detail at the temporal level. In conclusion, we have reason to believe that an expansion of our phonological accounts of prosody with the inclusion of the temporal dimension can be safely postponed until more compelling evidence is gathered.

6 Conclusion

In substance lies
A form that's pure
That is all lies
I'm not so sure

Nino Logoratti

 The working hypothesis which animated this book was that insights from research on phonetic detail at the prosodic level can be usefully incorporated into phonological models of intonation. This is consistent with our historist understanding of phonetic detail as systematically produced and perceived phonetic information which is not yet included in abstract phonological representations. Under such perspective, if phonological categories are flexible enough to be enriched with phonetic information which proves to be systematically produced and perceptually relevant, phonetic detail is not only consistent with exemplar-based approaches, but can also lead to a refinement of accounts based on abstractionist assumptions.
 In this book I explored whether and how one particular abstractionist model of intonation, the Autosegmental-Metrical (*AM*) framework, should account for detailed phonetic information in *f0* contours and durational patterns. The evidence gathered in the experimental chapters will be reviewed in the next section (Section 6.1), by grouping results according to their relevance to production or perception and to intonation or tempo (see Table 1.1 in Section 1.4). I will then provide a brief overview of the tools for the exploration of prosodic detail developed or fine-tuned across the various experimental chapters, thus grouping the methodological outcomes of this work in Section 6.2. I will conclude by discussing the wider theoretical implications of our findings and commenting on the polyvalence of prosodic detail, which can be accommodated in both exemplar-based (Section 6.3.1) and abstractionist (Section 6.3.2) accounts of prosody.

6 Conclusion

6.1 Summary of findings

Evidence from the experimental chapters points to the need of a partial enrichment of phonological categories in the AM framework. By examining functional contrasts between narrow focus questions and both partial topic statements (Section 2 and Section 3.2) and narrow focus statements (Section 3.3 and Sections 4–5), we have found that some phonetic detail in the shape of $f0$ contours should be included in abstract representations of tunes (Sections 2–3), whereas phonetic information about durational patterns can indeed be regarded as negligible detail (Sections 4–5), at least for this contrast and in this variety. In the following subsections, instead of presenting results for individual studies as in the experimental chapters, we group them according to the phonetic dimension involved (melodic detail, Sections 2–3, see Section 6.1.1; temporal detail, Sections 4–5, see Section 6.1.2) and to the mechanisms explored (production, Sections 2–4, and perception, Sections 3–5, see Section 6.1.3).

6.1.1 Intonation

In the AM framework, continuous phonetic information relative to $f0$ contours is discretized into phonological tunes. Tunes are composed by a series of tonal events, namely pitch accents and boundary tones, which are phonetically represented by points in the $f0$-time plane. As a result, $f0$ contours between such tonal events are considered as context-determined, inferable by rule, and, ultimately, phonologically irrelevant. However, we provided in Section 2 some evidence for systematically produced differences in the $f0$ contour between the two tones composing the nuclear pitch accents in narrow focus questions (*QNF*) and partial topic statements (*SPT*) in Neapolitan Italian (NI). Both pitch accents are realized phonetically as a rise which begins at stressed syllable onset and reaches its peak at the end of the stressed vowel. Alignment and scaling of rise start and end are not significantly different in the two contexts, but the $f0$ contour between the two is: the rise is more convex in QNF and more concave in SPT. If $f0$ contours had to be reduced to a sequence of points on the $f0$-time plane connected by irrelevant interpolations, there would be no way to account for these observed regularities in production.

As Section 3.2 shows, however, differences in $f0$ rise shape do not seem to be used as a perceptual cue to the contrast between QNF and SPT. We resynthesized stimuli at different points along a continuum of rise shape, ranging from very concave to very convex. Listeners' responses to a two-alternatives forced-choice identification task showed no correlation with stimulus manipulation. That is, it seems that differences in rise shape, while consistently produced, are not always used as a perceptual cue to pragmatic contrasts. Under these circumstances, pitch accent internal rise shape can not be considered as phonetic detail, and does not need to be included in the phonological representations of nuclear pitch accents in order to contrast QNFs and SPTs. Nuclear pitch accents in both contexts might use the prosodic transcription already suggested in the literature for QNF, namely L*+H. The contrast between the two contexts is rather expressed at the tune level, by different paradigmatic options in terms of boundary tones and postnuclear pitch accents.

The fact that rise shape does not play a perceptual role in contrasting QNF and SPT does not mean that rise shape is phonologically irrelevant altogether. In Section 3.3 we examined the perceptual role of rise shape differences in another pragmatic contrast, the one between QNF and narrow focus statements (SNF), whose nuclear rises are also more concave compared to questions. It has been long acknowledged that the contrast between QNF and SNF is primarily signalled by differences in tonal alignment - that is, in the synchronization of $f0$ movements with the segmental string. As we said above, in QNF the $f0$ peak is reached at the end of the stressed vowel; in SNF, on the other hand, the peak is reached around the stressed vowel midpoint, and the pitch accent is accordingly transcribed as L+H*. We hypothesized that, if alignment information were made ambiguous, rise shape could have been the only cue for listeners to rely on. A two-alternative forced choice identification task of stimuli with ambiguous alignment showed that listeners do use phonetic information in rise shape when categorizing (narrow focus) questions and statements.

These findings do not necessarily have to impact the conventions in use for prosodic transcription in the AM framework. We can still continue to label NI nuclear pitch accents as L*+H in questions and as L+H* in statements, as long as we acknowledge that these are used as shortcuts to richer phonetic descriptions. This might not always be the case, as shown by Petrone & D'Imperio's (2011) work on phonetic information in the prenuclear region, according to which a new structural position (a phrase accent) is required to account for sentence modality contrasts. It is important to stress that the exploration of melodic detail is consistent with different outcomes, ranging from the validation of information reduction (as we have seen in the case of QNF vs SPT rises) to an enrichment of phonetic representations which does not affect transcription conventions (as in the case of QNF vs SNF rises) and to the suggestion of different structural interpretations (as in the case of prenuclear falls across sentence modality). The interest of studying phonetic detail lies indeed in this rich range of solutions which can be suggested for the research questions it raises.

6 Conclusion

6.1.2 Tempo

Phonetic information fed into phonological categories in the AM framework is not only reduced with respect to the discretization of *f0* contours into a sequence of contrastive tonal events and irrelevant transition. Information is also reduced by concentrating on *f0* contours alone, thus discarding information on other dimensions, such as duration, intensity, voice quality and spectral proprieties. We thus tested whether sentence modality contrasts (again QNF vs SNF) are characterized acoustically by differences along other dimensions, and whether eventual differences are used as perceptual cues. We decided to focus on the temporal dimension, since in the last ten years the literature on sentence modality contrasts has shown that questions and statements often differ with respect to either global measures of speech rate or local measures in the duration of linguistic units of various sizes, ranging from segments to phonological words.

We thus collected two corpora of sentences uttered as both questions and statements, by controlling focus placement as well. Results of a first experiment (Section 4.3) show that global utterance duration and thus speech rate do not vary across sentence modality. Whereas van Heuven & van Zanten (2005) suggested that questions might display a universal trend to faster speech rate just as they show a trend to higher pitch, our findings are rather consistent with language-specific encoding of sentence modality contrasts. Differences between questions and statements along the temporal dimension, however, were found when analyzing our corpora in more detail. If overall utterance duration is the same, segmental durations have been found to vary in the two conditions. In particular, statements have longer initial segments, whereas the final segment (a vowel in our corpora) is systematically longer in questions. The magnitude of these effects is not negligible, especially for final vowel in questions, which are about 20 ms longer than in statements.

The existent differences in segmental duration within utterance of the same global duration suggested the use of an integrated metric for the evaluation of durational patterns. In a second experiment (Section 4.4) we thus adapted the algorithm proposed by Pfitzinger (2001) in order to capture local variations of speech rate. This allowed us to show that speech rate indeed follows different patterns across sentence modality, being globally increasing in statements and decreasing in questions.

A subsequent experiment (Section 5) was devised in order to establish whether durational differences at the segmental level were also consistently used as perceptual cues, in which case they should be considered as relevant prosodic detail and be somehow incorporated into phonological representations of sentence modality contrasts. We had to manipulate durational patterns independently of *f0* contours, which represent by themselves a very strong cue to sentence modality contrasts. As in the case of the perceptual study on melodic detail in QNF vs SNF pitch accents (Section 3.3), in which peak alignment information was made unavailable in order to evaluate the role of rise shape, in the study of durational patterns we manipulated the test stimuli so as to have an ambiguous *f0* contour. In addition, unlike the previous experiment on melodic detail, we also manipulated durational patterns in utterances with clear question or statement intonation. This enabled us to assess the perceptual importance of temporal information, by testing whether it is used constantly and independently (that is, in addition to intonational cues) or only when other primary cues are not available.

A two-alternative forced-choice identification task showed however that listeners' responses are not affected by manipulations of durational patterns, not even when intonation was made ambiguous. These results are not consistent with the hypothesis that temporal detail is evaluated as a perceptual cue in its own right. This finding has been replicated in a shorter experiment, in which subjects only listened to intonationally ambiguous stimuli, in order to maximize their attention on temporal cues. However, the fact that listeners responses are not affected by temporal manipulations does not entail that durational differences are not processed at all. Listeners might perceive durational information but ultimately discard it when intonational cues have been evaluated. For this reason, we measured reaction times to stimuli with either congruous or incongruous cues on the melodic and temporal level. Stimuli with congruous information (e.g. with statement-like *f0* contour and durational pattern) were predicted to elicit faster responses than stimuli with incongruous information (e.g. with statement-like *f0* contour and question-like durational pattern). However, this prediction was not borne out either. Reaction times are only slightly longer when intonation is ambiguous - a fact which contributes to show that, in NI sentence modality contrasts, durational information is negligible detail.

6.1.3 Production and perception

We are thus faced with an extremely interesting pattern of results, where production experiments show consistent acoustic differences in both melodic detail (between QNF and SPT nuclear rises) and temporal detail (in durational patterns across sentence modality), but perceptual experiments fail in attesting their use as perceptual cues. Of course, we cannot exclude that our negative results in perception are due to poor methodological choices in the set-up of the experiments. However, especially in the case of the perception of temporal detail, the

6 Conclusion

conditions for appropriate testing were probably met (see Sections 5.4.1–5.4.2 for discussion). According to Frick's (1995) "good effort criterion", we should even accept the null hypothesis of no durational information in phonological categories for sentence modality contrasts in NI, rather than simply stating that the alternative hypotheses are not supported. In any case, this does not allow us to conclude that durational patterns play no role at all in the perception of any contrast in any language, and thus we cannot exclude that phonetic information at the temporal level is stored and used in perception of post-lexical contrasts, as exemplar-based approaches would predict.

Our goal, however, is not to rule out the possibility of an "exemplar prosody" altogether. We rather aim to show that evidence from both production and perception is needed when working on prosodic detail, from either an abstractionist or an exemplarist viewpoint. Quite recently, Nguyen et al. (2009) observed that "much of the available evidence for long-term storage of FPD in the mental lexicon comes from studies of speech production". The observation is even more true for research on exemplar prosody, which deals exclusively with production data, as we will see shortly (Section 6.3.1). This is understandable, since research in this field is still very young. But when suggesting a new understanding of phonological structures, evaluating the impact of phonetic detail on perception is no less important. This is clearly shown, for example, by research on incomplete neutralization, dealing with allegedly neutralized phonological contrasts which are still reflected by surface phonetic differences.

For example, a devoicing process has been said to neutralize voicing contrasts in domain-final obstruents in German, thus making *Rat* (advice) and *Rad* (wheel) homophones.[1] However, subtle sub-phonemic durational differences can be found in speakers' production of underlying voiceless and devoiced obstruents. Along the phonetic continua of vowel duration, burst duration and closure voicing, devoiced obstruents are somewhere in between the extremes occupied by voiced and voiceless sounds. Crucially to our discussion, the perceptual role of this con-

---

[1] Among the vast bibliography on the topic, see Port et al. (1981); O'Dell & Port (1983); Charles-Luce (1985); Port & O'Dell (1985); Port & Crawford (1989); Port (1996); Kleber et al. (2010); Röttger et al. (2011); Winter & Röttger (forthcoming). Similar phenomena have been explored in other languages, such as Dutch (Warner et al. 2004, 2006; Ernestus & Baayen 2006), Russian (Pye 1986; Dmitrieva et al. 2010), Polish (Slowiaczek & Dinnsen 1985; Slowiaczek & Szymanska 1989) and Catalan (Dinnsen & Charles-Luce 1984; Charles-Luce & Dinnsen 1987). We exclude from our review the seminal paper by Dinnsen & Garcia Zamor (1971), which was unfortunately not available to us. Experimental results or theoretical arguments against incomplete neutralization are provided by Fourakis & Iverson (1984); Mascaró (1987); Jassem & Richter (1989); Kopkalli (1993); Manaster Ramer (1996).

sistently produced phonetic detail has been investigated since the very first studies on incomplete neutralization - that is, at least since Port et al. (1981). Constant methodological improvements enabled the exclusion of possible experimental confounds, as in the case of orthography-induced biases (Röttger et al. 2011). Likewise, determining whether such contrasts are perceptible is instrumental in deciding of their functional role: whereas Port et al. (1981) first thought that "this 'semicontrast' must be nearly useless in conversation", Ernestus & Baayen (2006) recently suggested that incomplete neutralization might be "a subphonemic cue to past-tense formation" in Dutch. Ultimately, it is this long-term exploration of both production and perception mechanisms which allowed researchers to recast the incomplete neutralization issue in abstractionist/exemplarist terms, as in Kleber et al. (2010). We hope that our investigation of prosodic detail, however far from conclusive, might at least demonstrate that the recent work on exemplar prosody based on production evidence (see Section 6.3.1) must be necessarily complemented by a thorough examination of perceptual mechanisms.

6.2 Tools for prosodic detail research

Besides suggesting a potentially interesting research topic, we also aimed at providing some experimental tools which might be useful in its exploration. This was particularly needed in the case of the study of temporal detail, which has not been analyzed in the literature as thoroughly as melodic detail. However, the tools briefly presented in the experimental chapters on temporal detail might also prove relevant in the study of prosodic detail in general.

6.2.1 Automatic Speech Segmentation for Italian

The study of temporal detail in production required the collection of a matrix with a great number of segment durations (Section 4.2.2). Pooling data from the *Orlando* and the *Danser* corpora (see Section 4.2.1), we had to segment 2376 utterances, each composed of 8 CV syllables. With more than 35.000 segmental boundaries to be placed, manual segmentation was simply not an option. However, tools for automatic segmentation of Italian were not available either.[2] Our solution has been to develop our own tool for Italian forced alignment, *ASSI* (Cangemi et al. 2011). In forced alignment, audio files are segmented according

---

[2] *EasyAlign* (Goldman 2011) only works with French, English, Brazilian Portuguese, Spanish and Taiwan Min, while *SPPAS* (Bigi & Hirst 2012), which works with French, English, Italian and Chinese, was only released after our experiment was planned, executed and published.

6 Conclusion

to an orthographic transcription and a phonetized lexicon provided by the user. The first is a plain text file containing for each row an audio file name and its orthographically transcribed content, as in (1) for the *Danser* transcription file:

(1) `Q1BD1.wav danilo_vola_da_roma`

The second contains for each row an orthographic word-form and a phonetic transcription of the expected pronunciation (variants are allowed), as in (2) for the *Orlando* lexicon file:

(2) `ralego r:a:l:[e:/E:]g:o:`

Forced alignment is especially suited for the segmentation of read speech, since for this kind of data the experimenter can provide an orthographic transcription with no effort. Moreover, when working on sentence modality and/or focus placement in NI, which only use prosodic cues to express these contrasts, the use of forced alignment is even more indicated: the same orthographic transcription based on the same phonetized lexicon can be used for a variety of experimental items. For example, the *Orlando* corpus contained three sentences composed by 16 segments. These were uttered in the six combinations between the two levels of the sentence modality factor (question, statement) and the three levels of the narrow focus placement factor (on subject, verb or object). Each of 30 speakers read three repetitions of three 16-segment sentences uttered in six contexts, thus requiring the extraction of 25.920 phone durations in total. This was accomplished by providing a single lexicon file with the phonetic transcription of *six* words, and a single transcription file containing orthographic transcriptions for *three* sentence types.

6.2.2 Multi-parametric continuous resynthesis

Whereas the exploration of temporal detail in production required a tool which merely speeded up an already existing procedure (viz. manual segmentation), to test our hypotheses on the perception of temporal detail we had to resynthesize stimuli using a new procedure altogether (see Section 5.2). The procedure is partly based on Gubian et al. (2010, 2011), and through a set of *Praat* (Boersma & Weenink 2008) and *R* (R Development Core Team 2008) scripts yields input files for the *PSOLA* (Moulines & Charpentier 1990) resynthesis engine in *Praat*. Given two utterances, the question and statement version of a same sentence, we needed to resynthesize each one using (1) durational patterns and/or *f0* contours of the other one (*cross-modality* resynthesis) and (2) ambiguous durational patterns and/or *f0* contours between the two (*ambiguous* resynthesis).

However, as we have seen discussing NI intonation (see 1.3.3), the synchronization of *f0* movements with the segmental string is crucial in signalling sentence modality contrasts. This means that, as far as cross-modality resynthesis is concerned, intonational and temporal cues must be jointly manipulated: one cannot simply extract the *f0* of the first utterance and use it to resynthesize the second. Similarly, segmental durations cannot be modified without transforming *f0* contours as well. Thus we extracted *f0* contours and segmental durations for each utterance, then the two *f0* contours were time-warped by aligning their corresponding segmental boundaries. This landmark registration procedure creates two intermediate contours having identical underlying phone durations. These intermediate contours can be combined with actual durational patterns and thus be ready to be resynthesized onto an actual utterance.

The results of cross-modality resynthesis are particularly satisfying. As we have seen in Section 5.4.1, listeners' responses to stimuli resynthesized by applying question *f0* contours onto statement bases are not significantly different from listeners' responses to natural questions. Informal testing shows encouraging results in the resynthesis of other contrasts as well, as for example in the case of focus placement, and even when the lexical material is different between the two sentences. For example, *f0* contour and durational pattern of a (prepositional) *object* narrow focus statement utterance of the sentence *Danilo vola da Roma* were used to resynthesize a *subject* narrow focus statement utterance of the sentence *Serena vive da Lara* (see Section 4.2.1.2), yielding a stimulus which was identified as having narrow focus on the object. In this case, performances could be even improved by adding manipulation of landmark-registered intensity contours, which could be easily included as an additional module in the resynthesis procedure. Of course, these excellent results are at least in part motivated by the use of sentences with identical metrical and syllable structures at both ends of the resynthesis procedure. However, we believe that very different sentences could also be used, if phonologically motivated assumptions guided the choice of the landmarks to be registered.

Our second goal was the creation of ambiguous stimuli, with respect to *f0* contours and/or durational patterns. This was achieved by averaging phone durations, in the case of durational patterns, and by averaging intermediate *f0* contours (i.e. landmark-registered contours expressed in normalized time with identical underlying phone durations), prior to resynthesis. By using a simple

6 Conclusion

average, we obtained *acoustically* ambiguous stimuli. These stimuli would have also been perceptually ambiguous only if the perceptual space between questions and statements was perfectly linear. Unsurprisingly, this proved not to be the case (for a discussion of how this affected the interpretation of our results, see Section 5.4.1): responses to stimuli with acoustically ambiguous intonation had a significant question bias, probably due to the postnuclear region.[3] What is relevant to the present discussion is that our resynthesis procedure allows us to address very explicitly the issue of the difference between acoustically and perceptually ambiguous stimuli in a multidimensional prosodic space. In this sense, this procedure could prove a useful tool in the investigation of questions which are not directly addressed in this book.

6.3 Theoretical implications

In this final section we interpret our findings on prosodic detail in Neapolitan Italian by discussing their relevance for recent exemplar-based approaches to prosody focussing on frequency effects in production (Section 6.3.1). We conclude by highlighting that a close examination of phonetic detail is necessary for the construction of phonologically adequate categories (Section 6.3.2): neither excessive unanalyzed phonetic information nor bony minimalist abstract categories are viable options when prosody is analyzed in production and perception.

6.3.1 Exemplar prosody

As we said in the introductory pages (Section 1.2.3), an exemplar-based approach to prosody would provide a natural setting for the accommodation of prosodic detail. Let us flesh out this statement in this section. According to Johnson,

> an exemplar is an association between a set of auditory properties and a set of category labels. The auditory properties are output from the peripheral auditory system, and the set of category labels includes any classification that may be important to the perceiver, and which was available at the time

---

[3] The subject narrow focus utterances used in the experiment have an audible fall in the question condition (see Figure 2.1, bottom panel) and flat $f0$ contour in the statement condition, which are respectively transcribed as !H* and !H+L*. However, in postnuclear position even slight $f0$ falls (as those in the acoustically ambiguous condition) can be salient, and thus bias the listener towards the question response. The impact of the postnuclear region on acoustical and perceptual ambiguity can thus be easily tested by using gated or object-focussed stimuli.

> that the exemplar was stored - for example, the linguistic value of the exemplar, the gender of the speaker, the name of the speaker, and so on. (Johnson 1997: 147)

As we explained above (see Section 1.2.1), in this approach the normalization phase is no longer necessary: new prompts activate both "linguistic value", thus feeding word recognition, and indexical information (e.g. the gender and name of the speaker), thus feeding talker recognition. But what happens if $f0$ contours are stored as part of the auditory properties set, and pragmatic or information structure contrasts are stored as part of the category labels set (specifically, its "linguistic value")? By enriching exemplars with information on both the substantial and the functional sides, the model could perform talker recognition, word recognition and extraction of post-lexical meaning at the same time.

Recent research has addressed the issue of whether $f0$ contours are stored into exemplars and connected to post-lexical meaning.[4] Most work has focussed on frequency effects in pitch accent production. Exemplar models have been extended to production since Pierrehumbert (2001). In her most basic model,

> the decision to produce a given category is realized through activation of that label. The selection of a phonetic target, given the label, may be modelled as a random selection of an exemplar from the cloud of exemplars associated with the label.(Pierrehumbert 2001: §3.1)

By positing activation of a region in the exemplar cloud rather than that of a single exemplar, the model can account for entrenchment effects, according to which productions become less variable with practice. In this case, phonetic variability is expected to decrease when the cloud is denser because the exemplars are produced and perceived with higher frequency.

Recent work by Katrin Schweitzer combines the hypothesis of $f0$ contour storage with predictions on entrenchment. In her model,

> during speech production a speaker selects a stored exemplar as a production target. Assuming that pitch accents can be stored with the word, the speaker would select an exemplar that matches not only the intended word but also the intended pitch accent. (Schweitzer et al. 2010b: 138)

If, instead of selecting a single exemplar, a whole region of exemplars is activated, as in Pierrehumbert's refined model, entrenchment would predict that more frequent pitch accents are less variable. In the last few years, a number of corpus

---

[4] For storage of fundamental frequency information connected to lexical contrasts, see Sekiguchi (2006).

6 Conclusion

studies has used parametrized descriptions of pitch accents (based on *PaIntE*, see Möhler & Conkie 1998; Möhler 2001) to explore whether phonetic variability is affected by frequency of occurrence. The results seem to provide mixed evidence, ranging from the absence of frequency effects in German (Walsh et al. 2008), to more prominent $f0$ movements in frequent word/pitch accent combinations (Schweitzer et al. 2010b) and to entrenchment in English collocations (Schweitzer et al. 2011). In sum, even if the authors conclude that "there is still a great deal to be understood about how lexicalised storage interacts with 'top-down' information in the production of prosody" (Schweitzer et al. 2011: 4), these results are taken as supporting an exemplar-based view of prosody.

6.3.2 Substance, form and function

This approach is surely intriguing, and we are persuaded that it will receive a great deal of attention in the coming years. Its elaboration, however, might benefit from a close inspection of its theoretical underpinnings, in order to rule out possible aporetic developments. At this point, it must be clear that in a model where exemplars are conceived as associations between $f0$ information and post-lexical function labels, there is no longer room for phonological representations, which are at best redundant. Substance is no longer linked to function by abstract forms, but rather through activation of exemplars using similarity functions. This is indeed the perspective of the so-called *functional* approaches to prosody (Shriberg et al. 1998; Noth et al. 2000; Batliner et al. 2001), which suggest that formal entities such as "the unfortunate notion of pitch accent" should be pruned by Occam's razor (Batliner & Möbius 2006: 25).

However, two possible objections arise at this point. The first is that, as Ladd (2008: 20) puts it, "whether we should adopt a 'phonological' approach to intonation is not primarily a matter of taste, but an *empirical question*". Or, in other words, in addition to dealing with previously unaccounted-for phenomena (such as frequency effects), an exemplar-based approach to prosody must also account for phenomena which have already been framed in phonological terms.[5] This objection, of course, is nothing more than an empirical argument: in Smith & Medin's (1981: 33) terms, "it is a statement about what has happened so far, not about what can happen". And since functional models have been seriously explored for only a decade, we surely cannot consider empirical arguments as conclusive.

---

[5] A few examples might be the role of accentedness in discourse structure (Hawkins & Warren 1991), the disentangling of linguistic and paralinguistic meaning (Scherer et al. 1984), and evidence from imitation studies (Cole & Shattuck-Hufnagel 2011).

The second objection is perhaps more cogent. It regards the covert use of phonological forms, even when the general system architecture is claimed to posit a direct link between phonetic substance and post-lexical meaning. In the discussion of frequency of usage in exemplar-based models of prosody, for example, we have seen that its effects have been explored in terms of phonetic variability of pitch accents. That is, even the arguments adduced in favour of exemplar dynamics eventually posit somehow abstract categories. At this point, it is unclear whether exemplars actually link phonetic substance to post-lexical categorical labels or rather to pitch accents - that is, forms which themselves bridge substance and functions.[6] An operationalized version of abstractions corresponding to pitch accents also seems to be required by current text-to-speech systems. In van Santen & Möbius' 2000: 278 quantitative model, for example, phonetic differences between *f0* contours interpreted as having the same function are accounted for by time warping of a common *template*.

It is unclear, at this point, whether formal representations of prosody can really be dismissed, even in exemplar-based approaches. Functional approaches criticize AM-like phonological approaches to intonation because

> The classical phonological concept of the Prague school has been abandoned in contemporary intonation models, namely that phonemes - be they segmental or suprasegmental - should only be assumed if these units make a difference in meaning. This functional point of view has given way to more formal criteria such as economy of description. Thus, the decision on the descriptive units is not based on differences in meaning but on formal criteria, and only afterwards are functional differences sought that can be described with these formal units. (Batliner & Möbius 2006: §1.1)

However, it is crucial to stress out that, in principle, "formal criteria" *include* consideration of contrasts in meaning. And that, in that very same Prague school, "phonemes - be they segmental or suprasegmental" are *formal* entities. In this sense, despite their claims, functional approaches do not actually advocate for the suppression of phonological representations and of inventories of formal units.

It is true that, in AM accounts of intonation, the mapping between forms and functions is often confusing. In discussing prenuclear fall shape across sentence modalities in NI (see Section 2.4.2) and German (see Section 3.1), we have seen a clear example of how meaningful phonetic detail can be accommodated by en-

---

[6] This state of affair is already exemplified by the titles of relevant studies in this perspective, such as "Relative frequency affects pitch accent realisation" (Schweitzer et al. 2010a) and "Frequency of occurrence effects on pitch accent realisation" (Schweitzer et al. 2010b).

6 Conclusion

riching either the tonal inventory or the sequential grammar. We agree with proponents of functional approaches that if a single pragmatic contrast is expressed by a given phonetic difference, having two competing phonological analyses is symptomatic of the unstable state of the formal descriptions available. But again, we must acknowledge that this objection is nothing more than an empirical argument: it does not prove that phonological representations are useless, but rather that they are not yet capable of providing a unified account.

Ultimately, the central point is that if decisions on the descriptive units must be based on differences in meaning, then we need to start from a catalogue of different functions. But as we have seen in the discussion of the gap between segmental and supra-segmental phonology (Section 2.4.3), there is no such thing as a theory-independent set of post-lexical functions. Moreover, individual theories of pragmatic and discourse meaning use as *explicans* the very same set of phenomena which is *explicandum* in a functional account of intonation.[7] The risk of circularity here is very high. Theories of intonation must acknowledge the need of a constant exchange between evidence provided by research on substance and by research on function: the formal level is indeed the central processor which permits the incorporation of insights coming from both directions.

Frequency effects on pitch accent variability shows that research on prosodic detail in production can provide arguments supporting an exemplar-based view of prosody, but also that no framework for the study of intonation has actually dismissed a somehow abstract level of representation altogether. Our results on the perception of prosodic detail support this view by showing that some consistently produced phonetic information does not function as a cue to some post-lexical contrasts. The strongest interpretation of these results is that an abstract representation in terms of phonological categories is useful and necessary in the study of intonation. However, current phonological models need to be refined with respect to both the richness of phonetic specification (as in the case of the nuclear rise shape across sentence modalities) and in the mechanisms used to link substance with function (as in the case of the competing analyses of prenuclear falls across sentence modalities). According to the minimalist interpretation, on the other hand, no inferences are drawn about the role of abstract forms in intonation, but whenever phonological categories are indeed assumed, they must be thoroughly explored in production and perception to rule out the exclusion of useful prosodic detail.

In any case, the exploration of prosodic detail appears to be crucial for both exemplar-based and abstractionist approaches to intonation, and will probably provide the common ground for their integration into a truly hybrid model.

---

[7] One example is the case of B-accents in Jackendoff (1972).

Bibliography

Abercrombie, David. 1967. *Elements of general phonetics*. Edinburgh: Edinburgh University Press.

Adjarian, Hrachia. 1899. Les explosives de l'ancien arménien étudiées dans les dialectes modernes. *La Parole: Revue internationale de Rhinologie, Otologie, Laryngologie et Phonétique expérimentale* 119–127.

Albano Leoni, Federico. 2006. Lo statuto del fonema. In Stefano Gensini & Martone Arturo (eds.), *Il linguaggio: Teorie e storia delle teorie. In onore di Lia Formigari*, 281–303. Napoli: Liguori.

Anderson, Mark, Janet Pierrehumbert & Mark Liberman. 1984. Synthesis by rule of English intonation patterns. In *Proceedings of 9th International Conference of Acoustics, Speech and Signal Processing*, vol. 9, 77–80. San Diego.

André, Carine, Alain Ghio, Christian Cavé & Bernard Teston. 2003. Perceval: A computer-driven system for experimentation on auditory and visual perception. In Daniel Recasens, Maria Josep Solé & Joaquín Romero (eds.), *Proceedings of the 15th International Congress of Phonetic Sciences*, 1421–1424. Barcelona.

Angelini, Bianca, Fabio Brugnara, Daniele Falavigna, Diegl Giuliani, Roberto Gretter & Maurizio Omologo. 1993. A baseline of a speaker independent continuous speech recognizer of Italian. In *Proceedings of the 3rd European Conference on Speech Communication and Technology*, 847–850. Berlin.

Arndt, Walter. 1960. Modal particles in Russian and German. *Word* 16. 323–336.

Atterer, Michaela & Robert Ladd. 2004. On the phonetics and phonology of segmental anchoring of F0: Evidence from German. *Journal of Phonetics* 32. 177–197.

Audacity Development Team. 2006. Audacity: Free audio editor and recorder. Computer program, retrieved from http://audacity.sourceforge.net/.

Avesani, Cinzia. 1990. A contribution to the synthesis of Italian intonation. In *Proceedings of the 1st International Conference on Spoken Language Processing*, 833–836. Kobe.

Balota, David. 1994. Visual word recognition. In Matthew Traxler & Morton Gernsbacher (eds.), *Handbook of psycholinguistics*, 334–357. San Diego: Academic Press.

Batliner, Anton & Batliner Möbius. 2006. Prosodic models, automatic speech understanding, and speech synthesis: Towards the common ground? In William Barry, Wim van Dommelen & Jacques Koreman (eds.), *The integration of phonetic knowledge in speech technology*, 21–44. Dordrecht: Kluwer.

Batliner, Anton, Bernd Möbius, Gregor Möhler, Antje Schweitzer & Elmar Nöth. 2001. Prosodic models, automatic speech understanding, and speech synthesis: Towards the common ground. In Paul Dalsgaard, Børge Lindberg & Henrik Benner (eds.), *Proceedings of the 7th European Conference on Speech Communication and Technology*, vol. 4, 2285–2288. Aalborg.

Beckman, Mary. 1996. The parsing of prosody. *Language and Cognitive Processes* 11(1-2). 17–68.

Beckman, Mary. 1997. A typology of spontaneous speech. In Yoshinori Sagisaka, Nick Campbell & Norio Higuchi (eds.), *Computing prosody: Computational models for processing spontaneous speech*, 7–26. Dordrecht, Heidelberg, London, New York: Springer.

Bigi, Brigitte & Daniel Hirst. 2012. SPeech Phonetization Alignment and Syllabification (SPPAS): A tool for the automatic analysis of speech prosody. In Qiuwu Ma, Hongwei Ding & Daniel Hirst (eds.), *Proceedings of the 5th International Conference on Speech Prosody*, vol. 1, 19–22. Shanghai: Tongji University Press.

Black, Alan & Andrew Hunt. 1996. Generating f0 contours from ToBI labels using linear regression. In *Proceedings of the 4th International Conference on Spoken Language Processing*, vol. 3, 1385–1388. Philadelphia.

Blesser, Barry. 1972. Speech perception under conditions of spectral transformation: I. Phonetic characteristics. *Journal of Speech and Hearing Research* 15(1). 5–41.

Boersma, Paul & David Weenink. 2008. Praat: Doing phonetics by computer. Computer program, retrieved from http://www.praat.org/.

Bolinger, Dwight. 1951. Intonation: Levels versus configurations. *Word* 7. 199–210.

Bolinger, Dwight. 1964. Intonation as a universal. In Horace Lunt (ed.), *Proceedings of the 9th International Congress of Linguists*, 833–848. The Hague: Mouton.

Bolinger, Dwight. 1989. *Intonation and its uses: Melody in grammar and discourse*. Palo Alto: Stanford University Press.

Brooks, Lee. 1978. Nonanalytic concept formation and memory for instances. In Eleanor Rosch & Barbara Lloyd (eds.), *Cognition and categorization*, 170–211. Hillsdale: Erlbaum.

Browman, Catherine & Louis Goldstein. 1986. Towards an articulatory phonology. *Phonology Yearbook* 3. 219–252.

Brunetti, Lisa, Mariapaola D'Imperio & Francesco Cangemi. 2010. On the prosodic marking of contrast in Romance sentence topic: Evidence from Neapolitan Italian. In *Proceedings of the 5th International Conference on Speech Prosody*, Chicago.

Bruni, Francesco. 1992. *L'italiano nelle regioni. Lingua nazionale e identità regionali.* Torino: Utet.

Büring, Daniel. 1997. *The meaning of topic and focus: The 59th street bridge accent.* London, New York: Routledge.

Bybee, Joan. 2001. *Phonology and language use.* Cambridge: Cambridge University Press.

Bybee, Joan. 2006. From usage to grammar: The mind's response to repetition. *Language* 82(4). 711–733.

Campbell, Nick & Parham Mokhtari. 2003. Voice quality: The 4th prosodic dimension. In Daniel Recasens, Maria Josep Solé & Joaquín Romero (eds.), *Proceedings of the 15th International Congress of Phonetic Sciences*, 2417–2420. Barcelona.

Cangemi, Francesco. 2009. Phonetic detail in intonation contour dynamics. In Stephan Schmid, Michael Schwarzenbach & Dieter Studer (eds.), *La dimensione temporale del parlato: Proceedings of the 5th Conference of Associazione Italiana di Scienze della Voce*, 325–334. Torriana: EDK.

Cangemi, Francesco, Francesco Cutugno, Bogdan Ludusan, Dino Seppi & Dirk Van Compernolle. 2011. Automatic Speech Segmentation for Italian (ASSI): Tools, models, evaluation and application. In Barbara Gili Fivela, Antonio Stella, Luigia Garrapa & Mirko Grimaldi (eds.), *Contesto comunicativo e variabilità nella produzione e percezione della lingua: Proceedings of the 7th Conference of Associazione Italiana di Scienze della Voce*, Roma: Bulzoni.

Cangemi, Francesco & Mariapaola D'Imperio. 2011a. Local speech rate differences between questions and statements in italian. In Wai-Sum Lee & Eric Zee (eds.), *Proceedings of the 17th International Congress of Phonetic Sciences*, 392–395. Hong Kong: City University of Hong Kong.

Cangemi, Francesco & Mariapaola D'Imperio. 2011b. Prosodia oltre la f0: Tempo e modalità. In Barbara Gili Fivela, Antonio Stella, Luigia Garrapa & Mirko Grimaldi (eds.), *Contesto comunicativo e variabilità nella produzione e percezione della lingua: Proceedings of the 7th Conference of Associazione Italiana di Scienze della Voce*, Roma: Bulzoni.

Cangemi, Francesco & Mariapaola D'Imperio. 2013. Tempo and the perception of sentence modality. *Laboratory Phonology* 4(1). 191–219.

Cangemi, Francesco & Mariapaola D'Imperio. forthcoming. Beyond f0: Sentence modality and speech rate. In Joaquín Romero & Maria Riera (eds.), *Selected papers from the 5th Conference on Phonetics and Phonology in Iberia, Amsterdam: John Benjamins.

Caputo, Maria Rosaria. 1994. L'intonazione delle domande sì/no in un campione di italiano parlato. In *Proceedings of the 4th Gruppo di Fonetica Sperimentale Workshop*, 9–18. Torino.

Caputo, Maria Rosaria. 1996. Presupposizione, fuoco, modalità e schemi melodici. In *Proceedings of the 24th National Congress of Associazione Italiana di Acustica*, 49–54. Trento.

Caputo, Maria Rosaria & Mariapaola D'Imperio. 1995. Verso un possibile sistema di trascrizione prosodica dell'italiano: Cenni preliminari. In *Proceedings of the 5th workshop of Gruppo di Fonetica Sperimentale*, 71–83. Trento.

Charles-Luce, Jan. 1985. Word-final devoicing in German and the effects of phonetic and sentential contexts. *Journal of Phonetics* 13. 309–324.

Charles-Luce, Jan & Daniel Dinnsen. 1987. A reanalysis of Catalan devoicing. *Journal of Phonetics* 15(2). 187–190.

Chomsky, Noam. 1965. *Aspects of the theory of syntax*. Cambridge: MIT Press.

Church, Barbara & Daniel Schacter. 1994. Perceptual specificity of auditory priming: Implicit memory for voice intonation and fundamental frequency. *Journal of Experimental Psychology: Learning, Memory, and Cognition* 20(3). 521–533.

Cole, Jennifer & Stefanie Shattuck-Hufnagel. 2011. The phonology and phonetics of perceived prosody: What do listeners imitate? In *Proceedings of the 12th Annual Conference of the International Speech Communication Association*, 969–972. Firenze.

Coleman, John. 2003. Discovering the acoustic correlates of phonological contrasts. *Journal of Phonetics* 31(3-4). 351–372.

Cooper, Franklin, Pierre Delattre, Alvin Liberman, John Borst & Louis Gerstman. 1952. Some experiments on the perception of synthetic speech sounds. *Journal of the Acoustical Society of America* 24(6). 597–606.

Cooper, William & Jeanne Paccia-Cooper. 1980. *Syntax and speech*. Cambridge: Harvard University Press.

Dahan, Delphine, Michael Tanenhaus & Craig Chambers. 2002. Accent and reference resolution in spoken-language comprehension. *Journal of Memory and Language* 47(2). 292–314.

De Dominicis, Amedeo. 2010. Interrogative e assertive in un corpus dialettale recuperato (Bomarzo). In Francesco Cutugno, Pietro Maturi, Renata Savy, Giovanni Abete & Iolanda Alfano (eds.), *Parlare con le persone, parlare alle macchine: La dimensione interazionale della comunicazione verbale: Proceedings of the 6th Conference of Associazione Italiana di Scienze della Voce*, Torriana: EDK.

De Mauro, Tullio. 1970. *Storia linguistica dell'Italia unita (nuova edizione)*. Laterza: Laterza.

Del Giudice, Alex, Ryan Shosted, Kathryn Davidson, Mohammad Salihie & Amalia Arvaniti. 2007. Comparing methods for locating pitch "elbows". In Jürgen Trouvain & William Barry (eds.), *Proceedings of the 16th International Congress of Phonetic Sciences*, 1117–1120. Saarbrücken.

Delattre, Pierre. 1966. Les dix intonations de base du français. *The French Review* 40(1). 1–14.

Delattre, Pierre, Alvin Liberman & Franklin Cooper. 1955. Acoustic loci and transitional cues for consonants. *Journal of the Acoustical Society of America* 27(4). 769–773.

D'Imperio, Mariapaola. 1995. Timing differences between prenuclear and nuclear pitch accents in Italian. *Journal of the Acoustical Society of America* 98(5). 2894.

D'Imperio, Mariapaola. 1996. Caratteristiche di timing degli accenti nucleari in parlato italiano letto. In *Proceedings of the 24th National Congress of Associazione Italiana di Acustica*, 55–60. Trento.

D'Imperio, Mariapaola. 1997a. Breadth of focus, modality, and prominence perception in Neapolitan Italian. *Working Papers in Linguistics – Ohio State University* 50. 19–39.

D'Imperio, Mariapaola. 1997b. Narrow focus and focal accent in the Neapolitan variety of Italian. In Antonis Botinis, Georgios Kouroupetroglou & George Carayiannis (eds.), *Intonation: Theory, models and applications. Proceedings of an European Conference on Speech Communication and Technology Workshop*, 87–90. Athens.

D'Imperio, Mariapaola. 1999. Tonal structure and pitch targets in Italian focus constituents. In John Ohala (ed.), *Proceedings of the 14th International Congress of Phonetic Sciences*, 1757–1760. San Francisco: University of California.

D'Imperio, Mariapaola. 2000. *The role of perception in defining tonal targets and their alignment*: Columbus: The Ohio State University dissertation.

D'Imperio, Mariapaola. 2001. Focus and tonal structure in neapolitan italian. *Speech Communication* 33(4). 339–356.

D'Imperio, Mariapaola. 2002. Italian intonation: An overview and some questions. *Probus* 14(1). 37–69.

D'Imperio, Mariapaola. 2003. Tonal structure and pitch targets in Italian focus constituents. *Catalan Journal of Linguistics* 2. 55–65.

D'Imperio, Mariapaola & Francesco Cangemi. 2009. The interplay between tonal alignment and rise shape in the perception of two Neapolitan rising accents. Talk presented at the 4th Conference on Phonetics and Phonology in Iberia, Gran Canaria, Spain.

D'Imperio, Mariapaola & Francesco Cangemi. 2011. Phrasing, register level downstep and partial topic constructions in Neapolitan Italian. In Christoph Gabriel

& Conxita Lleó (eds.), *Intonational phrasing in Romance and Germanic: Cross-linguistic and bilingual studies*, 75–94. Amsterdam: John Benjamins.

D'Imperio, Mariapaola, Francesco Cangemi & Lisa Brunetti. 2008. The phonetics and phonology of contrastive topic constructions in Italian. Poster presented at the 3rd Conference on Tone and Intonation in Europe, Lisbon, Portugal.

D'Imperio, Mariapaola, Gorka Elordieta, Sónia Frota, Pilar Prieto & Marina Vigàrio. 2005. Intonational phrasing in Romance: The role of syntactic and prosodic structure. In Sónia Frota, Marina Vigàrio & Maria Freitas (eds.), *Prosodies*, 59–97. Berlin, New York: Mouton de Gruyter.

D'Imperio, Mariapaola & Barbara Gili Fivela. 2003. How many levels of phrasing? Evidence from two varieties of Italian. In John Local, Richard Ogden & Rosalind Temple (eds.), *Papers in Laboratory Phonology*, vol. 6, 38–57. Cambridge: Cambridge University Press.

D'Imperio, Mariapaola & David House. 1997. Perception of questions and statements in Neapolitan Italian. In George Kokkinakis, Nikos Fakotakis & Evangelos Dermatas (eds.), *Proceedings of the 5th European Conference on Speech Communication and Technology*, 251–254. Rhodes.

D'Imperio, Mariapaola, Caterina Petrone & Noël Nguyen. 2007. Effects of tonal alignment on lexical identification in Italian. In Tomas Riad & Carlos Gussenhoven (eds.), *Tones and tunes: Experimental studies in word and sentence prosody*, vol. 2, 79–106. Berlin: de Gruyter.

Dinnsen, Daniel & Jan Charles-Luce. 1984. Phonological neutralization, phonetic implementation and individual differences. *Journal of Phonetics* 12(1). 49–60.

Dinnsen, Daniel & Maria Garcia Zamor. 1971. The three degrees of vowel length in German. *Research on Language & Social Interaction* 4(1). 111–126.

Dmitrieva, Olga, Allard Jongman & Joan Sereno. 2010. Phonological neutralization by native and non-native speakers: The case of Russian final devoicing. *Journal of Phonetics* 38(3). 483–492.

Dombrowski, Ernst & Oliver Niebuhr. 2005. Acoustic patterns and communicative functions of phrase-final f0 rises in German: Activating and restricting contours. *Phonetica* 62(2-4). 176–195.

Dryer, Matthew. 2011. Polar questions. In Matthew Dryer & Martin Haspelmath (eds.), *The World Atlas of Language Structures Online*, Munich: Max Planck Digital Library.

Duncan, Starkey. 1972. Some signals and rules for taking speaking turns in conversations. *Journal of Personality and Social Psychology* 23(2). 283–292.

Eefting, Wieke. 1991. The effect of "information value" and "accentuation" on the duration of Dutch words, syllables, and segments. *Journal of the Acoustical Society of America* 89(1). 412–424.

Elman, Jeffrey & James McClelland. 1988. Cognitive penetration of the mechanisms of perception: Compensation for coarticulation of lexically restored phonemes. *Journal of Memory and Language* 27(2). 143–165.

Ernestus, Mirjam. 2014. Acoustic reduction and the roles of abstractions and exemplars in speech processing. *Lingua* 142. 27–41.

Ernestus, Mirjam & Harald Baayen. 2006. The functionality of incomplete neutralization in Dutch: The case of past-tense formation. In Louis Goldstein, Douglas Whalen & Catherine Best (eds.), *Papers in Laboratory Phonology*, vol. 8, 27–49. Cambridge: Cambridge University Press.

Faber, Alice. 1992. Phonemic segmentation as epiphenomenon: Evidence from the history of alphabetic writing. In Pamela Downing, Susan Lima & Michael Noonan (eds.), *The linguistics of literacy*, 111–134. Amsterdam: John Benjamins.

Face, Timothy. 2001. Focus and early peak alignment in Spanish intonation. *Probus* 13(2). 223–246.

Farnetani, Edda & Shiro Kori. 1991. Rhytmic structure in Italian noun phrases: A study on vowel durations. *Phonetica* 47. 50–65.

Firth, John. 1948. Sounds and prosodies. *Transactions of the Philological Society* 47(1). 127–152.

Flemming, Edward. 1997. Phonetic detail in phonology: Towards a unified account of assimilation and coarticulation. In Keiichiro Suzuki & Dirk Elzinga (eds.), *Proceedings of the 1995 Southwestern Workshop in Optimality Theory (SWOT)*, Tucson.

Flemming, Edward. 2001. Scalar and categorical phenomena in a unified model of phonetics and phonology. *Phonology* 18(1). 7–44.

Fourakis, Marios & Gregory Iverson. 1984. On the 'incomplete neutralization' of German final obstruents. *Phonetica* 41(3). 140–149.

Frick, Robert. 1995. Accepting the null hypothesis. *Memory & Cognition* 23(1). 132–138.

Frota, Sónia, Mariapaola D'Imperio, Gorka Elordieta, Pilar Prieto & Marina Vigàrio. 2007. The phonetics and phonology of intonational phrasing in Romance. In Pilar Prieto, Joan Mascaró & Maria Josep Solé (eds.), *Segmental and prosodic issues in Romance phonology*, 131–154. Amsterdam: John Benjamins.

Fujisaki, Hiroya & Keikichi Hirose. 1982. Modelling the dynamic characteristics of voice fundamental frequency with application to analysis and synthesis of intonation. In Shiro Hattori & Kazuko Inoue (eds.), *Proceedings of 13th International Congress of Linguists*, 57–70. Tokyo.

Gili Fivela, Barbara. 2004. *The phonetics and phonology of intonation: The case of Pisa Italian*: Pisa: Scuola Normale Superiore dissertation.

Bibliography

Gili Fivela, Barbara. 2006. The coding of target alignment and scaling in pitch accent transcription. *Italian Journal of Linguistics* 18(1). 189–221.

Gili Fivela, Barbara. 2008. *Intonation in production and perception: The case of Pisa Italian*. Alessandria: Edizioni dell'Orso.

Gili Fivela, Barbara & Mariapaola D'Imperio. 2003. Tonal alignment of prenuclear accents in Italian. Poster presented at the 2nd Conference on Tone and Intonation in Europe, Santorini, Greece.

Goldinger, Stephen. 1996. Words and voices: Episodic traces in spoken word identification and recognition memory. *Journal of Experimental Psychology: Learning, Memory, and Cognition* 22(5). 1166–1183.

Goldinger, Stephen, David Pisoni & John Logan. 1991. On the nature of talker variability effects on recall of spoken word lists. *Journal of Experimental Psychology: Learning, Memory, and Cognition* 17(1). 152–162.

Goldman, Jean-Philippe. 2011. EasyAlign: An automatic phonetic alignment tool under Praat. In *Proceedings of the 12th Annual Conference of the International Speech Communication Association*, Firenze.

Grice, Martine. 1991. The intonation of interrogation in two varieties of Sicilian Italian. In *Proceedings of the 12th International Congress of Phonetic Sciences*, vol. 5, 210–213. Aix-en-Provence.

Grice, Martine. 1995. *The intonation of interrogation in Palermo Italian: Implications for intonation theory*. Tübingen: Niemeyer.

Grice, Martine & Stefan Baumann. 2002. Deutsche Intonation und GToBI. *Linguistische Berichte* 191. 267–298.

Grice, Martine, Stefan Baumann & Ralf Benzmülller. 2005a. German intonation in autosegmental-metrical phonology. In Sun-Ah Jun (ed.), *Prosodic typology: The phonology of intonation and phrasing*, 55–83. Oxford: Oxford University Press.

Grice, Martine, Mariapaola D'Imperio, Michelina Savino & Cinzia Avesani. 2005b. Towards a strategy for labelling varieties of italian. In Sun-Ah Jun (ed.), *Prosodic typology: The phonology of intonation and phrasing*, 362–389. Oxford: Oxford University Press.

Grice, Martine, Robert Ladd & Amalia Arvaniti. 2000. On the place of phrase accents in intonational phonology. *Phonology* 17(2). 143–185.

Gubian, Michele, Francesco Cangemi & Lou Boves. 2010. Automatic and data driven pitch contour manipulation with functional data analysis. In *Proceedings of the 5th International Conference on Speech Prosody*, Chicago.

Gubian, Michele, Francesco Cangemi & Lou Boves. 2011. Joint analysis of f0 and speech rate with functional data analysis. In *Proceedings of 36th International Conference of Acoustics, Speech and Signal Processing*, 4972–4975. Prague.

Gussenhoven, Carlos. 1984. *On the grammar and semantics of sentence accents.* Dordrecht: Foris.

Gussenhoven, Carlos. 2004. *The phonology of tone and intonation.* Cambridge: Cambridge University Press.

Gussenhoven, Carlos. 2006. Experimental approaches to establishing discreteness of intonational contrasts. In Stefan Sudhoff, Denisa Lenertová, Roland Meyer, Sandra Pappert, Petra Augurzky, Ina Mleinek, Nicole Richter & Johannes Schließer (eds.), *Methods in empirical prosody research*, 321–334. Berlin: De Gruyter.

Haan, Judith. 2002. *Speaking of questions.* Utrecht: LOT.

Harris, Zellig. 1955. From phoneme to morpheme. *Language* 31(2). 190–222.

Hawkins, Sarah. 2003. Roles and representations of systematic fine phonetic detail in speech understanding. *Journal of Phonetics* 31(3-4). 373–405.

Hawkins, Sarah. 2010. Phonetic variation as communicative system: Perception of the particular and the abstract. In Cécile Fougeron, Barbara Kühnert, Mariapaola D'Imperio & Nathalie Vallée (eds.), *Papers in Laboratory Phonology*, vol. 10, 479–510. Cambridge: Cambridge University Press.

Hawkins, Sarah. 2011. Does phonetic detail guide situation-specific speech recognition? In Wai-Sum Lee & Eric Zee (eds.), *Proceedings of the 17th International Congress of Phonetic Sciences*, 9–18. Hong Kong: City University of Hong Kong.

Hawkins, Sarah & Noël Nguyen. 2003. Effects on word recognition of syllable-onset cues to syllable-coda voicing. In John Local, Richard Ogden & Rosalind Temple (eds.), *Papers in Laboratory Phonology*, vol. 6, 38–57. Cambridge: Cambridge University Press.

Hawkins, Sarah & Noël Nguyen. 2004. Influence of syllable-coda voicing on the acoustic properties of syllable-onset /l/ in English. *Journal of Phonetics* 32(2). 199–231.

Hawkins, Sarah & Rachel Smith. 2001. Polysp: A polysystemic, phonetically-rich approach to speech understanding. *Italian Journal of Linguistics* 13. 99–188.

Hawkins, Sarah & Paul Warren. 1991. Factors affecting the given-new distinction in speech. In *Proceedings of the 12th International Congress of Phonetic Sciences*, 66–69. Aix-en-Provence: Université de Provence.

Heinrich, Antje, Yvonne Flory & Sarah Hawkins. 2010. Influence of english r-resonances on intelligibility of speech in noise for native English and German listeners. *Speech Communication* 52(11). 1038–1055.

Henriksen, Nicholas. 2012. The intonation and signaling of declarative questions in Manchego Peninsular Spanish. *Language and Speech* 55(4).

Hintzman, Douglas. 1986. Schema abstraction in a multiple-trace memory model. *Psychological Review* 93(4). 411–428.

Hirschberg, Julia & Gregory Ward. 1992. The influence of pitch range, duration, amplitude and spectral features on the interpretation of the rise-fall-rise intonation contour in English. *Journal of Phonetics* 20. 241–251.

Hooper, Joan. 1976. Word frequency in lexical diffusion and the source of morphophonological change. In William Christie (ed.), *Current progress in historical linguistics. Proceedings of the 2nd International Conference on Historical Linguistics*, 96–105. Amsterdam: North-Holland.

House, David. 1990. *Tonal perception in speech*. Lund: Lund University Press.

House, David. 1997. Perceptual thresholds and tonal categories. *Phonum* 4. 179–182.

Hualde, José. 2002. Intonation in Spanish and the other Ibero-Romance languages: Overview and status quaestionis. In Caroline Wiltshire & Joaquim Camps (eds.), *Romance phonology and variation*, 101–116. Amsterdam: John Benjamins.

Huddleston, Rodney. 1994. The contrast between interrogatives and questions. *Journal of Linguistics* 30(2). 411–39.

Institut für Phonetik und digitale Sprachverarbeitung. 1994. The Kiel Corpus of Read Speech. CD rom.

Isačenko, Aleksandr & Hans Joachim Schädlich. 1970. *Untersuchungen über die deutsche Satzintonation*. Berlin: Mouton.

Jackendoff, Ray. 1972. *Semantic interpretation in generative grammar*. Cambridge: MIT Press.

Jakobson, Roman, Gunnar Fant & Morris Halle. 1952. Preliminaries to speech analysis: The distinctive features. MIT Acoustics Laboratory technical report.

Jassem, Wiktor & Lutosława Richter. 1989. Neutralization of voicing in Polish obstruents. *Journal of Phonetics* 17(4). 317–326.

Johnson, Keith. 1997. Speech perception without speaker normalization. In Keith Johnson & John Mullennix (eds.), *Talker variability in speech processing*, 145–165. San Diego: Academic Press.

Johnson, Keith & John Mullennix. 1997. Complex representations used in speech processing. In Keith Johnson & John Mullennix (eds.), *Talker variability in speech processing*, 1–8. San Diego: Academic Press.

Jun, Sun-Ah. 1993. *The phonetics and phonology of Korean prosody*: Columbus: The Ohio State University dissertation.

Jusczyk, Peter & Paul Luce. 2002. Speech perception and spoken word recognition: Past and present. *Ear and Hearing* 23(1). 2–40.

Kelly, John & John Local. 1986. Long-domain resonance patterns in English. In *Proceedings of the International Conference on Speech Input/Output, Techniques and Applications*, 304–308. London.

Kirsner, Robert, Vincent van Heuven & Renée van Bezooijen. 1994. Interaction of particle and prosody in the interpretation of factual Dutch sentences. In Reineke Bok-Bennema & Crit Cremers (eds.), *Linguistics in the Netherlands*, 107–118. Amsterdam: John Benjamins.

Klatt, Dennis. 1973. Discrimination of fundamental frequency contours in synthetic speech: Implications for models of pitch perception. *Journal of the Acoustical Society of America* 53(1). 8–16.

Klatt, Dennis. 1979. Speech perception: A model of acoustic-phonetic analysis and lexical access. *Journal of Phonetics* 7. 279–312.

Kleber, Felicitas, Tina John & Jonathan Harrington. 2010. The implications for speech perception of incomplete neutralization of final devoicing in German. *Journal of Phonetics* 38(2). 185–196.

Kohler, Klaus. 1987. Categorical pitch perception. In *Proceedings of the 11th International Congress of Phonetic Sciences*, vol. 5, 331–333. Tallin: Academy of Sciences.

Kohler, Klaus. 1991. A model of German intonation. *Arbeitsberichte des Instituts für Phonetik der Universität Kiel* 25. 295–360.

Kopkalli, Handan. 1993. *A phonetic and phonological analysis of final devoicing in Turkish*: Ann Arbor: University of Michigan dissertation.

Kretschmer, Paul. 1938. Der Ursprung des Fragetons & Fragesatzes. In *Scritti in onore di alfredo trombetti*, 27–50. Milano: Hoepli.

Kruschke, John. 1992. ALCOVE: An exemplar-based connectionist model of category learning. *Psychological Review* 99(1). 22–44.

Ladd, Robert. 1996. *Intonational phonology*. Cambridge: Cambridge University Press.

Ladd, Robert. 2008. *Intonational phonology (2nd edition)*. Cambridge: Cambridge University Press.

Ladd, Robert & Astrid Schepman. 2003. "Sagging transitions" between high pitch accents in English: Experimental evidence. *Journal of Phonetics* 31(1). 81–112.

Ladefoged, Peter. 2000. *A course in phonetics (4th edition)*. Boston: Heinle & Heinle.

Ladefoged, Peter & Donald Broadbent. 1957. Information conveyed by vowels. *Journal of the Acoustical Society of America* 29(1). 98–104.

Lehiste, Ilse. 1970. *Suprasegmentals*. Cambridge: MIT Press.

Levi, Susannah & Jennifer Bruno. 2010. Priming at the level of phonetic detail: Evidence from voice onset time. *Journal of the Acoustical Society of America* 127(3). 1853.

Liberman, Mark. 1979. *The intonational system of English*. New York: Garland.

Bibliography

Licklider, Joseph. 1952. On the process of speech perception. *Journal of the Acoustical Society of America* 24(6). 590–594.

Lindgren, Nilo. 1965. Machine recognition of human language. *Spectrum* 2(3). 114–136.

Lisker, Leigh. 1986. Voicing in English: A catalogue of acoustic features signaling /b/ versus /p/ in trochees. *Language and Speech* 29. 3–11.

Lisker, Leigh & Arthur Abramson. 1964. A cross-language study of voicing in initial stops: Acoustical measurements. *Word* 20(3). 384–422.

Local, John. 2003a. Phonetics and talk-in-interaction. In Daniel Recasens, Maria Josep Solé & Joaquín Romero (eds.), *Proceedings of the 15th International Congress of Phonetic Sciences*, 115–118. Barcelona.

Local, John. 2003b. Variable domains and variable relevance: Interpreting phonetic exponents. *Journal of Phonetics* 31(3-4). 321–339.

Luce, Paul & Conor McLennan. 2005. Spoken word recognition: The challenge of variation. In David Pisoni & Robert Remez (eds.), *The handbook of speech perception*, 590–609. Hoboken: Wiley-Blackwell.

Luce, Paul, Conor McLennan & Jan Charles-Luce. 2003. Abstractness and specificity in spoken word recognition: Indexical and allophonic variability in long-term repetition priming. In Jeffrey Bowers & Chad Marsolek (eds.), *Rethinking implicit memory*, 145–165. Oxford: Oxford University Press.

Lyberg, Bertil. 1981. Some observations on the vowel duration and the fundamental frequency contour in Swedish utterances. *Journal of Phonetics* 9. 261–272.

Lyons, John. 1977. *Semantics*. Cambridge: Cambridge University Press.

Magno Caldognetto, Emanuela, Franco Ferrero, Carlo Lavagnoli & Kyriaki Vagges. 1978. F0 contours of statements, yes-no questions, and wh-questions of two regional varieties of Italian. *Journal of Italian Linguistics* 3(1). 57–66.

Manaster Ramer, Alexis. 1996. A letter from an incompletely neutral phonologist. *Journal of Phonetics* 24(4). 477–489.

Marchese, Lynell. 1978. *Atlas linguistique Kru: Essai de typologie*. Abidjan: Institut de Linguistique Appliquée.

Marslen-Wilson, William & Lorraine Tyler. 1980. The temporal structure of spoken language understanding. *Cognition* 8(1). 1–71.

Marslen-Wilson, William & Alan Welsh. 1978. Processing interactions and lexical access during word recognition in continuous speech. *Cognitive Psychology* 10(1). 29–63.

Mascaró, Joan. 1987. Underlying voicing recoverability of finally devoiced obstruents in Catalan. *Journal of Phonetics* 15. 183–186.

Matthews, Peter. 1993. *Grammatical theory in the United States from Bloomfield to Chomsky*. Cambridge: Cambridge University Press.

Maturi, Pietro. 1988. L'intonazione delle frasi dichiarative ed interrogative nella varietà napoletana dell'italiano. *Rivista Italiana di Acustica* 12. 13–30.

McClelland, James. 1981. Retrieving general and specific information from stored knowledge of specifics. In *Proceedings of the 3rd Annual Conference of the Cognitive Science Society*, 170–172. Berkeley.

McClelland, James & Jeffrey Elman. 1986. The TRACE model of speech perception. *Cognitive Psychology* 18(1). 1–86.

McClelland, James & David Rumelhart. 1985. Distributed memory and the representation of general and specific information. *Journal of Experimental Psychology: General* 114(2). 159–197.

Medin, Douglas & Marguerite Schaffer. 1978. Context theory of classification learning. *Psychological Review* 85(3). 207–238.

Michelas, Amandine. 2011. *Caractérisation phonétique et phonologique du syntagme intermédiaire en français: De la production à la perception*: Aix-en-Provence: Université de Provence dissertation.

Möhler, Gregor. 2001. Improvements of the PaIntE model for f0 parametrization. Research Papers from the Phonetics Lab, IMS Universität Stuttgart.

Möhler, Gregor & Alistair Conkie. 1998. Parametric modeling of intonation using vector quantization. In *Proceedings of the 3rd ESCA Workshop on Speech Synthesis*, 311–316. Jenolan Caves.

Moulines, Eric & Francis Charpentier. 1990. Pitch-synchronous waveform processing techniques for text-to-speech synthesis using diphones. *Speech Communication* 9(5). 453–467.

Nash, Rose & Anthony Mulac. 1980. The intonation of verifiability. In Linda Waugh & Cornelis van Schoonevenld (eds.), *The melody of language: Intonation and prosody*, 219–242. Baltimore: University Park Press.

Neukom, Lukas. 1995. *Description grammaticale du nateni (Bénin): Système verbal, classification nominale, phrases complexes, textes*. Zürich: Universität Zürich.

Nguyen, Noël, Sophie Wauquier & Betty Tuller. 2009. The dynamical approach to speech perception: From fine phonetic detail to abstract phonological categories. In François Pellegrino, Egidio Marsico, Ioana Chitoran & Christophe Coupé (eds.), *Approaches to phonological complexity*, 193–217. Berlin: Mouton de Gruyter.

Niebuhr, Oliver. 2007. Categorical perception in intonation: A matter of signal dynamics? In Cyril Goutte, Nicola Cancedda, Marc Dymetman & George Foster (eds.), *Proceedings of the 8th Annual Conference of the International Speech Communication Association*, 642–645. Antwerp.

Niebuhr, Oliver & Gilbert Ambrazaitis. 2006. Alignment of medial and late peaks in German spontaneous speech. In Rüdiger Hoffmann & Hansjörg Mixdorff (eds.), *Proceedings of the 3rd International Conference on Speech Prosody*, 161–164. Dresden.

Niebuhr, Oliver, Mariapaola D'Imperio, Barbara Gili Fivela & Francesco Cangemi. 2011. Are there "shapers" and "aligners"? Individual differences in signalling pitch accent category. In Wai-Sum Lee & Eric Zee (eds.), *Proceedings of the 17th International Congress of Phonetic Sciences*, 120–123. Hong Kong: City University of Hong Kong.

Niebuhr, Oliver & Hartmut Pfitzinger. 2010. On pitch-accent identification: The role of syllable duration and intensity. In *Proceedings of the 5th International Conference on Speech Prosody*, Chicago.

Nosofsky, Robert. 1986. Attention, similarity, and the identification–categorization relationship. *Journal of Experimental Psychology: General* 115(1). 39–61.

Nosofsky, Robert. 1988. Exemplar-based accounts of relations between classification, recognition, and typicality. *Journal of Experimental Psychology: Learning, Memory, and Cognition* 14(4). 700–708.

Noth, Elmar, Anton Batliner, Andreas Kießling, Ralf Kompe & Heinrich Niemann. 2000. Verbmobil: The use of prosody in the linguistic components of a speech understanding system. *Speech and Audio Processing* 8(5). 519–532.

O'Dell, Michael & Robert Port. 1983. Discrimination of word-final voicing in German. *Journal of the Acoustical Society of America* 73. S31.

Ohala, John. 1983. Cross-language use of pitch: An ethological view. *Phonetica* 40(1). 1–18.

Ohala, John. 1984. An ethological perspective on common cross-language utilization of f0 of voice. *Phonetica* 41(1). 1–16.

Ohala, John. 1990. There is no interface between phonology and phonetics: A personal view. *Journal of Phonetics* 18(2). 153–172.

Oldfield, Richard. 1966. Things, words and the brain. *The Quarterly Journal of Experimental Psychology* 18(4). 340–353.

Osgood, Charles, George Suci & Percy Tannenbaum. 1957. *The measurement of meaning*. Urbana: University of Illinois Press.

Palmeri, Thomas, Stephen Goldinger & David Pisoni. 1993. Episodic encoding of voice attributes and recognition memory for spoken words. *Journal of Experimental Psychology: Learning, Memory, and Cognition* 19(2). 309–328.

Pandelaere, Mario & Siegfried Dewitte. 2006. Is this a question? Not for long: The statement bias. *Journal of Experimental Social Psychology* 42(4). 525–531.

Peterson, Gordon. 1952. The information-bearing elements of speech. *Journal of the Acoustical Society of America* 24(6). 629–637.

Peterson, Gordon & Harold Barney. 1952. Control methods used in a study of the vowels. *Journal of the Acoustical Society of America* 24(2). 175–184.

Petrone, Caterina. 2008. *Le rôle de la variabilité phonétique dans la représentation des contours intonatifs et de leur sens*: Aix-en-Provence: Université de Provence dissertation.

Petrone, Caterina & Mariapaola D'Imperio. 2008. Tonal structure and constituency in Neapolitan Italian: Evidence for the accentual phrase in statements and questions. In Plinio Barbosa, Sandra Madureira & César Reis (eds.), *Proceedings of 4th International Conference on Speech Prosody*, 301–304. Campinas.

Petrone, Caterina & Mariapaola D'Imperio. 2009. Is tonal alignment interpretation independent of methodology? In Maria Uther, Roger Moore & Stephen Cox (eds.), *Proceedings of the 10th Annual Conference of the International Speech Communication Association*, 2459–2462. Brighton.

Petrone, Caterina & Mariapaola D'Imperio. 2011. From tones to tunes: Effects of the f0 prenuclear region in the perception of Neapolitan statements and questions. In Sónia Frota, Gorka Elordieta & Pilar Prieto (eds.), *Prosodic categories: Production, perception and comprehension*, 207–230. Dordrecht, Heidelberg, London, New York: Springer.

Petrone, Caterina & Oliver Niebuhr. 2014. On the intonation in German intonation questions: The role of the prenuclear region. *Language and Speech* 57(1). 108–46.

Pfitzinger, Hartmut. 2001. *Phonetische Analyse der Sprechgeschwindigkeit*: Munich: Ludwig-Maximilians-Universität München dissertation.

Pierrehumbert, Janet. 1980. *The phonology and phonetics of English intonation*: Cambridge, MA: Massachussets Institut of Technology dissertation.

Pierrehumbert, Janet. 1981. Synthesizing intonation. *Journal of the Acoustical Society of America* 70(4). 985–995.

Pierrehumbert, Janet. 1990. Phonological and phonetic representation. *Journal of Phonetics* 18(3). 375–394.

Pierrehumbert, Janet. 2001. Exemplar dynamics: Word frequency, lenition and contrast. In Joan Bybee & Paul Hopper (eds.), *Frequency and the emergence of linguistic structure*, 137–158. Amsterdam: John Benjamins.

Pierrehumbert, Janet & Mary Beckman. 1988. *Japanese tone structure*. Cambridge: MIT Press.

Pierrehumbert, Janet, Mary Beckman & Robert Ladd. 2000. Conceptual foundations of phonology as a laboratory science. In Noel Burton-Roberts, Philip

Carr & Gerard Docherty (eds.), *Phonological knowledge: Conceptual and empirical issues*, 273–303. Oxford: Oxford University Press.

Pierrehumbert, Janet & Julia Hirschberg. 1990. The meaning of intonational contours in the interpretation of discourse. In Philip Cohen, Jerry Morgan & Martha Pollack (eds.), *Intentions in communication*, 271–311. Cambridge: MIT Press.

Pierrehumbert, Janet & Shirley Steele. 1989. Categories of tonal alignment in English. *Phonetica* 46(3). 181–196.

Pike, Kenneth. 1945. *The intonation of American English*. Ann Arbor: University of Michigan Press.

Podi, Napo. 1995. *Esquisse comparative de l'akasilimi et du basaal*: Grenoble: Université de Grenoble III dissertation.

Port, Robert. 1996. The discreteness of phonetic elements and formal linguistics: Response to A. Manaster Ramer. *Journal of Phonetics* 24(4). 491–512.

Port, Robert. 2006. The graphical basis of phones and phonemes. In Murray Munro & Ocke-Schwen Bohn (eds.), *Second language speech learning: The role of language experience in speech perception and production*, 349–365. Amsterdam: John Benjamins.

Port, Robert & Penny Crawford. 1989. Incomplete neutralization and pragmatics in German. *Journal of Phonetics* 17(4). 257–282.

Port, Robert, Fares Mitleb & Michael O'Dell. 1981. Neutralization of obstruent voicing in German is incomplete. *Journal of the Acoustical Society of America* 70. S13.

Port, Robert & Michael O'Dell. 1985. Neutralization of syllable-final voicing in German. *Journal of Phonetics* 13(4). 455–471.

Prieto, Pilar, Mariapaola D'Imperio & Barbara Gili Fivela. 2005. Pitch accent alignment in Romance: Primary and secondary associations with metrical structure. *Language and Speech* 48(4). 359–396.

Pye, Susan. 1986. Word-final devoicing of obstruents in Russian. *Cambridge Papers in Phonetics and Experimental Linguistics* 5. 1–10.

R Development Core Team. 2008. R: A language and environment for statistical computing. Computer program, retrieved from http://www.R-project.org/.

Repp, Bruno. 1979. Relative amplitude of aspiration noise as a voicing cue for syllable-initial stop consonants. *Language and Speech* 22(2). 173–189.

Rialland, Annie. 1984. Le fini/l'infini ou l'affirmation/l'interrogation en moba (langue voltaïque parlée au Nord-Togo). *Studies in African Linguistics* supp. 9. 258–261.

Rialland, Annie. 2007. Question prosody: An African perspective. In Tomas Riad & Carlos Gussenhoven (eds.), *Tones and tunes: Experimental studies in word and sentence prosody*, vol. 2, 35–62. Berlin: de Gruyter.

Rietveld, Toni & Carlos Gussenhoven. 1987. Perceived speech rate and intonation. *Journal of Phonetics* 15(3). 273–285.

Rossi, Mario. 1971. Le seuil de glissando ou seuil de perception des variations tonales pour les sons de la parole. *Phonetica* 23(1). 1–33.

Röttger, Timo, Bodo Winter & Sven Grawunder. 2011. The robustness of incomplete neutralization in German. In Wai-Sum Lee & Eric Zee (eds.), *Proceedings of the 17th International Congress of Phonetic Sciences*, 1722–1725. Hong Kong: City University of Hong Kong.

Ryalls, John, Guylaine Le Dorze, Nathalie Lever, Lisa Ouellet & Céline Larfeuil. 1994. The effects of age and sex on speech intonation and duration for matched statements and questions in French. *Journal of the Acoustical Society of America* 95(4). 2274–2276.

Sabatini, Francesco. 1985. L'italiano dell'uso medio: Una realtà tra le varietà linguistiche italiane. In Günter Holtus & Edgar Radtke (eds.), *Gesprochenes Italienisch in Geschichte und Gegenwart*, 154–184. Tübingen: Gunter Narr.

Sadock, Jerrold & Arnold Zwicky. 1985. Speech act distinctions in syntax. In Timothy Shopen (ed.), *Language typology and syntactic description*, 155–196. Cambridge: Cambridge University Press.

Savino, Michelina. 1997. *Il ruolo dell'intonazione nell'interazione comunicativa: Analisi strumentale delle domande polari in un corpus di dialoghi spontanei (varieta' di Bari)*: Bari: Università/Politecnico di Bari dissertation.

Savino, Michelina. 2012. The intonation of polar questions in Italian: Where is the rise? *Journal of the International Phonetic Association* 42. 23–48.

Savy, Renata & Francesco Cutugno. 2009. CLIPS: Diatopic, diamesic and diaphasic variations in spoken Italian. In *Proceedings of the 5th Corpus Linguistics Conference*, Liverpool.

Schacter, Daniel & Barbara Church. 1992. Auditory priming: Implicit and explicit memory for words and voices. *Journal of Experimental Psychology: Learning, Memory, and Cognition* 18(5). 915–930.

Scherer, Klaus, Robert Ladd & Kim Silverman. 1984. Vocal cues to speaker affect: Testing two models. *Journal of the Acoustical Society of America* 76(5). 1346–1356.

Schouten, Marten Egbertus Hendrik. 1985. Identification and discrimination of sweep tones. *Attention, Perception, & Psychophysics* 37(4). 369–376.

Schweitzer, Katrin, Sasha Calhoun, Hinrich Schütze, Antje Schweitzer & Michael Walsh. 2010a. Relative frequency affects pitch accent realisation: Evidence for exemplar storage of prosody. In Marija Tabain, Janet Fletcher, David Grayden, John Hajek & Andy Butcher (eds.), *Proceedings of the 13th Australasian International Conference on Speech Science and Technology*, 62–65. Melbourne.

Bibliography

Schweitzer, Katrin, Michael Walsh, Sasha Calhoun & Hinrich Schütze. 2011. Prosodic variability in lexical sequences: Intonation entrenches too. In Wai-Sum Lee & Eric Zee (eds.), *Proceedings of the 17th International Congress of Phonetic Sciences*, 1778–1781. Hong Kong: City University of Hong Kong.

Schweitzer, Katrin, Michael Walsh, Bernd Möbius, Arndt Riester, Antje Schweitzer & Hinrich Schütze. 2009. Frequency matters: Pitch accents and information status. In Diana McCarthy & Shuly Wintner (eds.), *Proceedings of the 12th Conference of the European Chapter of the Association for Computational Linguistics*, 728–736. Athens.

Schweitzer, Katrin, Michael Walsh, Bernd Möbius & Hinrich Schütze. 2010b. Frequency of occurrence effects on pitch accent realisation. In Takao Kobayashi, Keikichi Hirose & Satoshi Nakamura (eds.), *Proceedings of the 11th Annual Conference of the International Speech Communication Association*, 138–141. Makuhari.

Sekiguchi, Takahiro. 2006. Effects of lexical prosody and word familiarity on lexical access of spoken Japanese words. *Journal of Psycholinguistic Research* 35(4). 369–384.

Sergeant, Russell & Donald Harris. 1962. Sensitivity to unidirectional frequency modulation. *Journal of the Acoustical Society of America* 34(10). 1625–1628.

Shattuck-Hufnagel, Stefanie & Alice Turk. 1996. A prosody tutorial for investigators of auditory sentence processing. *Journal of Psycholinguistic Research* 25(2). 193–247.

Sheffert, Sonya, David Pisoni, Jennifer Fellowes & Robert Remez. 2002. Learning to recognize talkers from natural, sinewave, and reversed speech samples. *Journal of Experimental Psychology: Human Perception and Performance* 28(6). 1447–1469.

Shriberg, Elizabeth, Andreas Stolcke, Daniel Jurafsky, Noah Coccaro, Marie Meteer, Rebecca Bates, Paul Taylor, Klaus Ries, Rachel Martin & Carol Van Ess-Dykema. 1998. Can prosody aid the automatic classification of dialog acts in conversational speech? *Language and Speech* 41(3-4). 443–492.

Slowiaczek, Louisa & Daniel Dinnsen. 1985. On the neutralizing status of Polish word-final devoicing. *Journal of Phonetics* 13(3). 325–341.

Slowiaczek, Louisa & Helena Szymanska. 1989. Perception of word-final devoicing in Polish. *Journal of Phonetics* 17(3). 205–212.

Smith, Caroline. 2002. Prosodic finality and sentence type in French. *Language and Speech* 45(2). 141–178.

Smith, Edward & Douglas Medin. 1981. *Categories and concepts*. Cambridge: Harvard University Press.

Smith, Rachel, Rachel Baker & Sarah Hawkins. 2012. Phonetic detail that distinguishes prefixed from pseudo-prefixed words. *Journal of Phonetics* 40(5). 689–705.

Smith, Rachel & Sarah Hawkins. 2000. Allophonic influences on word-spotting experiments. In Anne Cutler, James McQueen & Rian Zondervan (eds.), *ISCA Tutorial and Research Workshop on Spoken Word Access Processes*, 139–142. Nijmegen: Max-Planck-Gesellschaft zur Förderung der Wissenschaften.

Sobrero, Alberto. 1992. *L'italiano di oggi*. Roma: Istituto della Enciclopedia Italiana.

Standing, Lionel, Jerry Conezio & Ralph Haber. 1970. Perception and memory for pictures: Single-trial learning of 2500 visual stimuli. *Psychonomic Science* 19(2). 73–74.

Stevens, Kenneth. 1960. Toward a model for speech recognition. *Journal of the Acoustical Society of America* 32(1). 47–55.

Stevens, Kenneth. 2004. Invariance and variability in speech: Interpreting acoustic evidence. In Janet Slifka, Sharon Manuel & Melanie Matthies (eds.), *Proceedings of From Sound to Sense Workshop*, vol. B, 77–85. Cambridge: MIT Press.

Swerts, Marc, Cinzia Avesani & Emiel Krahmer. 1999. Reaccentuation or deaccentuation: A comparative study of Italian and Dutch. In John Ohala (ed.), *Proceedings of the 14th International Congress of Phonetic Sciences*, 1541–144. San Francisco: University of California.

't Hart, Johan. 1976. Psychoacoustic backgrounds of pitch contour stylisation. *IPO – Annual Progress Report* 11. 11–19.

't Hart, Johan, Rene Collier & Antonie Cohen. 1990. *A perceptual study of intonation: An experimental-phonetic approach*. Cambridge: Cambridge University Press.

Taljaard, Petrus & Sonja Bosch. 1988. *Handbook of Isizulu*. Hatfield, Pretoria: J.L. van Schaik.

Tenpenny, Patricia. 1995. Abstractionist versus episodic theories of repetition priming and word identification. *Psychonomic Bulletin & Review* 2(3). 339–363.

Theodore, Rachel. 2009. *Some characteristics of talker-specific phonetic detail*: Boston: Northeastern University dissertation.

Trager, Leonard & Henry Smith. 1951. *An outline of English structure*. Norman: Battenburg Press.

Trouvain, Jürgen. 2004. *Tempo variation in speech production: Implications for speech synthesis*: Saarbrücken: Saarland University dissertation.

Trubetzkoy, Nikolaus. 1939. *Grundzüge der Phonologie*. Prag: Travaux du cercle linguistique de Prague.

Bibliography

Turk, Alice, Satsuki Nakai & Mariko Sugahara. 2006. Acoustic segment durations in prosodic research: A practical guide. In Stefan Sudhoff, Denisa Lenertová, Roland Meyer, Sandra Pappert, Petra Augurzky, Ina Mleinek, Nicole Richter & Johannes Schließer (eds.), *Methods in empirical prosody research*, 1–28. Berlin: De Gruyter.

Uldall, Elizabeth. 1964. Dimensions of meaning in intonation. In David Abercrombie (ed.), *In honour of Daniel Jones*, 271–279. London: Longmans.

van Alphen, Petra & James McQueen. 2006. The effect of voice onset time differences on lexical access in Dutch. *Journal of Experimental Psychology: Human Perception and Performance* 32(1). 178–196.

van Heerden, Charl Johannes & Etienne Barnard. 2007. Speech rate normalization used to improve speaker verification. *South African Institute of Electrical Engineers* 98(4). 136–140.

van Heuven, Vincent & Judith Haan. 2000. Phonetic correlates of statement versus question intonation in Dutch. In Antonis Botinis (ed.), *Intonation: Analysis, modelling and technology*, 119–144. Dordrecht: Kluwer.

van Heuven, Vincent & Judith Haan. 2002. Temporal distribution of interrogativity markers in Dutch: A perceptual study. In Carlos Gussenhoven & Natasha Warner (eds.), *Papers in Laboratory Phonology*, vol. 7, 61–86. Berlin: Mouton de Gruyter.

van Heuven, Vincent & Ellen van Zanten. 2005. Speech rate as a secondary prosodic characteristic of polarity questions in three languages. *Speech Communication* 47(1). 87–99.

van Santen, Jan & Bernd Möbius. 2000. A quantitative model of f0 generation and alignment. In Antonis Botinis (ed.), *Intonation: Analysis, modelling and technology*, 269–288. Dordrecht: Kluwer.

Walsh, Michael, Katrin Schweitzer, Bernd Möbius & Hinrich Schütze. 2008. Examining pitch-accent variability from an exemplar-theoretic perspective. In Janet Fletcher, Deborah Loakes, Roland Gocke, Denis Burnham & Michael Wagner (eds.), *Proceedings of the 9th Annual Conference of the International Speech Communication Association*, 877–880. Brisbane.

Warner, Natasha, Erin Good, Allard Jongman & Joan Sereno. 2006. Orthographic vs. morphological incomplete neutralization effects. *Journal of Phonetics* 34(2). 285–293.

Warner, Natasha, Allard Jongman, Joan Sereno & Rachèl Kemps. 2004. Incomplete neutralization and other sub-phonemic durational differences in production and perception: Evidence from Dutch. *Journal of Phonetics* 32(2). 251–276.

Wells, Rulon. 1945. The pitch phonemes of English. *Language* 21. 27–39.

West, Paula. 1999. Perception of distributed coarticulatory properties of english /l/ and /r/. *Journal of Phonetics* 27(4). 405–426.

Wheeler, Daniel. 1970. Processes in word recognition. *Cognitive Psychology* 1(1). 59–85.

Williams, Carl & Kenneth Stevens. 1972. Emotions and speech: Some acoustical correlates. *Journal of the Acoustical Society of America* 52(4). 1238–1250.

Winter, Bodo & Timo Röttger. forthcoming. The nature of incomplete neutralization in German: Implications for laboratory phonology. *Grazer Linguistische Studien* .

Wood, Sidney. 1973. Speech tempo. In *Working papers*, vol. 9, 99–147. Lund: Department of Linguistics, Lund University.

Xu, Yi. 2005. Speech melody as articulatorily implemented communicative functions. *Speech Communication* 46(3). 220–251.

Zeng, XiaoLi, Philippe Martin & Georges Boulakia. 2004. Tones and intonation in declarative and interrogative sentences in Mandarin. In *Proceedings of the International Symposium on Tonal Aspects of Languages*, 235–238. Beijing.

Name index

Abercrombie, David, 29
Abramson, Arthur, 14
Adjarian, Hrachia, 14
Albano Leoni, Federico, 8
Ambrazaitis, Gilbert, 61
Anderson, Mark, 35
André, Carine, 74, 96, 125
Angelini, Bianca, 98
Arndt, Walter, 19
Arvaniti, Amalia, 35, 44
Atterer, Michaela, 61
Audacity Development Team, 98
Avesani, Cinzia, 22–25, 41, 64

Baayen, Harald, 144, 145
Baker, Rachel, 12, 15
Balota, David, 9
Barnard, Etienne, 93
Barney, Harold, 9
Bates, Rebecca, 150
Batliner, Anton, 150, 151
Baumann, Stefan, 21, 56
Beckman, Mary, 14, 16, 22, 27
Benzmülller, Ralf, 21
Bigi, Brigitte, 98, 145
Black, Alan, 35
Blesser, Barry, 9
Boersma, Paul, 44, 75, 83, 98, 127, 146
Bolinger, Dwight, 21, 115
Borst, John, 8
Bosch, Sonja, 92
Boulakia, Georges, 63

Boves, Lou, 93, 107, 127, 131, 146
Broadbent, Donald, 9
Brooks, Lee, 10
Browman, Catherine, 8
Brugnara, Fabio, 98
Brunetti, Lisa, 22, 35, 42, 43, 80
Bruni, Francesco, 19
Bruno, Jennifer, 14
Büring, Daniel, 39
Bybee, Joan, 13, 16

Calhoun, Sasha, 16, 150, 151
Campbell, Nick, 28
Cangemi, Francesco, 22, 23, 35, 37, 41–43, 53, 72, 73, 78, 80, 92–94, 98, 107, 117, 120, 127, 131, 145, 146
Caputo, Maria Rosaria, 22
Cavé, Christian, 74, 96, 125
Chambers, Craig, 68
Charles-Luce, Jan, 8, 11, 12, 144
Charpentier, Francis, 75, 83, 146
Chomsky, Noam, 8
Church, Barbara, 10, 27
Coccaro, Noah, 150
Cohen, Antonie, 21
Cole, Jennifer, 150
Coleman, John, 13
Collier, Rene, 21
Conezio, Jerry, 10
Conkie, Alistair, 150
Cooper, Franklin, 8

Name index

Cooper, William, 17
Crawford, Penny, 144
Cutugno, Francesco, 94, 98, 145

Dahan, Delphine, 68
Davidson, Kathryn, 44
De Dominicis, Amedeo, 94, 100
De Mauro, Tullio, 19
Del Giudice, Alex, 44
Delattre, Pierre, 8, 21, 34
Dewitte, Siegfried, 80
D'Imperio, Mariapaola, 22–25, 35, 38, 41–45, 53, 55, 56, 58, 59, 64, 68, 70, 72, 73, 78, 80, 86, 89, 92, 117, 120, 141
Dinnsen, Daniel, 144
Dmitrieva, Olga, 144
Dombrowski, Ernst, 35, 38, 46, 47, 53, 54, 59, 64
Dryer, Matthew, 19
Duncan, Starkey, 93

Eefting, Wieke, 93
Elman, Jeffrey, 9, 15
Elordieta, Gorka, 42
Ernestus, Mirjam, 13, 144, 145

Faber, Alice, 8
Face, Timothy, 35
Falavigna, Daniele, 98
Fant, Gunnar, 14
Farnetani, Edda, 107
Fellowes, Jennifer, 88
Ferrero, Franco, 22
Firth, John, 8
Flemming, Edward, 14
Flory, Yvonne, 13, 15, 27, 28
Fourakis, Marios, 144
Frick, Robert, 144

Frota, Sónia, 42
Fujisaki, Hiroya, 17

Garcia Zamor, Maria, 144
Gerstman, Louis, 8
Ghio, Alain, 74, 96, 125
Gili Fivela, Barbara, 19, 22, 24, 27, 53, 55, 59, 117
Giuliani, Diegl, 98
Goldinger, Stephen, 10
Goldman, Jean-Philippe, 145
Goldstein, Louis, 8
Good, Erin, 144
Grawunder, Sven, 144, 145
Gretter, Roberto, 98
Grice, Martine, 19, 21–25, 35, 41, 56, 64
Gubian, Michele, 93, 107, 127, 131, 146
Gussenhoven, Carlos, 20, 21, 58, 65, 68, 115

Haan, Judith, 31, 93
Haber, Ralph, 10
Halle, Morris, 14
Harrington, Jonathan, 144, 145
Harris, Donald, 67
Harris, Zellig, 8
Hawkins, Sarah, 12, 13, 15, 27, 28, 150
Heinrich, Antje, 13, 15, 27, 28
Henriksen, Nicholas, 94
Hintzman, Douglas, 10
Hirose, Keikichi, 17
Hirschberg, Julia, 62, 89
Hirst, Daniel, 98, 145
Hooper, Joan, 13
House, David, 22, 49, 68
Hualde, José, 35
Huddleston, Rodney, 31
Hunt, Andrew, 35

Name index

Isačenko, Aleksandr, 21
Iverson, Gregory, 144

Jackendoff, Ray, 152
Jakobson, Roman, 14
Jassem, Wiktor, 144
John, Tina, 144, 145
Johnson, Keith, 8, 10, 15, 34, 149
Jongman, Allard, 144
Jun, Sun-Ah, 58
Jurafsky, Daniel, 150
Jusczyk, Peter, 7, 8

Kelly, John, 13
Kemps, Rachèl, 144
Kießling, Andreas, 150
Kirsner, Robert, 68
Klatt, Dennis, 9, 68
Kleber, Felicitas, 144, 145
Kohler, Klaus, 53, 68
Kompe, Ralf, 150
Kopkalli, Handan, 144
Kori, Shiro, 107
Krahmer, Emiel, 23
Kretschmer, Paul, 30
Kruschke, John, 10

Ladd, Robert, 14, 16, 17, 20, 21, 28, 35, 61, 119, 121, 150
Ladefoged, Peter, 9, 12
Larfeuil, Céline, 93, 94, 100
Lavagnoli, Carlo, 22
Le Dorze, Guylaine, 93, 94, 100
Lehiste, Ilse, 29, 92, 103, 121, 122
Lever, Nathalie, 93, 94, 100
Levi, Susannah, 14
Liberman, Alvin, 8
Liberman, Mark, 16, 35
Licklider, Joseph, 9

Lindgren, Nilo, 9
Lisker, Leigh, 14, 124
Local, John, 12, 13, 15
Logan, John, 10
Luce, Paul, 7–9, 11, 12
Ludusan, Bogdan, 94, 98, 145
Lyberg, Bertil, 28
Lyons, John, 30

Magno Caldognetto, Emanuela, 22
Manaster Ramer, Alexis, 144
Marchese, Lynell, 92
Marslen-Wilson, William, 9
Martin, Philippe, 63
Martin, Rachel, 150
Mascaró, Joan, 144
Matthews, Peter, 8
Maturi, Pietro, 22, 93, 94, 99, 100, 106
McClelland, James, 9, 10, 15
McLennan, Conor, 8, 9, 11, 12
McQueen, James, 14
Medin, Douglas, 10, 150
Meteer, Marie, 150
Michelas, Amandine, 58
Mitleb, Fares, 144, 145
Möbius, Batliner, 150, 151
Möbius, Bernd, 16, 149–151
Möhler, Gregor, 150
Mokhtari, Parham, 28
Moulines, Eric, 75, 83, 146
Mulac, Anthony, 68
Mullennix, John, 8, 34

Nakai, Satsuki, 93
Nash, Rose, 68
Neukom, Lukas, 92
Nguyen, Noël, 13, 15, 22, 27, 144
Niebuhr, Oliver, 35, 38, 46, 47, 53, 54, 56, 59–61, 64, 68, 70, 72, 80,

Name index

86, 89, 117
Niemann, Heinrich, 150
Nosofsky, Robert, 10, 11
Nöth, Elmar, 150

O'Dell, Michael, 144, 145
Ohala, John, 14, 58, 115
Oldfield, Richard, 9
Omologo, Maurizio, 98
Osgood, Charles, 68
Ouellet, Lisa, 93, 94, 100

Paccia-Cooper, Jeanne, 17
Palmeri, Thomas, 10
Pandelaere, Mario, 80
Peterson, Gordon, 9
Petrone, Caterina, 22–24, 38, 44, 53, 55, 56, 58, 60, 61, 64, 68, 70, 72, 73, 78, 80, 93, 94, 99, 100, 141
Pfitzinger, Hartmut, 86, 89, 107, 142
Pierrehumbert, Janet, 14, 16, 17, 20, 22, 23, 33, 35, 62, 68, 149
Pike, Kenneth, 21
Pisoni, David, 10, 88
Podi, Napo, 92
Port, Robert, 8, 144, 145
Prieto, Pilar, 22, 24, 42
Pye, Susan, 144

R Development Core Team, 46, 108, 127, 146
Remez, Robert, 88
Repp, Bruno, 18
Rialland, Annie, 91, 93, 94, 100
Richter, Lutosława, 144
Ries, Klaus, 150
Riester, Arndt, 16
Rietveld, Toni, 115

Rossi, Mario, 68
Röttger, Timo, 144, 145
Rumelhart, David, 10
Ryalls, John, 93, 94, 100

Sabatini, Francesco, 19
Sadock, Jerrold, 30
Salihie, Mohammad, 44
Savino, Michelina, 19, 22–25, 41, 42, 64
Savy, Renata, 98
Schacter, Daniel, 10, 27
Schädlich, Hans Joachim, 21
Schaffer, Marguerite, 10
Schepman, Astrid, 35
Scherer, Klaus, 150
Schouten, Marten Egbertus Hendrik, 68
Schütze, Hinrich, 16, 149–151
Schweitzer, Antje, 16, 150, 151
Schweitzer, Katrin, 16, 149–151
Sekiguchi, Takahiro, 149
Seppi, Dino, 94, 98, 145
Sereno, Joan, 144
Sergeant, Russell, 67
Shattuck-Hufnagel, Stefanie, 20, 21, 28, 150
Sheffert, Sonya, 88
Shosted, Ryan, 44
Shriberg, Elizabeth, 150
Silverman, Kim, 150
Slowiaczek, Louisa, 144
Smith, Caroline, 93, 94, 100
Smith, Edward, 150
Smith, Henry, 21
Smith, Rachel, 12, 15, 27
Sobrero, Alberto, 19
Standing, Lionel, 10
Steele, Shirley, 68

Name index

Stevens, Kenneth, 9, 15, 93
Stolcke, Andreas, 150
Suci, George, 68
Sugahara, Mariko, 93
Swerts, Marc, 23
Szymanska, Helena, 144

't Hart, Johan, 21, 68
Taljaard, Petrus, 92
Tanenhaus, Michael, 68
Tannenbaum, Percy, 68
Taylor, Paul, 150
Tenpenny, Patricia, 10
Teston, Bernard, 74, 96, 125
Theodore, Rachel, 14
Trager, Leonard, 21
Trouvain, Jürgen, 29
Trubetzkoy, Nikolaus, 14
Tuller, Betty, 13, 15, 27, 144
Turk, Alice, 20, 21, 28, 93
Tyler, Lorraine, 9

Uldall, Elizabeth, 68

Vagges, Kyriaki, 22
van Alphen, Petra, 14
van Bezooijen, Renée, 68
Van Compernolle, Dirk, 94, 98, 145
Van Ess-Dykema, Carol, 150
van Heerden, Charl Johannes, 93
van Heuven, Vincent, 68, 93, 94, 100, 105, 115, 116, 142
van Santen, Jan, 151
van Zanten, Ellen, 93, 94, 100, 105, 115, 116, 142
Vigàrio, Marina, 42

Walsh, Michael, 16, 149–151
Ward, Gregory, 89

Warner, Natasha, 144
Warren, Paul, 150
Wauquier, Sophie, 13, 15, 27, 144
Weenink, David, 44, 75, 83, 98, 127, 146
Wells, Rulon, 21
Welsh, Alan, 9
West, Paula, 13, 27
Wheeler, Daniel, 9
Williams, Carl, 93
Winter, Bodo, 144, 145
Wood, Sidney, 29

Xu, Yi, 17

Zeng, XiaoLi, 63
Zwicky, Arnold, 30

Subject index

abstractionism, 1, 14
ASSI, 98, 145
autosegmental-metrical
        intonation, 20, 33, 58, 121

categorization, 4
compositionality, 64, 79
curve index, 46, 51

elbow detection, 44
English, 94
exemplar prosody, 16, 148
exemplarism, 5, 10, 34

f0 dynamics, 38, 53, 67, 72, 86, 140
French, 34, 94
frequency code, 115, 142

German, 53, 56, 70
good effort, 134, 144

incomplete neutralization, 144
intonational inventory, 33, 58
Italian, 18, 94

Kiel Intonation Model, 53, 59

Local Phone Rate, 107, 142

Manado Malay, 94
Mandarin Chinese, 63
Moba, 91

narrow focus, 39, 72, 80, 107, 114

Nateni, 92
Ncam, 92
Neapolitan Italian, 18, 22, 55, 68

partial topic, 39, 72, 79, 140
perception of speech, 7
phonetic detail, 7, 11, 27, 139
phonological contrast, 62
pitch accent, 41, 72, 141, 150
prosodic detail, 15, 86, 116

resynthesis, 68, 75, 80, 83, 91, 127, 131, 143, 146

sentence modality, 29, 68, 91, 99, 114, 141
Spanish, 94
speech rate, 93

tempo, 29, 92, 116, 121, 142

Wobé, 92

Subject index